GUIDE TO ANALYSING COMPANIES

OTHER ECONOMIST BOOKS

Guide to Business Modelling
Guide to Business Planning
Guide to Cash Management
Guide to Commodities
Guide to Country Risk
Guide to Decision Making
Guide to Economic Indicators
Guide to Emerging Markets
Guide to the European Union
Guide to Financial Management
Guide to Financial Markets
Guide to Hedge Funds
Guide to Investment Strategy
Guide to Management Ideas and Gurus
Guide to Managing Growth
Guide to Organisation Design
Guide to Project Management
Guide to Supply Chain Management
Numbers Guide
Style Guide

Book of Business Quotations
Book of Isms
Brands and Branding
Business Consulting
Business Strategy
Buying Professional Services
The Chief Financial Officer
Economics
Managing Talent
Managing Uncertainty
Marketing
Marketing for Growth
Megachange – the world in 2050
Modern Warfare, Intelligence and Deterrence
Organisation Culture
Successful Strategy Execution
Unhappy Union

Directors: an A–Z Guide
Economics: an A–Z Guide
Investment: an A–Z Guide
Negotiation: an A–Z Guide

Pocket World in Figures

The
Economist

GUIDE TO ANALYSING COMPANIES

(6th Edition)

Bob Vause

PUBLICAFFAIRS
New York

Typeset in EcoType by MacGuru Ltd
info@macguru.org.uk

Library of Congress Control Number: 2014950431
ISBN 978-1-61039-478-9 (PB)
ISBN 978-1-61039-479-6 (EB)

First Edition

10 9 8 7 6 5 4 3 2 1

Contents

List of figures

Introduction

THE AIM OF THIS BOOK is to provide an understanding of how to analyse and assess the performance and financial position of a company from the various sources of information available. Financial analysis is as much an art as it is a science. Combine any two figures from an annual report and a ratio is produced; the real skill is in deciding which figures to use, where to find them and how to judge the result.

Before attempting to analyse a company, a sound grasp of financial terminology and presentation is required. Part 1 of this book explains the content and intent of the main financial statements appearing in a company's annual report: the statement of financial position (balance sheet); the income statement (profit and loss account); and the statement of cash flows. Two newcomers, the statement of comprehensive income and the statement of changes in equity, are also covered.

All countries and companies share the basic accounting framework used in the preparation of financial statements, but their presentation is not yet completely standardised. Adjustments may have to be made, but the outline in Part 1 is applicable to most companies and countries. Reference is made to UK and US GAAP (generally accepted accounting principles) as well as the appropriate International Accounting Standards or International Financial Reporting Standards (IAS or IFRS), but there is no attempt at a detailed interpretation of their application. This is an area of study you may move on to after this book.

As far as possible, the examples given have been kept simple in order to emphasise or reinforce the subject matter; once the fundamental theory and practice are grasped there should be no problem in moving to more detailed and sophisticated analysis. In general, the book's examples focus on retail, service and manufacturing companies rather than banks and other financial services companies, which are subject to a different set of legal and reporting requirements.

Part 2 deals with the analysis of the different aspects of corporate performance and position. Three important ground rules apply:

1 Never judge a company on the basis of one year's figures. Always look at three, or, ideally, five years' figures.

2 Never judge a company in isolation. Always compare its performance with others of the same size and/or in the same business sector and/or country.

3 When comparing companies always make sure, as far as you can, that you are comparing like with like – in other words, that the basis of the data being analysed is consistent.

Profit and finance are the two broad strands interwoven in the overall management of successful business organisations today. They also provide the basis for the analysis of a company. Each strand is equally important and both must be followed. Analysing a company's profitability without any reference to its financial position is of little value. Similarly, there is little point in completing a detailed analysis of a company's financial structure without reference to its performance. Profit is not sufficient on its own; a company must have the resources to allow it to continue in business and to flourish.

A common corporate objective is to achieve a level of profit necessary to satisfy shareholders' requirements – to add value to their investment. Without profit there can be no dividend or share value improvements, or reinvestment for future growth and development. A substantial part of this book focuses on various ways of identifying and measuring profitability. Shareholder value is more than just annual profit, and not everything is capable of quantification. Future expectations of a company's performance outweigh its historical track record in determining its share price – which probably offers as good an indicator as any of shareholder satisfaction. Chapter 5 offers some general guidelines for undertaking practical analysis.

When the analysis of a company is completed, the tables in Appendix 1 offer some benchmarks against which the ratios explained in Part 2 can be tested and compared. This reinforces the last lesson of financial analysis: comparison. Producing a series of ratios for one company can be useful in indicating trends in its performance, but it cannot confirm whether this is good, bad or indifferent. That can only be determined by applying the three rules stated earlier.

An important lesson from the downturn in the 1990s and the 2008 global financial crisis is to invest in a company only when you are absolutely certain you understand the business and sector within which it operates. If you cannot see where the profits are coming from, don't invest. If you cannot understand what the company does, don't invest. In all probability it is not a failure of your analytic ability but someone practising corporate legerdemain.

The question of whether to use rules or principles as the basis guidance in the preparation and presentation of financial statements appears to have been answered. Financial reporting now operates under a set of mainly principles-based accounting standards kept on the straight and narrow by additional guidance and professional auditors as necessary. The main objective of the International Accounting Standards Board (IASB) is "to develop, in the public interest, a single set of high quality, understandable and enforceable global accounting standards", and it is working with the Financial Accounting Standards Board (FASB) towards this.

Despite recent changes, the terminology of accounting and financial reporting remains much the same, though the importance attached to some has changed. Understanding the meaning of the terms "recognition", "fair value", "present value", "faithful representation" and others is essential to reading a set of accounts. This book is not intended to provide a detailed toolkit for financial report preparation but, rather, to give you confidence in using the information contained in an annual report. Throughout the book the FASB or IASB statements and terminologies are selected as being the most appropriate to clarify the item or topic being discussed. This is not a textbook. The aim is to provide you with some confidence in reading the accounts, and moving to the next level in your financial analysis and management competence.

As far as possible the book is written with a light touch. It is not intended to be read from start to finish – dip in as appropriate. If you find a section hard going – move on; it will be my fault not yours.

Companies get their momentum from people, and financial analysis of their activities is an art. Art combined with people should be fun: if it is not, you should leave it to those who enjoy it.

Bob Vause
August 2014

PART 1

Understanding the basics

1 The annual report – and what underlies it

AN ANNUAL REPORT contains two distinct types of information: quantitative – the financial statements; and qualitative – various reports and a management commentary. These are complex documents and often impenetrable – sometimes intentionally so. The increasing volume and detail of legislation, regulation, rules, accounting standards and codes of practice all contribute to this. The annual report tends to be too long and too complex, using mainly financial information that is unhelpful to the average reader. Accountants are acutely aware of these problems.

The main challenge facing the accounting profession is not just to continue to ensure that the balance sheet balances, but also to help companies in the production of an integrated annual report focusing as much on the quality of management's current and future involvement in the social, environmental, economic and ethical aspects of their business as on the bottom line of the income statement.

Each time there is a major corporate fraud or mismanagement, or a severe economic crisis, there is pressure either for a change in the role, duties and responsibilities of auditors or directors, or for the disclosure of additional or more detailed information. Deloitte Touche Tohmatsu, one of the "Big Four" professional services firms, estimated that in 1996 the average company report contained some 45 pages; today it is over 100 pages. In 2012 two UK-based banks, HSBC and Royal Bank of Scotland (RBS), published annual reports of more than 500 pages. A typical listed company can be expected to publish a 150-page report which takes more than two months to prepare and approve. There is ever-increasing emphasis on the internet as a means of paperless communication.

In December 1983 the Financial Accounting Standards Board (FASB) issued Statement of Financial Accounting Concept (SFAC) 5, "The Recognition and Measurement in Financial Statements of Business Enterprise", which stated that a full set of financial accounts of a company should consist of statements of:

- financial position at the end of the period;
- earnings in the period;
- comprehensive income for the period;
- cash flows during the period;
- investments by and distributions to owners during the period.

In 2013 the Financial Reporting Council (FRC) issued three Financial Reporting Standards (FRS), which, in effect, replaced all previous UK reporting standards and UK generally accepted accounting principles (GAAP) for non-listed companies. FRS 102 includes a description of the financial statements to be provided. International Accounting Standard (IAS) 1, "Presentation of Financial Statements", issued in 1997 and reviewed in 2011, was adopted by the International Accounting Standards Board (IASB) in 2001. This requires companies' annual reports to contain a:

- statement of financial position (balance sheet);
- statement of comprehensive income (profit and loss account);
- statement of changes in equity;
- statement of cash flows.

These four statements will be found in the annual reports of almost all listed companies. There will also be, where appropriate, comparative figures for the previous year. The financial statements produced by US companies follow US GAAP. UK and listed companies will comply with the IASB's International Financial Reporting Standards (IFRS).

Information on a company's financial position is mainly derived from the balance sheet and cash flow statement. The three basic accounting elements related to the balance sheet – assets, liabilities and equity – are discussed in Chapter 2. An assessment of company performance will focus on the income statement and the statement of changes in equity. Income and expense, the two basic elements involved in performance measurement from the income statement, are discussed in Chapter 3.

The annual report comprises three elements: narrative reporting, including the strategic report and the directors' report; governance statements, including those from the chairman and the directors' remuneration committee, nominations committee and the audit committee; and the financial statements and allied notes. A typical company annual report will contain:

- summary information or highlights;
- the chairman's statement;
- the chief executive officer's review of the business;
- a strategy review and directors' report;
- a corporate governance statement;
- a directors' remuneration report;
- a statement of directors' responsibilities;
- a nominations committee report;
- an audit committee report;
- an auditor's report;
- the financial statements;
- a statement of accounting policies;
- segmental information;
- a five-year history;
- shareholder information;
- notes to the financial statements.

UK companies should now provide a strategic report – previously there were requirements for the publication of an operating and financial review (OFR) or business review (BR). The strategic report is the equivalent to the management discussion and analysis of financial condition and result of operations (MD&A) statement appearing in US company reports. For UK companies the 2006 Companies Act, as amended in 2013, sets out company financial reporting requirements. Everything is covered, from the maintenance of the necessary financial records, application of accounting standards, the presentation of a "true and fair view" and the necessary audit requirements, to the issue and distribution of the annual report. The act allows companies to continue calling the statement of financial position the balance sheet. It also requires a strategic report to be published detailing company objectives, strategies and performance. You will probably find the full strategic report on a company's website with an edited version included in the annual report. Shareholders who opt not to receive a company's full annual report will often be sent the strategic review as an alternative source of information.

It is recognised that if the cost of collecting the information is greater than the benefit of providing it, it is not worth it. The report is expected to be timely. If information takes too long to collect, the report may lose its relevance. A listed company will normally publish its annual report within two months of the financial year end.

To read and use an annual report effectively, you need some understanding of the broad theory and the framework of financial accounting. In 1966 the American Accounting Association defined accounting as:

> *The process of identifying, measuring and communicating economic information to permit informed judgments and decisions by users of the information.*

The mechanics of double entry book-keeping do not need to be mastered. It is extremely unusual for a listed company to run into problems with debit and credit. The book-keeping process required to arrive at a statement of financial position that balances – a balance sheet – can be taken for granted. However, some background might be useful.

Double entry book-keeping

Italy claims to have been the first country in Europe to adopt double entry book-keeping. Luca Pacioli has the accolade of being the first to publish on the subject. In 1494 he wrote *De Computis et Scripturis*. Little is known of him beyond that he was an itinerant mathematics teacher, an unsuccessful gambler and ended up in a monastery. His book included, for the first time, details of the double entry book-keeping (debits and credits) system being used in Italy.

Under this system, sometimes referred to as "duality", every transaction has two entries in the books of account. Whatever amount is entered on the right-hand side (credit) of one account, the same amount is entered on the left-hand side (debit) of another account. This guarantees that at the end of the financial year it is possible to produce an income statement (profit and loss account) disclosing the profit or loss for the year and a balance sheet (statement of financial position) with assets (debit balances) equalling liabilities (credit balances). If whatever was entered on the left-hand side was also entered on the right-hand side, the total of the two sides of all the accounts must equal each other. The books must balance. In 1673 France had legislation requiring companies to prepare an annual balance sheet. It was not until the industrial revolution that book-keeping and financial reporting gained real impetus in Europe.

Who publishes accounts?

Every commercial business must prepare a set of accounts in order to agree its tax liability. The term "entity" is now used to describe any company or other business organisation. Even when the entity is a charity or otherwise tax exempt, accounts must still be prepared to allow those interested in its activities to assess the adequacy and probity of the management of its operations and assets. All public or nationalised enterprises are expected to produce and publish accounts in order to report not only to the state but also to the people. Any company in which the public has been invited to become involved must publish an annual report containing a set of financial statements (accounts). All other companies with limited liability submit accounts to the tax authorities each year and file them, thus making them available for public scrutiny.

Limited liability

Most trading companies have limited liability. This was introduced in the 1860s to provide shareholders with some protection against a company's creditors. Shareholders (stockholders) providing a company with capital, through the purchase of stocks and shares, cannot be forced to contribute any further money to the company or its creditors. Having paid the $1 or £1 for a share or unit of stock, they need pay no more. Should the company fail they can lose no more than the $1 or £1 invested; their liability is limited to this amount.

The corporate persona

A company is a legal entity separate from its managers and owners and is referred to as an entity in most accounting standards. It can make contracts, sue and be sued as an individual can. Financial statements are prepared as if the company were an individual. For the purposes of law and accounting, it owns assets and incurs liabilities. This is why the shareholders' stake in a company is shown as a liability. A company's net worth or equity is the amount the company owes to its shareholders. After having realised all assets and repaid all loans and creditors, the last act of a company, before it ceases to exist, is to pay what remains to the shareholders – the net worth of the company.

Private and public companies

A quoted or listed company is one whose shares can be bought and sold on a stock exchange. In the UK this is a public limited company (plc). The term "public" refers to the size of the share capital of the company, so a plc does not necessarily have its shares quoted on the stock exchange. Unquoted limited liability companies have "limited" (ltd) in their name. Most countries provide a distinction between public and private companies. For example, in France it is SARL and SA; Germany AG and GmBH; Italy Spa and Srl; the Netherlands NV and BV; Belgium NV and SPRL; Spain SA and SL. In the US various states have their own requirements, but most commonly "corporation" (Corp or Inc) is used for listed companies.

A quoted company must publish more information than a private company. This is to satisfy legislation and the requirements of the listing stock exchange. A private company cannot offer its shares for sale to the public, so different safeguards and reporting requirements apply compared with those for public or stock exchange listed companies. Private companies can be large organisations. In 2013 in the US there were 100 private companies with annual sales in excess of $4 billion, including Mars ($33 billion), which has "freedom" as one of its five key principles.

Listed companies usually give a preliminary statement of the year's financial performance within a few weeks of the end of their financial year; formal publication of the annual report follows soon after. For private companies, there can often be a considerable delay after the year end before a set of accounts is made public. This can make relevant analysis and comparisons difficult.

Ownership and management

Shareholders or stockholders of a private company are often directly involved in its management, often with members of the family acting as directors. Shareholders of a public company are much less likely to be directly involved in its management. The management of a public company, its directors and managers, is normally clearly separated from the owners of the company, its shareholders. The directors act as stewards of their shareholders' investment in the company and each year report the result of their management and the financial position of the company. In the UK "stewardship" was commonly used to describe the directors' relationship with their shareholders, but problems arose in translating this into other languages. "Accountability" is now the preferred term. At the annual general meeting (AGM) directors present the annual report and accounts to shareholders.

Consolidated accounts

Where one company, the parent company, has a controlling interest in other companies, its subsidiaries, it is necessary to prepare consolidated or group accounts. These incorporate all the activities of all the companies in the group to provide a set of consolidated accounts, including an income statement, statement of financial position and cash flow statement. Since the 1900s, UK and US companies have been required to publish consolidated or group accounts. The Seventh Directive on European harmonisation, revised in 2013, deals with group accounts, and since 1970 they have been mandatory for all EU companies. The objective of a set of consolidated accounts is to ensure that shareholders and others interested in the group of companies have adequate information upon which to assess its operations and financial position. IFRS 3 and IAS 27 deal with business combinations and consolidated financial statements.

In addition to the consolidated statement of financial position, UK groups must provide one for the parent company, though this is often relegated to the notes accompanying the annual report. There is no requirement to provide an income statement. The presentation of a parent statement of financial position is not required in the US.

Non-controlling interest

Where a subsidiary is not 100% owned, the non-controlling interest (NCI), outside or minority interest (MI) – the proportion of the subsidiary owned by those other than the parent company – is shown separately in the financial statements. Inevitably, some problems may arise in identifying ownership and control when there are pyramid structures of shareholdings.

All intra-group trading is eliminated to avoid double counting of profits, so only revenue from dealing with customers outside the group of companies is recognised in the income statement. However, non-controlling interests must be credited with their proportion of any profits flowing from intra-group trading. What remains belongs to the parent company.

Details of subsidiaries

With a group of companies, the annual report should provide full details of all subsidiaries. The name, business, geographic location and the proportion of voting or other shares owned by the parent company should be disclosed. If, during the year, a subsidiary has been sold or otherwise disposed of, details should be reported as part of the notes to the accounts on discontinued operations. Any gain or loss on disposal will also be disclosed separately.

Other influences on the annual report

EU Directives

In the UK and the US it is the accounting profession that oversees the development and implementation of accounting rules. In most of continental Europe a country's government takes on this role. In 1957 the Treaty of Rome set out the objectives for what has become the European Union (EU). Directives are issued which member countries are expected to incorporate into their own legislation. The Fourth Directive (1978) dealt with accounting principles, financial statements and allied information and imposed a standard format for the income statement and balance sheet. It also contained the true and fair view requirement in the preparation of the annual report. The Seventh Directive (1983) dealt with public quoted companies and the presentation of consolidated or group accounts, including the treatment of goodwill. This was adopted in the 1989 Companies Act in the UK. In 2013 the two Directives were consolidated. Since 2005 all EU listed companies have had to use IFRS as the basis for their financial reporting.

Stock exchange listing requirements

In the US the Securities and Exchange Commission (SEC) imposes reporting and disclosure requirements on all listed (quoted) companies, including the filing of 10-K reports (see below). In 2012 the Financial Conduct Authority (FCA) took over this responsibility in the UK.

The stock exchange also reinforces the application of accounting standards by requiring companies to provide a compliance statement and an explanation of any material deviations. The overall objective is to ensure that investors have appropriate information for their buy-hold-sell decisions. China has two stock exchanges, Shanghai (established in 1891) and Shenzhen. In 2005 the first Chinese company was listed on London's Alternative Investment Market (AIM).

Every company listed on a stock exchange must comply with its listing requirements. This may call for revision of the presentation and content of the financial statements. In 1993 Daimler-Benz complied with US GAAP when it became the first German company to be listed in New York. Today the adoption of IFRS provides an acceptable basis for a stock-exchange listing.

Companies with assets over $75m must file a 10-K report within 60 days of the year end. The SEC (www.sec.gov) provides a good introduction to the content of a 10-K report, *How to Read a 10-K*. The 10-K often contains more information and financial data than the traditional annual report – with no pictures or graphics to distract the reader – and is presented in a standardised format. In it are the audited financial statements together with a detailed overview of the business and its financial condition. Item 6, "Selected Financial Data", provides five-year financial information, linking with the more detailed three-year data in Item 8.

There is also a general description of the development of the business noting any material changes in the manner in which it is run. Item 7, "Management Discussion and Analysis of Financial Condition and Results of Operations", includes a discussion of management's view of the key risks the facing the business. There will also be a detailed segment analysis by product and/or geographical area, including the naming of any customer accounting for more than 10% of revenues.

The objectives of the annual report

The annual report was designed primarily to satisfy the information needs of existing and possible future shareholders. The financial reports are intended to assist and support their decision-making and to provide the basis for assessing the directors' management of their investment in the company. Financial statements are not only a historical review; they also aim to assist users to predict the timing, nature and risks of future cash flows.

The annual report is an important document, containing not only the statutory financial statements, tables, notes and management reports but also anything else that the company may wish to disclose. It is the formal report by directors to their shareholders of their performance during the year and the financial position of the company at the year end. It also has an important public relations role.

A listed company may have many thousands of shareholders,

and, though only a few hundred are likely to turn up for the AGM where the accounts are formally presented to shareholders, all will receive a copy or, more likely, have access to an electronic copy on the internet. Anyone else interested in the company may also request a copy. Producing the annual report, which is often supported by audio-visual materials and internet access, is therefore a significant cost; a listed company typically spends between $500,000 and $1m on this publication.

In 2010 the IASB approved *The Conceptual Framework for Financial Reporting (The Framework)*, replacing the one issued in 1989, which defined the prime objective of financial reporting as being:

> *To provide financial information about the reporting entity that is useful to existing and potential investors, lenders, and other creditors in making decisions about providing resources to the entity. These decisions involve buying, selling, or holding equity and debt instruments and providing or settling loans and other forms of credit.*

A company's annual report is also expected to provide information on the following:

- Economic resources, claims and changes in these. This enables users to assess current and future financial strengths and weaknesses, liquidity and solvency issues, and to predict future cash flows.
- Financial performance indicated by accrual accounting. This provides a better basis for assessing performance than simple cash in and cash out reporting.
- Performance reflected by past cash flows. This provides a sound basis for assessing performance and position and predicting future cash flows.
- Changes in economic resources and claims not resulting from financial performance. For example, if a company has issued shares during the year this will affect its economic resources, and users should be made aware of this.

Obtaining an annual report

The UK Companies Act requires listed companies to place their annual accounts on their website "as soon as reasonably practicable". The simplest way to obtain an annual report is to visit a company's website. All listed companies have one, usually with a separate "investor relations" section which includes financial information. There are also agencies offering to provide either hard-copy or downloaded annual reports. In the UK the *Financial Times* (annual report service) offers a user-friendly service at www.ft.com/annual reports.

Annual reports are filed by government agencies. All SEC listed companies in the US file their financial reports and other required information using Edgar (www.sec.gov/edgar.shtml) – a website that provides free access to all such information with the valuable ability to import the data directly into a spreadsheet (see Chapter 10).

In the UK, Companies House (www.companieshouse.gov.uk) collects company statutory accounts and associated information. A company's annual filing can be downloaded for a nominal £1 fee. In 2013 some 3.1m accounts were on file with more than 76% of companies providing information electronically. Companies House has launched the Free Accounts Data Product to assist public access to company information. Though not yet as user-friendly as Edgar, it will eventually offer a similar service.

Who uses annual reports?

The Framework says that financial reports are "prepared for users who have a reasonable knowledge of business and economic activity and who review and analyse the information diligently". Seven major users of the annual report can be identified. Companies are expected to provide information on their financial performance and position, the generation and use of cash, and financial adaptability in order to satisfy the information requirements of each user group.

Investors and their advisers

Probably the best concise explanation of the function of the annual report is found in the 2013 FRC *Guidance on the Strategic Report*:

The purpose of the annual report is to provide shareholders with relevant information that is useful for making resource allocation decisions and assessing management's stewardship.

Investors – shareholders or stockholders – are the principal target for annual reporting. The annual report is expected to provide them with a basis for assessing the current performance and position of their company as well as giving them some insight into its future prospects. It should also contain information on the strategy being adopted by the company to achieve its objectives including a description of its business model and its governance.

Shareholders range from individuals owning a few shares to institutions owning a large number, and it is a mistake to assume that the requirements of the two groups for information about the company are the same. Meeting the requirements of financial advisers, security analysts and shareholders in a single publication is a difficult task.

Although they own the company, shareholders do not have access to its internal management information systems. They have to rely on published reports to discover how their investment has been managed by directors during the previous year. Shares are normally acquired and retained for future income and capital growth. The annual report provides the basis for assessing past trends, but shareholders will be more interested in the level of dividends and capital growth they are likely to see in the future. In assessing this they will look at a range of measuring sticks covered in Part 2, including dividend cover, rate of return and debt/equity ratios.

The people who advise shareholders, those who earn a living on the strength of their analyses and forecasts of company performance, will look at a wider range of measures and focus closely on indicators of the potential risk of investing in the company. They are generally most interested in the likely future of the company.

Shareholders and power

The majority of shareholders in a typical listed company may make up to 60–80% of the total number of shareholders but own less than 10% of the issued shares. The bulk of the shares – and therefore effective control of the company – is almost always in the hands of a group of institutional shareholders, usually a few hundred. These will include insurance companies, trust and pension funds, banks, private equity funds and other financial institutions. In the UK individuals hold just over 10% of shares. Foreign investors now own close to 50% of UK and US equities.

It is not necessary to own 50% of the shares to control a company. In practice, holding 20% or more of a public company's shares provides a high degree of control over its actions. Typically, the term "controlling shareholder" is used to refer to a holding of more than 20% of a company's shares. US GAAP uses 20% equity ownership to define a "significant interest" (see Chapter 2). Details of anyone, excluding directors, owning more than 3% of a company's equity shares will be found in the annual report, and any transactions with a controlling shareholder will be described.

When a group of institutional shareholders get together to tackle a company they wield formidable power that cannot be ignored by even the most autocratic CEO or chairman. These are the shareholders that the directors must listen to and try to satisfy. They have a significant interest in the company. They are usually well informed and highly competent in financial analysis, and so are generally in a better position to know what is going on than small shareholders.

Lenders

Lenders – providers of long-term and short-term finance to a company – include not only banks, other institutions and wealthy individuals but also suppliers offering goods and services to a company on credit terms. They have strong incentives to assess the company's performance. They need to be assured that the company can meet the interest payments due on borrowed funds and that the loans they have advanced will be repaid when due. They are therefore likely to focus on profit and cash flow generating capability, and measures of liquidity, solvency and gearing (see Chapters 8 and 9). In assessing this, a company's creditors often rely on professional credit-rating agencies. There are three major agencies – Fitch, Standard & Poor's and Moody's – offering company and country ratings.

Credit ratings for a company can run from AAA (the highest rating) through BBB (adequate) to BB (speculative) to CCC (currently vulnerable) ending with C (bankrupt). A few months before Enron's collapse, Standard and Poor's gave the company's debt an AAA rating. Part of the fallout from the 2008 global financial crisis has been a further denting of credit agencies' reputations. In 2008 the International Organization of Securities Commissions (IOSCO) published a voluntary code of practice for credit-rating agencies. Gradually the agencies are winning back confidence – companies maintain a careful watch on their rating.

Suppliers

Suppliers need to satisfy themselves that if they provide goods or services on credit to a company they will receive payment. If the company is a major customer, it is important to gain some indication as to its long-term prospects and survival.

Employees and unions

Employees and their advisers or representatives turn to the annual report to help them assess a company's ability to continue to offer employment and the wages it can afford to pay. Employees who do not turn immediately to the pages detailing the directors' remuneration usually show greatest interest in information concerning the particular part of the business – the division, factory, section or department – in which they work. Evidence suggests they have less direct interest in, or sympathy for, the company as a whole.

Generally, employees have difficulty reading an annual report, which can create problems for corporate communication. Companies are therefore increasingly providing employees with a separate report, briefing, or audio-visual presentation that provides a clear summary of important matters.

Government and the taxman

Annual reports and the information filed with them may be used by the government for statistical analysis. Regulators will have an interest in the annual reports of companies under their control.

Company and personal taxation are often based on the statement of accounting profit given in annual reports. However, in most countries a company's tax liability is not fixed on the basis of the annual report but on a separate set of accounts and calculations produced for tax purposes and agreed with the tax authority. One exception to this is Germany, where a company's tax liability is fixed on the basis of the published accounts, and *Massgeblichkeitsprinzip* (the principle of congruency and bindingness) is the basis for net income definition. As a result, German companies can be expected to favour understating profits in the income statement, and understating assets and overstating liabilities in their financial statements.

Customers

Customers of a company will use its annual report to look for reassurance that it will be in business long enough to fulfil its side of any contracts it has with them. This can be particularly important in the case of, say, a large construction project or the installation of a complex management information system spanning several years, or the provision of a product or service where future continuity of delivery and quality is essential. The failure of a major supplier could have serious cost implications for the customer.

The public

The general public can also be expected to show interest in a company's annual report. They may be interested in the company's products or services, local investment and activities, or be considering taking employment with it.

Underlying the annual report

Before reading an annual report, it is sensible to have some appreciation of the basis upon which it has been prepared. Traditionally financial accountants, particularly auditors, were trained to be:

- Careful
- Cautious
- Conservative

- Consistent
- Correct
- Conscientious

These six Cs are still evident in the preparation and presentation of the annual report. Financial accounting and reporting are governed by what are referred to as assumptions, concepts, principles, conventions, elements and rules. These have evolved over many years. They have been moulded by experience and linked together to provide the framework for the construction of a set of financial statements. They are applicable to every country and company. The underlying assumptions in the preparation of an annual report are as follows.

Money quantification

If it is impossible to reliably place a monetary value on a transaction or an event, it cannot be recorded in the books of account. A rule of thumb for accountants is "if you can't measure it, ignore it". This is one reason accountants have such difficulties with intangibles (goodwill, brand names) or the qualitative aspects of a business. For example, the cost of a board of directors can be quantified to two decimal places and appear in the annual report each year. However, the question of what the directors are worth to the company is, at least for the accountant, impossible to answer and so they never appear in the balance sheet, as either an asset or a liability.

Accountants can be cautious in the treatment of intangibles or when quantifying difficult aspects of business costs and expenses. However, if it proves necessary for a measuring rod to be placed against anything, an accountant will prove well up to the task. For example, a company's employees could be quantified for inclusion in the balance sheet using human-asset accounting, and there is increasing pressure to quantify and report on the environmental aspects of a business.

Going concern

Each year financial statements are prepared on the assumption that they will form part of a continuing flow of such accounts. For all companies it can be assumed that the financial statements have been prepared on the going-concern basis. Directors consider that their company will continue trading for at least the next 12 months. In other words, it is a going concern. UK Listing Rules and the UK Corporate Governance Code require the annual report to contain a statement from the directors, checked by the auditors, that they consider their company to be a going concern.

Accrual

Merely looking at cash movements during the year and year-end cash balances will not provide a useful basis for assessing either performance or position. The income statement shows the revenue generated during the year and matches it with the costs and expenses incurred in producing it. Income and expenses are included in the income statement at the time the transaction or event took place. This is usually when an invoice is raised, not when the cash relating to the transaction is received or paid. An item is recognised – brought into the accounts – when it occurs, not when cash is received or paid. This is accrual accounting.

The accrual basis of accounting matches income and expenses for the financial year in the income statement without reference to their cash impact. The difference between the timing of the transaction and its translation into a cash movement is shown either as an accrual (money to be paid in a future time period) or a prepayment (money paid in advance for future benefit). This approach provides a much better basis for performance and position analysis and is the basis for all corporate reporting.

Recognition

Accounting standards refer to "recognition", meaning that an item has been entered in a company's financial records, the income statement or the balance sheet. Until an event or transaction has actually taken place it should not be taken into account (or recognised) in arriving at the profit or loss for the year. A major customer may, at the end of a company's financial year, promise a large order. This is good news for the company. It will be recorded in the management information and control systems, and plans may be made to adjust the order book and production schedules. However, until a formal and legally binding agreement is made and executed, nothing has occurred as far as the financial accounting system is concerned. No revenue can be brought into this year's account. The transaction has not yet taken place and so is quite correctly ignored in the financial statements. Profit is made or realised only when the transaction is completed. For example, a sale is recognised only when the transaction is completed by ownership of the goods passing to the customer.

An asset is recognised in the balance sheet only when its cost or value can be accurately measured and it is expected to provide future economic benefits to the company. A liability must be capable of measurement and an outflow of economic benefits will occur on its settlement.

Asset values may increase as a result of inflation or market changes. This is beneficial for the company but it cannot claim that it has made a profit. Unless the asset is sold, any increase in value must be retained in the balance sheet as part of the shareholders' equity. A profit can be recognised in the income statement only when the asset is sold.

The elements of financial statements

In 1985 FASB issued SFAC 6, which listed the ten elements relating to corporate financial statements. These still represent the building blocks used in the preparation and presentation of the annual report:

- assets, liabilities and equity;
- investments by and distributions to owners;
- comprehensive income;
- revenues and expenses;
- gains and losses.

It is easy to consider the term "comprehensive income" as a

relatively recent addition to financial reporting terminology. As the FASB's list above shows, this is not the case.

Generally accepted accounting principles

Over a number of years the accounting profession developed rules and guidelines of best practice, but it was not until the 1930s that these began to be written down and codified. Every country has developed a set of generally accepted accounting principles (GAAP), consisting of a mixture of legislation, stock exchange rules, accounting standards, conventions, concepts and practice. The aim of GAAP is to ensure that the preparation and presentation of financial statements conform to the current best accounting practice. A good source of information on different countries' GAAP is the Institute of Chartered Accountants in England and Wales (ICAEW) library (www.icaew.com/en/library).

The important words are "generally accepted" and "principles". GAAP do not comprise an unchanging set of written rules; they provide the skeleton upon which the financial statements must be fleshed out. As circumstances and theory and practice change so do GAAP. The People's Republic of China is developing its own GAAP. But most countries are now using IFRS and their individual GAAP have less relevance.

Who sets the standards for the UK and US?

Accounting standards in the US began to be developed in 1936 when, encouraged by the SEC, the American Institute of Certified Public Accountants (AICPA) set up the Committee of Accounting Procedures (CAP). In 1973 the FASB (www.fasb.org) replaced the CAP as the source of US financial accounting standards (FAS). The SEC supports these standards for adoption by all listed companies.

The FASB has the task of establishing and communicating US GAAP. Until 2009, US GAAP incorporated the FASB standards, technical bulletins, Emerging Issues Task Force (EITF) statements and interpretation guides. There were also AICPA research bulletins, interpretations and statements of position, and the Accounting Principles Board (APB) opinions. In 2009 the FASB initiated a major restructuring of reporting standards with the Accounting Standards

Codification (ASC) "to integrate and synthesize existing US GAAP and offer an online database" – the Codification Research System (CRS). In 2013 the US GAAP Financial Reporting Taxonomy (UGT), based on computer-readable Extensible Business Reporting Language (XBRL) tags (see Chapter 10), was issued. The FASB now provides listed companies in the US with a comprehensive online source of guidance for their financial reporting – the only source of US GAAP.

The ICAEW (www.icaew. com) began to issue Recommendations on Accounting Principles for the UK in 1942. In 1970 the Accounting Standards Committee (ASC) was set up, and its first Statement of Standard Accounting Practice (SSAP) issued in 1971. Between 1971 and 1990 24 SSAPs were issued. In 1990 the Financial Reporting Council (FRC – www.frc.org.uk) was established with its subsidiary, the Accounting Standards Board (ASB), replacing the ASC as the UK accounting and auditing standards setter, and was recognised under the 1985 Companies Act for this purpose. In January 2014 the FRC restated its mission as being "to promote high-quality corporate governance and reporting". The FRC co-operates with the IASB on the development of international financial reporting standards.

The FRC was reorganised in 2012. It now sets UK accounting standards – Financial Reporting Standards (FRS) – and is recognised by UK company law. It has two main committees. The Codes and Standards Committee provides advice on the maintenance of an effective framework of UK codes and standards and on corporate governance issues; it also co-operates with the various international accounting standards setters. The Conduct Committee monitors companies to ensure they comply with the 2006 Companies Act and FRS in their reporting. There are currently 30 FRS in issue. The aim is to promote and police high-quality corporate reporting. Companies may be required to amend their accounts if they do not satisfy the FRC. Financial Reporting Standards for Smaller Entities (FRSSE) are also issued.

FRS 102

The FRC recognised that there was little sense in having two separate sets of accounting standards: UK GAAP and IFRS. In March 2013 it published FRS 102, "The Financial Reporting Standard applicable in the UK and Republic of Ireland", updating and consolidating UK accounting standards. It is intended to ensure that a company's financial statements provide a true and fair view and became effective from 2014.

FRS 102 goes a long way towards bringing UK GAAP and IFRS into line. The fact that it is only some 300 pages long, compared with nearly 3,000 pages of UK GAAP, is impressive. It provides a much needed reference work for the preparation of financial statements. It will be revised as necessary every three years.

FRS 100 gives an overview of the financial reporting framework and FRS 101 deals with reduced disclosure by qualifying entities. From 2014 listed companies may choose to adopt FRS 101 and 102 in their reporting or continue with IFRS guidance.

International accounting standards

In 1973 the professional accounting bodies of Australia, Canada, France, Germany, Japan, Mexico, the Netherlands, the UK and the US formed the International Accounting Standards Committee (IASC). Over its lifetime it issued 41 International Accounting Standards (IAS – see list below).

In 2000 the SEC, the IOSCO and the EU endorsed the use of international accounting standards in company financial reporting. In 2001 the International Financial Reporting Standards Foundation was established and the International Accounting Standards Board (IASB) replaced the IASC as the international standard-setting body. The IASB is an independent private institution that issues international financial reporting standards (IFRS – see list below). The IFRS Foundation's objective is "to develop a single set of high-quality, understandable, enforceable and globally accepted International Financial Reporting Standards (IFRS) through its standard-setting body, the International Accounting Standards Board (IASB)".

The original objective of the IASB was to bring about the international convergence and harmonisation of corporate reporting through the adoption of a set of global standards. In 2006 the chairman of the IASB stated:

A common financial language, applied consistently, will enable investors to compare the financial results of companies operating in different jurisdictions more easily and provide more opportunity for investment and diversification. The removal of a major investment risk – the concern that the nuances of different national accounting regimes have not been fully understood – should reduce the cost of capital and open new opportunities for diversification and improved investment returns.

The IASB is supported by a technical advisory body, the Accounting Standards Advisory Forum (ASAF), which aims to improve global co-operation between standard setters and to advise the IASB as it develops IFRS. The International Financial Reporting Issues Committee (IFRIC) – previously named the Standing Interpretations Committee (SIC) – assists with the practical interpretation of IFRS. The EU and more than 100 countries apply IFRS.

The IASB website (www.iasb.org) contains detailed information on IFRS. Deloitte offers a useful website (www.iasplus.com) as does KPMG (www.KPMG.com/global). It is worth having a look at any of the large accounting firms' websites to see what is available and which you find easiest to work with.

Adopting IFRS

National GAAP still exist in Europe, but the EU has endorsed IFRS for listed companies – more than 7,000 now use these. US companies still look to the FASB for reporting guidance and some 15,000 listed companies apply US GAAP. In 2002 the IASB and the FASB signed the Norwalk Agreement to work together to improve financial reporting standards and eventually to achieve convergence – aligning US accounting standards with IFRS. The aim is to provide a basis for the provision of a "cohesive financial picture" of a company.

In 2013 the ASAF was set up to assist the IASB in its collaboration with FASB in the production of a set of globally accepted financial reporting standards. The word "convergence" is no longer used; the emphasis has shifted to the development of global standards.

From November 2007 foreign companies have been exempt from reconciling their accounts with US GAAP as long as they have

International Accounting Standards (IAS)

IAS 1   Presentation of Financial Statements
IAS 2   Inventories
IAS 7   Cash Flow Statements
IAS 8   Accounting Policies
IAS 10   Events after the Balance Sheet Date
IAS 11   Construction Contracts
IAS 12   Income Taxes
IAS 16   Property, Plant and Equipment
IAS 17   Accounting for Leases
IAS 18   Revenue
IAS 19   Employee Benefits
IAS 20   Accounting for Government Grants
IAS 21   The Effects of Changes in Foreign Exchange Rates
IAS 23   Borrowing Costs
IAS 24   Related-Party Disclosures
IAS 26   Accounting and Reporting by Retirement Benefit Plans
IAS 27   Consolidated and Separate Financial Statements
IAS 28   Accounting for Investment in Associates
IAS 29   Financial Reporting in Hyperinflationary Economies
IAS 31   Financial Reporting of Interests in Joint Ventures
IAS 32   Financial Instruments
IAS 33   Earnings Per Share
IAS 34   Interim Financial Reporting
IAS 36   Impairment of Assets
IAS 37   Provisions, Contingent Liabilities, and Contingent Assets
IAS 38   Intangible Assets
IAS 39   Financial Instruments: Recognition and Measurement
IAS 40   Investment Property
IAS 41   Agriculture

International Financial Reporting Standards (IFRS)

IFRS 1   First-Time Adoption of IFRS
IFRS 2   Share-Based Payment
IFRS 3   Business Combinations
IFRS 4   Insurance Contracts
IFRS 5   Non-current Assets Held for Sale and Discontinued Operations
IFRS 6   Exploration for and Evaluation of Mineral Resources
IFRS 7   Financial Instruments: Disclosures
IFRS 8   Operating Segments
IFRS 9   Financial Instruments
IFRS 10   Consolidated Financial Statements
IFRS 11   Joint Arrangements
IFRS 12   Disclosure of Interest in other Entities
IFRS 13   Fair Value Measurement
IFRS 14   Regulatory Deferral Accounts
IFRS 15   Revenue from Contracts with Customers

complied with IFRS. This has considerably eased the complexity and cost of listing for these companies.

A conceptual framework

The accounting standards setters are to be congratulated. Wading through a terrifying mix of linguistics and semantics, accounting theory and practice, national and professional body pressures, with big business and political "assistance" always available, they have managed to produce a usable framework for future international developments. A former chairman of the IASC made the case for accounting standards: "In a rapidly globalising world, it only makes sense that the same economic transactions are accounted for in the same manner."

In 1989 the IASC published the *Framework for the Preparation and Presentation of Financial Statements* (the Framework) to provide the basis for company reports and the principles upon which future accounting standards would be based. It was not an accounting standard but was intended to be the base reference point for all IFRS. This relieved individual accounting standards of the burden of restating definitions, principles or assumptions. The Framework, for the first time, provided definitions of asset, liability, income and expense. The underlying assumptions and qualitative characteristics of financial statements were also dealt with. In 2001 the Framework was adopted by the IASB to form the basis for its work in developing IFRS.

In 2004, following on from the 1989 Framework, the IASB and the FASB jointly began work on a conceptual framework for financial reporting. The first stages were published in September 2010 when the FASB issued SFAC 8, "The Objective of General Purpose Financial Reporting and Qualitative Characteristics of Useful Financial Information" replacing SFAC 1 and 2. The IASB published the same document as *The Conceptual Framework for Financial Reporting 2010.*

Progress on the joint FASB and IASB activity then slowed down and in 2012 the IASB decided to continue working alone. In 2013 a discussion paper of over 200 pages was published to provide the basis for the revision and amendment of the Framework, hopefully to be completed by the end of 2015. This was followed in January 2014 with a *Review of the Conceptual Framework for Financial Reporting*.

The FASB has been rules-based, producing detailed standards to be followed exactly by companies. Each time a standard was revised to overcome a specific problem it was not long before companies developed new means of avoiding its impact. The IASB has been more principles-based, with standards indicating the way to provide financial information rather than specific instructions. Paul Boyle of the FRC summed it up: "If you have a precise rule it also makes it possible to design something that is precisely just outside the rule."

The Framework provides the basic concepts that underlie the preparation of financial statements and allows standards to be principles-based rather than a set of detailed rules. There are pros and cons to both approaches. The collapse of Enron showed the shortcomings of the FASB approach, and the IASB's non-specific standards may make international comparisons difficult. Also the lack of precise guidelines can place auditors under considerable pressure. Neither approach is foolproof: and combining the two is taking time.

Fundamental qualitative characteristics

In the Framework, the IASB and the FASB identified two fundamental qualitative characteristics of financial information: relevance and faithful representation. If the financial information provided by a company is to be useful to investors, lenders and other creditors, it must incorporate these two characteristics.

Relevance and materiality

The information contained in the annual report must be relevant to users' needs. A company may show an asset in the balance sheet at a cost-based valuation. Cost is easy to find and reliable. However, the current market value of the asset – its fair value – is probably more relevant to those using the financial statements of the company. SFAC 8 and the IASB Framework see relevance and faithful representation as being the fundamental qualitative characteristics of a financial report. Relevance is defined as: "Relevant financial information is capable of making a difference in the decisions made by users."

Materiality is seen as one factor contributing to relevance. Only items of sufficient importance to influence the decisions the users of financial statements might take need to be disclosed. The intention is to ensure that all appropriate information is made available to such users. Materiality is not quantified by the IASB but left to the company to decide. This is a further example of principles-based rather than rules-based accounting standards:

> *Information is material if omitting it or misstating it could influence the decisions that users make on the basis of the financial information about a specific reporting entity.*

The 10% rule offers a rough guide to materiality in terms of size. For example, in segmental reporting, if a classification of sales revenue represents more than 10% of total revenues, it should be reported separately. IAS 1 makes clear that all material items, or classes of items (aggregation), should be shown separately in the financial statements. It also provides limitations to the "offsetting" (netting) of revenue and expenses or assets and liabilities, this being allowed only in limited cases.

Faithful representation

In the UK both the 1947 and the 1985 Companies Act make reference to the true and fair view requirement of financial reporting. The term was adopted in the EU's Fourth Directive but is not to be found in US GAAP. A definition of true and fair has never been provided in either UK legislation or EU Directive, but for some 50 years it remained the prime objective of company reporting. It was assumed that everyone knew what it meant.

In 2008 the FRC took a legal opinion that confirmed the overriding importance of the true and fair view in financial statements. Now, if a recently qualified accountant were asked to define the objective of an annual report, the reply would almost certainly include reference to "faithful representation" rather than a "true and fair view". FRS 102 explains that fair presentation or faithful representation is beginning to replace true and fair view.

The IASB and the FASB use the term "faithful representation" as the overriding objective of financial reporting. The application of US GAAP or IFRS, with additional disclosure when necessary, is presumed to result in a set of financial statements that achieve a faithful representation. This requires that the information contained in the financial statements should be accurate, timely, error free, unbiased and complete, and should clearly reflect the substance rather than the form of transactions and events.

It has long been agreed that financial statements should always adopt substance over form – "it's not what I say but what I mean". Merely to follow the legal form may not fully explain the commercial or business implications of what has occurred. It is more important for the basics of a transaction or event to be understood. FRS 102 and the 2006 Companies Act require that a company's financial statements should clearly reflect the economic reality of any material transaction or event that has taken place during the year. This is an essential contributor to faithful representation: "Transactions and other events should be accounted for and presented in accordance with their substance and not merely their legal form."

The annual report has a variety of users each with differing interests. It may be used as a basis for buying or selling a company's shares or even the company itself, or granting credit to, purchasing a product from, taking a job with, or lending money to a company. Because it is impossible in a single set of financial statements to meet all the requirements of all users, it is best for accountants to be cautious in presenting the figures. The 1989 Framework included "prudence" as a qualitative characteristic of financial reports.

To help avoid overoptimistic definitions of profit in the income statement or asset valuation in the balance sheet, accountants developed the rule of prudence, caution, or conservatism. Profit or asset values should never knowingly be overstated. For financial accounting and reporting this was condensed to:

- when in doubt take the lower of two available values;
- if still in doubt write it off.

The Framework made clear that prudence should never give rise to hidden reserves or excessive provisions – creative accounting. However, prudence in preparing and presenting the figures appearing in financial statements was seen as important. For example:

- value inventory at the lower of cost or fair value;
- write off potential bad debts immediately, not when all hope of collecting the money has evaporated;
- if there is any doubt about revenue, recognise it only when it is collected in cash;
- do not anticipate events – only include profits that have been realised during the year;
- take care to provide for all known liabilities and losses to date, although not to the extent of creating hidden reserves;
- recognise losses as soon as they are known, not when they happen.

The Framework does not include prudence as a separate characteristic of financial information. The argument is that using prudence to reflect conservative estimates of asset values is applying a bias and conflicts with neutrality:

> Understating assets or overstating liabilities in one period frequently leads to overstating financial performance in later periods – a result that cannot be described as prudent or neutral.

Faithful representation requires the information to be complete, neutral and free from error.

Enhancing qualitative characteristics

The Framework defines the four enhancing qualitative characteristics necessary for preparation of a relevant and faithfully presented financial report.

Comparability

A major dilemma for accountants is that accounting problems rarely have a single solution; usually there are several perfectly acceptable alternatives. This has given rise to the apocryphal story of a chief executive who is said to have advertised for an accountant with only one arm as he was tired of being told "on the one hand ... but then on the other hand ...".

The treatment of items in the preparation of a financial report is expected to be consistent, and thereby comparable, from year to year. A company could massage its profits for the year simply by changing its accounting policy: for example, by adjusting the inventory valuation or depreciation method. What may appear to be in the best interests of the company one year may not be in the next. If companies were allowed each year to change their methods of asset valuation and depreciation charging or the treatment of costs and expenses, it would be impossible to compare previous years' financial statements with the current ones. These financial statements would be of little value in comparing the performance and financial position of a company over a number of years and with that of other companies. Without consistency in presentation there can be no comparability.

Unless there is a statement to the contrary, it can be assumed that the underlying accounting policies for the preparation of this year's financial statements are the same as for the previous year. As far as possible, from one year to the next, there should be consistency of terminology, calculation and presentation of all items included in the financial statements to allow comparisons to be made.

Companies can of course correctly decide to change an accounting policy in order to improve the quality of information being provided. When this occurs the notes in the annual report should clearly state the nature of the change and the reasons for it. SFAC 8 provides the guidelines for changing an accounting policy.

Verifiability

For users of a financial report to have confidence in its content they must be sure that the information it contains is capable of independent verification. Two equally competent users of a financial report should reach similar conclusions, though not necessarily complete agreement, as to whether or not they have been given a faithful representation upon which to base their analysis.

Timeliness

If the information is to provide any real benefit to users it must be available in time for them to incorporate it in their decision-making.

Understandability

The Framework sees the typical user of an annual report as having "a reasonable knowledge of business and economic activities", and who "reviews and analyses the information diligently". The annual report should be prepared with a view to being readable by the average user – small-print notes can meet the needs of experts.

Cost constraints in financial reporting

It will never be possible to fulfil all users' information requirements in a single annual report. Weighing cost against benefit will always be important. It is recognised that information has an associated cost – and this is the overriding constraint in information provision. If the cost of gathering or presenting the information is greater than the benefits of its availability, it is not worth the effort.

Statement of accounting policies

When reading the financial statements in an annual report it can be assumed that all the appropriate assumptions and qualitative characteristics have been applied. The overriding requirement for financial statements, and the objective of accounting standards, is to give a faithful representation. IAS 1 requires companies to explain the measurement basis used in preparing the financial statements and also to disclose anything else relevant to understanding them. IAS 8 states that "the specific principles, bases, conventions, rules and practices applied to an entity in preparing and presenting financial statements" should be described in the accounting policies statement.

For each major item companies are expected to comply with GAAP and with all applicable accounting standards. A statement of compliance is normally found within the accounting policies statement. Where there is no applicable standard, management is expected to use appropriate judgment in the selection of the accounting policy to apply in its presentation and to disclose this.

A statement of accounting policies will normally include:

- the basis of preparation of consolidated financial statements;
- conformity with appropriate accounting standards;

- foreign currency translation;
- the treatment of intangible assets;
- the valuation of non-current assets;
- employee benefit calculations;
- income tax calculations;
- details of financial instruments.

It can be assumed that a company's accounting policies will be applied consistently from year to year. A company can change an accounting policy if this is required by a new standard, or the change will improve the relevance or reliability of the information being presented. Any changes in accounting policies will be set out in the annual report. When a company makes any such change, you should read the auditor's report to see if it gives the company a clean bill of health. If the auditors believe that some aspect of the financial statements does not comply with legislation, accounting standards or GAAP, they have a duty to make this clear in their report to shareholders.

Auditors

Every listed company must employ an independent professional auditor. Auditing developed in the 19th century to protect shareholders' interests. Auditors are professional accountants who check the accounting records and all other relevant sources of data and information, and report that the financial statements give a true and fair view or faithful presentation, and have been properly prepared in accordance with all relevant legislation, IFRS and appropriate GAAP – the financial reporting framework.

Auditors are independent of management. They are employed by the shareholders, not the directors of the company. They report directly to shareholders at the AGM. In the UK, the main professional body is the ICAEW, and in the US it is the AICPA.

All countries have many firms of auditors dealing with small and medium-sized companies, but for listed companies, particularly if they are multinational, there are only a few suitable auditing firms. These are capable of offering full professional services anywhere in the world. They are as multinational as any company they may deal with and their names are well known. The largest, "the Big Four", and their 2013 fee income are:

- Deloitte Touche Tohmatsu ($32.4 billion);
- PricewaterhouseCoopers ($32.1 billion);
- Ernst & Young ($25.8 billion);
- KPMG ($23.4 billion).

Size is important. A small firm of auditors, threatened with losing the business of a major company, might find the prospect made it more amenable to management's wishes. A large firm might not like losing the account any more than a small one, but it would not miss the income to the same degree. Bernard Madoff's $50 billion hedge fund relied on being audited by a three-person firm: a 78-year-old retiree and two assistants. This fact alone should have set alarm bells ringing well before the fraud was discovered at the end of 2008.

However, experience of corporate misadventure through the 1990s and the 2008 global financial crisis cast doubt on the effectiveness of large auditing firms as a safeguard to shareholders. One particular problem in the 1990s was that, in general, for every $1 charged to a company for audit fees, professional firms seemed to generate more than $1 of non-audit-related income. Can complete independence be guaranteed if the auditing firm is reliant on consultancy or other fees from the same company?

Sarbanes-Oxley Act

In 1996 Alan Greenspan, then chairman of the US Federal Reserve, warned investors against "irrational exuberance", and in 2002 he warned them of "infectious greed". At the start of the new millennium there were a number of financial reporting frauds, the most infamous being Enron, a US energy and commodities company. In October 2001 Enron declared that as a result of "accounting errors", it was reducing after-tax net income by $544m and stockholders' equity by $1.2 billion. A further restatement was offered in November with bankruptcy coming in December. In one year, Arthur Andersen, then one of the largest international audit firms, received $25m for audit-related activities from Enron and $27m for consultancy work. In June 1999 Rite Aid, a US drugstore chain, where the SEC found "widespread accounting fraud schemes" resulting in an overstatement of profits between 1997 and 1999 of some $1 billion, paid its auditors $1.5m in consultancy contracts.

In 2002 186 large US companies filed for bankruptcy, with WorldCom owing over $100 billion. And, not to be outdone, in 2003 Italy contributed Parmalat, a multinational dairy and food company, to the list of giant companies failing in questionable circumstances in Europe's largest ever bankruptcy. In 2002 the Public Company Accounting Reform and Investor Protection Act, referred to as the Sarbanes-Oxley Act (SOX), was passed. Self-regulation ended for the auditing profession. The Dodd-Frank Act of 2010 set up the Financial Stability Oversight Council (FSOC), which has the task of promoting financial stability for banks and other financial institutions.

The SOX created the Public Company Accounting Oversight Board (PCAOB) to protect investors and ensure full, transparent corporate reporting and the application of the highest auditing standards. To achieve this audit reports are expected to be "informative, accurate and independent". With the support of the SEC, the PCAOB sets the standards for auditing (AS) and auditors, and oversees the Generally Accepted Auditing Standards (GAAS). Firms are banned from undertaking non-audit work for companies they audit. The PCAOB is working towards the improvement of both auditing standards and the content of the auditor's report.

In the UK the FRC contributes to the development and application of auditing standards through the Auditing Practices Board (APB). In 2012 it published *The Auditor's Report on Financial Statements* to support the move towards expanding the auditor's report to include more positive information to assist the understanding of a company's financial statements.

Most countries have a set of auditing standards that are mandatory for members of the auditing and assurance profession. The Auditing Standards Board (ASB) has this role in the US and the FRC provides standards and guidance for UK auditors.

Auditor's report

The purpose of an audit is to provide an expert and independent view of a company's financial statements. It is primarily designed for the shareholders. The auditor's report normally describes the respective responsibilities of management and the auditor for the preparation and presentation of the financial statements, and the basis upon which the audit was conducted, and ends with a formal opinion. The auditor's opinion is the item of prime interest in an audit report – do the financial statements give a true and fair view? Does the auditor give the company a clean bill of health or is there any cause for concern?

If appropriate there will also be discussion of any key (IAASB) or critical (PCAOB) audit matters (KAM or CAM) representing the significant issues arising during the audit. The audit report should confirm that the financial statements have been prepared properly in accordance with an appropriate financial reporting framework – IFRS, GAAP – and any relevant legislation. There should also be some information on the approach taken by the auditor in completing the audit. ISA 700 requires auditors to describe any material risks they saw as having an impact on their audit strategy.

ISA 700, "Forming an Opinion and Reporting on Financial Statements", is the primary guide for auditor reporting standards in the UK. Auditors learn a considerable amount about the company they are auditing. It would obviously be beneficial if this information were shared with users of the financial statements. Since 2014 the UK audit report has become a more valuable document. Auditors are encouraged to prepare an "Auditor's Commentary". This should explain the work they carried out and describe the key points they discovered that have a bearing on the understanding of the financial statements.

The auditor's report will include an opinion on the accounts. In the US the audit report is likely to include the following: "In our opinion the financial statements present fairly, in all material matters, the financial position of the company, and the result of its operations and its cash flows for the year in conformity with US GAAP." A typical UK report will contain: "In our opinion, the financial statements give a true and fair view of [or present fairly, in all material aspects] the financial position of the company ... and the results of operations and its cash flows for the year in accordance with IFRS or GAAP." The report will also comment on the appropriateness of management's use of the going-concern assumption in preparing the financial statements.

For a UK listed company the audit can be expected to take, on average, some 60 days to complete. The annual report will include details of the auditor's fees for the statutory audit and any non-audit fees. The statutory audit fees for a large multinational company can range from $5m to $50m. In 2012 the top four UK banking groups all paid more than £20m for their audit, with Barclays heading the list at £35m. Royal Dutch Shell paid £28m, GlaxoSmithKline £14m, Diageo £6m and Marks & Spencer £2m.

In 2014, to comply with the UK Corporate Governance Code, PricewaterhouseCoopers, which had been Marks & Spencer's auditor since 1926, handed over to Deloitte. Its final audit report provides a good example of the new format.

With the changes made to ISA 700 it is worth reading the auditor's report. Auditors have welcomed the opportunity to share their knowledge of a company's operations and explain what work they have carried out. The auditor's report may contain some useful information to assist your understanding of the company and in the framing of your analysis of the financial statements.

Qualified report

Always read the auditor's report. It is extremely important. An independent professional accountancy firm has studied the preparation and presentation of the company's financial statements and provided an opinion as to the level of confidence you can place in them. When auditors feel it necessary to make public any concerns they have this should influence any view taken of the company, its management and its future. If auditors are not satisfied with any aspect of the information provided to them or in the preparation and presentation of the financial statements, they have a duty to draw this to shareholders' attention. They qualify their report.

The auditors will detail the area of concern and indicate how this may influence the standing of the company. A qualified report on the application of an accounting standard or a change in accounting policy may reflect nothing more than a basic disagreement on principle between auditor and management and is not necessarily a serious problem. However, an auditor might state, for example: "This indicates the existence of a material uncertainty, which may cast significant doubt on the company's ability to continue as a going concern."

This is about as bad as it can get, and makes the auditor's report the most important page in the annual report. In effect, the auditor is saying, there is a likelihood that this company will fail.

The last resort of an auditor is to resign. In 2008 the third largest travel operator in the UK, XL Leisure Group, failed, leaving thousands of people stranded abroad, and many thousands more lost their pre-booked and paid-for holidays. In 2006 the auditors had resigned from the audit of one of the main XL subsidiaries after deciding there were "material errors" in the financial statements and warned that as a result these did not "give a true and fair view of the profit and state of affairs of the company".

Auditors and fraud

It is a common misapprehension that the auditor's main role is to search for fraud. The detection of fraud is the responsibility of management and others involved in the governance of the company. An 1896 legal case in the UK provided a useful definition of the auditor as "a watchdog not a bloodhound". That a company has a clean audit report does not guarantee that there has been no fraud or, indeed, that the company will not fail the day after the annual report is published. In 2006 the Association of Certified Fraud Examiners (ACFE) published research suggesting that only 10% of fraud was initially detected by auditors, whereas 40% was disclosed by whistle-blowers. Traditionally, auditors were employed only to ensure the presentation of a set of financial statements that provided a true and fair view.

The IAASB recommends that auditors should maintain a healthy level of scepticism as they endeavour to "identify and assess the risks of material misstatement of the financial statements due to fraud". In the US auditors have responsibility for designing and completing an audit that gives "reasonable assurance that the financial statements are free from material misstatement either by fraud or error".

Auditors must satisfy themselves that the company's internal control systems are adequate. It was a combination of less-than-effective auditing and sloppy internal management control that led to the demise of Barings Bank in 1995.

Directors are required to make clear that they have complete confidence in their internal control systems, and that they consider the financial statements free from fraud and material misstatement. Auditors also make sure that the information contained in the directors' report is consistent with the financial statements.

From the end of 2014 it is likely that companies will have to change auditors at least every ten years. This will help avoid auditors becoming too cosy with their clients. In Italy auditors must change every nine years. When Deloitte took over the audit of Parmalat the company's financial problems were soon recognised, leading to Europe's biggest corporate bankruptcy.

Bannerman and liability limitation

Bannerman Johnstone Maclay was the auditor of a company that failed in 1998 owing some £13m to RBS. In 2002 RBS sued the auditor, claiming that the financial accounts had misstated the true position of the company. This proved to be an important case (referred to as Bannerman) defining the duties and liabilities of auditors. The auditor claimed there was no duty of care to third parties, but lost the case. The judge ruled that as the auditor had not made it clear it was denying any duty of care to third parties using the audit report, it could be assumed that this duty was accepted. The absence of any disclaimer was the key. An appeal in 2005 was dismissed. Following the Bannerman ruling PricewaterhouseCoopers was the first major firm to change its audit opinion statement to include: "We do not, in giving this opinion, accept or assume responsibility for any other purpose or to any other person to whom this report is shown or in whose hands it may come save where expressly agreed by our prior consent in writing."

Most audit reports now contain a "Bannerman disclaimer" – the auditors do not accept any responsibility to third parties using the annual report.

It is now common for auditors, in agreement with a company's directors and shareholders, to set limits to their liability. In the UK they are allowed to apply to shareholders for a liability limitation agreement (LLA). Most EU countries have some form of limit to auditors' liability.

Management accountability for information disclosure and control

The chief executive and chief financial officer must certify that they consider the financial statements to be accurate and that they have established, maintained and evaluated all appropriate disclosure controls and procedures. Directors are expected to take responsibility for the effectiveness of the internal control system, and each year to review and report on it in the annual report. They should report that "the financial statements, and other financial information included in the report, fairly present in all material respects the financial condition and result of operations".

UK Listing Rules require directors to provide a going-concern statement. This indicates that they consider their company will continue in business for at least the next year and that they have no intention of liquidation. If this were not the case, the valuation of assets and liabilities in the balance sheet could change dramatically. In 2009 the FRC supported the view that the going-concern concept underlies all the financial statements and offered guidance to companies on its application.

Directors have accepted responsibility for full disclosure in financial reports and are personally responsible. Auditors require a guarantee of the quality of the information provided to them.

Corporate governance

The annual report often contains examples of senior managers in photogenic poses together with an organisation chart, but these are of little practical assistance in understanding how the company is actually being managed. What are its strategic objectives and how are they to be achieved? Answers to these questions are needed before reaching any conclusions based on quantitative analysis of the financial statements. In the 1990s, after a series of examples of blatant mismanagement (if not fraud) in public companies, corporate governance became a major issue in both the UK and the US. Additional disclosure was demanded so that shareholders and others interested in a company might gain confidence in its management and likely future viability.

In the UK in 1998 the Hampel Committee concluded that a board of directors should always act in the best interests of its shareholders and in doing so adopt the highest principles of corporate governance. Hampel reinforced and expanded on the recommendations of the Committee on the Financial Aspects of Corporate Governance (Cadbury Code, 1992) and the Greenbury Code (1996). The result was the publication of the Combined Code on Corporate Governance. This was followed in 1999 by the Turnbull Committee, which dealt with the internal control of companies, the Higgs Committee (2003), which looked at the effectiveness of non-executive directors, and the Smith Committee (2003), which dealt with audit committees.

Corporate governance encompasses how a company is managed, its operational framework, accountability and responsibilities, its interaction with society, and what dictates its behaviour. Probably the best definition of corporate governance was produced by the Cadbury Committee – "the system by which companies are directed and controlled".

Boards of directors are responsible for the governance of their companies. The shareholders' role in governance is to appoint the directors and the auditors, and to satisfy themselves that an appropriate governance structure is in place. The responsibilities of the board include setting the company's strategic aims, providing the leadership to put them into effect, supervising the management of the business and reporting to shareholders on their stewardship. The board's actions are subject to laws, regulations and the shareholders in general meeting.

In 2012 the FRC published the UK Corporate Governance Code, replacing the Combined Code, which was applicable to all UK listed companies from October that year. The UK Stewardship Code, which provides guidance on good practice for communication between directors and investors, should be seen as a companion to this code. It is aimed at institutional investors in an attempt to improve their role as active participants in the corporate governance of their investments and their stewardship responsibilities.

To find out how a company is managed, and how well it is doing, read the information provided to comply with the code. If a company is not complying with the code, it must explain why – "comply or explain". The code is reviewed every two years. It is not a set of rules but is based on principles, offering a guide to best practice, and has five main sections. In its 2011 and 2012 annual reports Marks & Spencer, a multinational retailer, made good use of these as the framework for its management discussion. The five sections are as follows:

- **Leadership.** The chairman is responsible for leading and running an effective board with clearly identified roles – including non-executives – which has collective responsibility for the achievement of the company's long-term goals and success.

- **Effectiveness.** The board should have the appropriate set of skills and experience necessary to successfully run the company. Each year directors are evaluated as to their competence and contribution. The appointment of new directors and re-elections should be transparent.

- **Accountability.** Each year the board should confirm that the company is a going concern and, identifying the main risks to be faced, present a "fair, balanced and understandable" description of the company's position and future prospects. This should allow understanding of how the company intends to generate or preserve value in the long term. The company's business model and the strategy to be followed to deliver its objectives should be made clear.

- **Remuneration.** The executive remuneration packages should be transparent and the level and components of remuneration clearly defined. Any performance-related benefits should directly assist the achievement of the long-term objectives of the company. Everything relating to this now somewhat contentious issue should be dealt with in a separate report from the remuneration committee, which should comprise a least three independent non-executive directors.

■ **Investor relations.** The chairman is expected to lead the board in a continuing dialogue and interaction with investors. The senior non-executive director should also be involved in the communication to major shareholders of the company's governance and strategy.

Audit committee

In 1999 the New York Stock Exchange (NYSE) and the National Association of Securities Dealers Automated Quotations (NASDAQ) made independent audit committees a requirement for all listed companies, reinforced in 2002 by the Sarbanes-Oxley Act. In 2006 the EU's Eighth Directive followed the same pattern. The UK's Corporate Governance Code has a similar requirement for the establishment of an audit committee. In 2012 the FRC issued detailed guidance on the process of working with the auditor. The annual report should contain a report from the audit committee on its activities during the year. Full information, including its terms of reference, will probably be found on a company's website. In the UK, shareholders are given the opportunity to vote on whether they consider the audit committee's report provides sufficient information. The audit committee has taken over from management the responsibility of overseeing the appointment, remuneration and terms of reference of the auditor.

The chairman's report

Each year the chairman is expected to publish a report. A chairman can say whatever he or she wants, and this is not subject to strict audit. It is a personal statement in which almost anything goes, from attacking the government to spreading a little homespun philosophy. It is unusual for it to take up more than two pages at the beginning of the annual report. Whatever the company's performance, the language used is normally biased towards the positive in an attempt to give a good impression; this is referred to as the "Pollyanna effect".

If things are going well, this can be claimed as the result of positive management action and the language is clear and simple. When performance has been poor the language is more technical, with blame placed on the environment or other non-controllable factors.

The UK Corporate Governance Code encourages the chairman to describe how the principles of the code have been applied to the role and effectiveness of the board in running the company. There is normally an overview of performance, often with only the bright spots highlighted, and a comment on the general business outlook. It is rarely found to be downbeat and is almost certain to be biased – so read it with caution and healthy scepticism. A chairman's performance at the AGM is likely to be more significant than the written report. It should be possible to watch this on the company's website.

The directors' report

The directors' report normally provides personal details of each director and details of any changes to the board during the year (new appointments or retirements). At the AGM directors will be put forward in rotation for re-election with a formal vote by shareholders taking place at the meeting.

Directors are accountable to shareholders. They have overall responsibility for the management of all a company's assets and equity. Part of their responsibility involves providing shareholders with not only financial statements but also adequate information on the principal aspects of the business. The director's report will give details of the principal activities of the company. The dividend to be proposed at the AGM will also be disclosed. At the AGM shareholders have the opportunity to raise any questions they wish. One of the principal tasks of a company's chairman is to manage the AGM.

Management commentary

The annual report should include a management commentary (MC), referred to as the strategic report (SR) in the UK and the management discussion and analysis (MD&A) statement in the US. The MD&A became an SEC requirement in 1980, the intention being to allow investors to see the company "through the eyes of management".

Companies listed in the US must also file an annual 10-K report, which may be used as an alternative to the full annual report. It contains the MD&A, 3–5 years' selected financial data, a listing of the important risk factors facing the company and details of the auditors and their fees.

Following amendments to the UK Companies Act in 2013, the SR replaced the business review and the operating and financial review (OFR) for UK listed companies. The SR should offer a fair, balanced and comprehensive review of the company's business and analysis of performance during the year. A description of the principal risks and uncertainties being faced should also be included. If the directors consider that there is anything that might affect the company's future development, performance and position, they should draw this to shareholders' attention. The auditor's only duty is to ensure that the SR is consistent with the financial statements.

The SR is seen as a way of helping investors form a view as to the competence and success of the directors in running the business during the year and the viability of the year-end financial position (see Chapter 10 for more details).

Key performance indicators (KPIs) may be used to assist in understanding a company's activity and performance. These can be financial or non-financial measures used in the management of operations. Financial measures are typically defined in terms of profit, revenue, return on capital, shareholders' return and cash flow. Non-financial measures may be concerned with customer satisfaction, product lines, environmental issues, health and safety.

The MC is a good starting point for studying a company. Though aimed at shareholders, it is intended to be read and understood by anybody and therefore is relatively free of specialist terminology and jargon. If figures are included, such as those concerned with gearing or earnings per share, they should be clearly linked with those appearing in the financial statements. There should be a reference to accounting policies with a full discussion of any changes in the way in which the financial statements have been prepared or presented. Increasingly, companies are moving beyond explaining what they do and beginning to explain and discuss their business objectives and business model. The business model describes how a company creates value; you will find a good example in Marks & Spencer's 2012 annual report.

The MC should not just focus on good news and victories, as is so often the case with statements by the chairman or CEO. It should provide a basis for assessing how successful a company's strategy has been and what the likely prospects are for the future. It would be unreasonable to expect a company to publish its corporate plan, but it should discuss business trends. Each year the MC sets out the historical performance and activity of the company together with some indication of management's view of likely future developments. Any major deviation from these should be explained the following year. It is intended to "assist the user's assessment of the future performance of the reporting entity by setting out the directors' analysis of the business".

Ideally, there are three sections offering a description of the business, its objectives and overall strategy; its actual performance; and its financial position. The qualities of comprehensibility and comparability should be evident.

The AICPA set up a committee to study the relevance and usefulness of business reporting. The Jenkins Report, published in 1994, offered six broad headings for the MD&A:

- Financial information
- Operating data
- Management analysis of the business
- Forward-looking information
- Information about management and shareholders
- Company background, objectives and strategy

The intention is to produce a plain-language report incorporating the basic qualitative financial information attributes already described in this chapter for financial reporting.

The MC should be based on the information used internally by management in running the company, with the main focus on how it intends to create long-term value for shareholders. It should be forward-looking and directly related to management's plans describing the opportunities, risks and uncertainties the company faces. Non-financial measures supporting a view of performance should be incorporated.

Pro-forma figures

When faced with uncertainty, poor performance, or the need to hide incompetence or fraud, directors may be attracted to presenting "pro-forma" figures in their reports to investors. They develop their own measures of performance that do not necessarily correlate with the published financial statements or support objective analysis.

If the terms "adjusted", "normalised" or "underlying" are used in the review of a company's performance, be on your guard. Examples of such measures may be found in the use of earnings before interest, taxation, depreciation and amortisation (EBITDA – see Chapter 6). A company showing a loss in its published income statement could produce a positive EBITDA figure. If in the discussion of performance management choose to use a measure other than one firmly based on the reported financial figures and GAAP, a clear explanation must be provided.

The hindsight factor

There is only one attribute needed to ensure perfect financial analysis and investment: hindsight. A few days after a major event anyone can articulate precisely what occurred and the impact it had on a company and its share price. Parmalat is an example. In its annual report in one year it claimed to have sold enough milk powder to Cuba to provide more than 50 gallons of milk for every person in the country. After the event it is difficult to see how this was not questioned. But as it was published by a large and historically successful company, perhaps not – there was no reason to even think about doubting the figures.

It is easy to criticise the annual report as an ineffectual document. There are numerous examples of companies failing shortly after publishing apparently healthy figures. With hindsight there may have been clear evidence of directors' incompetence, if not misrepresentation and fraud. It is often the poor auditors who bear the brunt of criticism over their apparent inability to discover and draw attention to the real situation before shareholders lose their investment. However, the annual report is all we have, so we have to make the best use of it that we can.

2 The statement of financial position

THE BASIS OF FINANCIAL ANALYSIS is the ability to read the accounts. This is a necessary skill for any manager and essential for those with ambitions for a seat on the board. The balance sheet is one of the key financial statements provided by a company in its annual report. It is sometimes called a statement of assets and liabilities. Recent accounting standards and company legislation have introduced the title "statement of financial position", but it seems likely that balance sheet will continue to be used for some time yet. Those with little or no financial knowledge often view it as a puzzle, and one best left alone. Others see it as the pinnacle of the accountant's necromantic art, with some spectacular effects but no real substance.

The balance sheet provides much of the data and information necessary to support the analysis of a company's performance and position. It is the starting point for an assessment of a company's liquidity and solvency (Chapter 8), gearing (Chapter 9) and the calculation of rates of return on assets, capital or investment (Chapter 6).

Presentation
Proof of the book-keeping

Originally, a balance sheet was prepared at the end of the financial year to provide proof of the accuracy of the double entry book-keeping system. It listed all the balances in the books of account at the end of the year – hence the name. If the two sides of the account balanced, with assets (debit balances on the left-hand side) equalling liabilities (credit balances on the right-hand side), it could be assumed that proper records had been maintained throughout the year.

The statement of financial position can be viewed as a set of old-fashioned kitchen scales. On one side is a bowl containing the assets (items of value a company owns or has a right to receive in the future), and on the other side is a bowl containing the liabilities (amounts a company owes to its shareholders and others providing finance and credit). For any business, one side of the scales represents what it has got and the other where it got the money from. The two sides must balance. It is not possible for a business to have more assets than sources of finance, to use more money than is available, or to have more finance available than is used.

The year-end position

The balance sheet originated as the final statement in the book-keeping process and was never intended to show the value of a business. It was one of a continuing chain of year-end accounts. The statement of financial position continues to fulfil its role as the final proof of the books of account, but in recent years it has gained a more central role in financial reporting.

The balance sheet can be seen as presenting the fair value of assets and liabilities at the end of the year; the income statement contains the changes in them over the year. Changes in shareholders' equity are dealt with separately. The income statement shows the change in the wealth of the company from year to year; the balance sheet, taking into account all income and value changes, shows its financial position at the end of each year. FRS 102 states that the "financial position of an entity is the relationship of its assets, liabilities and equity as of a specific date". This financial statement provides a snapshot of the financial state of a company at the year end, setting out is financial position on the last day of the financial year. The basic equation is:

$$\text{Assets} = \text{liabilities}$$

In the 2010 Conceptual Framework the IASB defined an asset as "a resource controlled by the entity as a result of past events and from which future economic benefits are expected to flow to the entity". A liability was defined as "a present obligation of the entity arising from past events, the settlement of which is expected to result in an outflow from the entity of resources embodying economic benefits".

Under the rules of double entry book-keeping, assets appear on the left side of the balance sheet and liabilities on the right. The UK was an exception to this rule, with companies displaying assets on the right-hand side of the balance sheet. This idiosyncratic behaviour dated back to the 1860s, when a civil servant made an error in the example of balance sheet presentation incorporated in a Companies Act. Assets were shown on the right instead of the left, and UK accountants followed the letter of the law for more than 100 years.

What to show

Traditionally, attention focused on the income statement as disclosing the profit or loss for the year. Income and expenses were matched for the year and any "leftovers" taken to the balance sheet. It was the calculation of the profit or loss for the year that was seen as most important. The balance sheet took second place as a less important statement.

The emphasis on fair value reporting has meant that the balance sheet has gained importance in a move to show the current year-end value of the assets and liabilities employed. The FASB and the IASB favour a balance-sheet-first approach to arrive at income for the year. A profit or loss may be recognised – brought into the financial statements – when there is an increase or decrease in an asset or a liability.

It is not necessary to prepare an income statement to discover the change in shareholders' interest (profit or loss) for the year. If, at the end of the year, all the assets of the company are set down on one side of the page and all the liabilities on the other, the two sides will not balance. The difference represents the profit or loss for the year that will appear in the income statement. If net assets (shareholders' funds, equity) have increased, a profit has been achieved; if they have decreased, there has been a loss. When the income statement is prepared the final figure (profit for the year or net income) will provide the necessary "proving" balancing figure for the statement of financial position. The current trend is to focus on taking the change in balance sheet net assets, termed "comprehensive income", to represent company performance for the year (see Chapter 3).

Fair value

An important issue is what value to place on the assets and liabilities in the statement of financial position. Traditionally, a balance sheet has accepted different valuation methods for separate classes of assets and liabilities: their cost, written down value, replacement cost or fair (market) value. The cost of an asset can be defined with some accuracy, but its true value is uncertain until it is sold. Whatever method of valuation is adopted, any changes in the value of assets and liabilities occurring during the year will have an impact on the shareholders' stake in the business. The figures appearing in any statement of financial position are a mixture of cost and some estimate of current market value. In recent years there has been a positive move towards using fair value as the basis for statement of financial position presentation.

There is general agreement among accountants that it is best if asset values are based on their fair or true current worth. In IFRS 13, the IASB defined fair value as: "The price that would be received to sell an asset or paid to transfer a liability in an orderly transaction between market participants at the measurement date."

The market is assumed to be operating between two unrelated, knowledgeable and willing parties. The entry price is that for buying the asset and the exit price is that received on its sale. This is similar to the US GAAP definition provided in the 2006 FAS 157. Fair value represents the current exchange price for an asset or liability. The intention is that the balance sheet should, as far as possible, reflect the current market values of a company's assets and liabilities. This can only improve the understanding of a company's financial position and performance.

Deciding when to take a profit is comparatively simple compared with dealing with a loss. The treatment of falling asset values in the 2008 global financial crisis was a major problem for accountants. If the fall in asset value was treated in the same way as an increase in value – ignore it until realisation occurs when it is sold – everything would be fine. The boat would not be rocked and no one would be upset. Accountants have faced severe criticism for pressurising banks and other financial institutions to apply fair value accounting during the financial crisis. Rather than, as previously, showing their assets – including subprime loans – at historical cost, companies were encouraged to show them at their current market value. The result was a substantial write-down of asset values, which, it was argued, added momentum to the financial crisis and the loss of confidence in the banking sector. Whether financial reporting does significantly contribute to the business cycle (pro-cyclicality) is uncertain, but the debate is sure to continue.

Statement of financial position building blocks

A balance sheet normally consists of five basic building blocks. These are provided for any company, irrespective of the nature of the business or the country or countries within which it operates. The way in which the five building blocks are set out depends partly on what is common practice or legally required within a particular business sector or country.

For most companies and countries the balance sheet displays a figure for total assets and total liabilities. IAS 1 requires that these are classified as either "current" or "non-current" depending on their expected life span. Current assets and liabilities are short-term and circulate as part of the operating cycle of the business. It is assumed they are received or paid in cash within a year. Any other assets or liabilities are defined as non-current. The long-term assets and liabilities employed in the business are defined as non-current – they are not expected to be paid or received within one year.

On one side of the statement, non-current assets added to current assets gives the total assets employed at the end of the year.

	$
Non-current assets	90
Current assets	60
Total assets	**150**

There are only three possible sources of funds that can be applied to finance total assets. Shareholders provide funds (equity) by purchasing shares or stock and allowing the company to retain profit. The company may undertake long-term borrowing (non-current liabilities) or use short-term borrowing and creditors (current liabilities) to finance the business. These sources of finance are set out on the other side of the balance sheet.

	$
Equity or shareholders' funds (capital and reserves)	100
Non-current liabilities (long-term creditors and borrowing)	20
Current liabilities (short-term creditors and borrowings)	30
Total liabilities	**150**

How these three sources are combined to finance the total assets employed is central to understanding the financial structure – the gearing or leverage – of a company. In assessing the adequacy or safety of a company's balance sheet, the proportion of finance provided by the shareholders is compared with that derived from other sources: outside borrowings, loan or debt, and short-term creditors. In China up until the 1990s there was only one shareholder: the state. Assets were financed by the state's investment of fixed, current and specific funds. The terminology may be different but the basic balance sheet formulas cannot change.

Total assets = total liabilities

Non-current assets + current assets =
equity + non-current liabilities + current liabilities

UK presentation

Having proved their obstinacy on the question of which side of the balance sheet to place assets, UK accountants remained out of step with those in other countries. The traditional horizontal presentation of the balance sheet (see Figure 2.1) was replaced by a vertical one that linked current assets and current liabilities to highlight net current assets (see Figure 2.2). Net current assets are defined as current assets less current liabilities. The fact that a company had more short-term

FIG 2.1 **Alternative formats for the horizontal balance sheet**

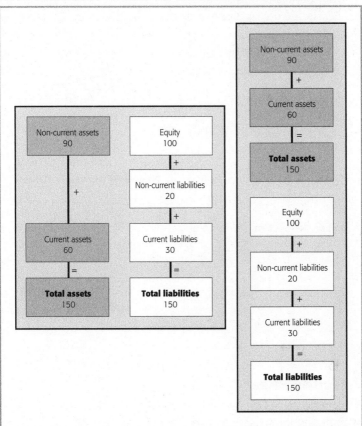

assets than short-term liabilities was taken as a simple indicator of financial health and solvency – the ability to pay creditors.

Highlighting net current assets was seen as providing useful information on the extent to which a company could, if necessary, quickly pay its short-term creditors by using its short-term assets. Current assets, if not already in the form of cash balances, are assumed to be capable of being turned into cash within the company's normal operating cycle (12 months). Current liabilities are creditors due for payment within 12 months.

FIG 2.2 **The vertical balance sheet presentation adopted in the UK in the 1970s**

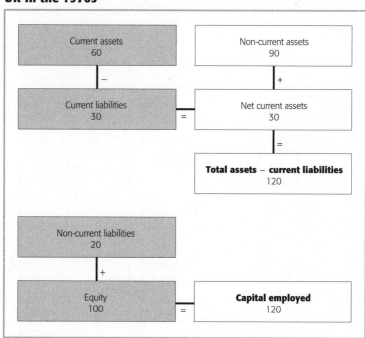

Net current assets

If a company is to pay its creditors within the next few months, where might it find the necessary cash? It would not be expected either to sell any non-current assets or to borrow long-term to pay short-term creditors. For most companies it would be reasonable to expect this cash to be generated from within the current asset building block.

In paying creditors, a company would first use available cash balances, then collect cash owed to it by customers (receivables), and lastly turn its inventory into cash. A surplus of current assets over current liabilities – net current assets – in the balance sheet indicates that a company has more short-term assets that can be turned into cash reasonably quickly than short-term liabilities that require cash for payment in the same timescale.

IAS 1 statement of financial position format

The format is guided by IAS 1, which provides for the classification of assets and liabilities as either current or non-current. IAS 1 does not precisely define the form of presentation, but it does set out the items that appear as individual lines in a statement of financial position, including:

Non-current assets
Property, plant and equipment
Investment property
Intangible assets
Investments valued using the equity method

Current assets
Inventories
Trade and other receivables
Cash and cash equivalents

TOTAL ASSETS

Current liabilities
Trade and other payables
Short-term borrowings
Taxes payable

Non-current liabilities
Deferred tax

TOTAL LIABILITIES

Equity
Share capital
Retained earnings
Other reserves
Minority interest

TOTAL EQUITY AND LIABILITIES

This is the most common format for a statement of financial position. Total assets match total liabilities and shareholders' equity. In the UK, some companies show net assets balanced against shareholders' equity.

Net assets = (total assets − total liabilities) = **shareholders' equity**

Equity

This building block in the statement indicates the amount of finance shareholders (stockholders) have provided for the company. This can have a variety of titles – capital and reserves, shareholders' funds, stockholders' interest, net worth – but equity is the most likely. Equity is what is left when liabilities are deducted from assets. This defines, in balance sheet terms, what is left for shareholders after all the external liabilities are settled.

Equity = total assets − total liabilities = net assets or net worth

The term net worth is a good basis for understanding what this building block represents. If the company with the example statement of financial position used above were to close down and turn its assets into cash (a process known as liquidation), there would be $150 cash available. It would repay its borrowings and long-term creditors (non-current liabilities) $20, and short-term creditors (current liabilities) $30, leaving $100 in the bank. This $100 is the net worth or equity of the company. After all borrowings and creditors (liabilities) have been paid, what is left belongs to the shareholders. The final step, before the company ceased to exist, would be to repay to the shareholders the $100, representing their investment or stake.

Share capital and retained earnings will normally provide the largest contribution to the figure for equity. The section of a company's statement of financial position giving details of equity normally contains four main headings:

- Called-up share capital
- Share premium account
- Other reserves
- Retained earnings

Shareholders have acquired the issued shares or stock of the company and are its owners. The shareholders' stake represents a long-term source of finance (capital) to the company. The two principal items are share capital (the shares issued to shareholders) and retained earnings, representing the profit retained (ploughed back) over the life of the company.

Statement of changes in equity

The income statement matches all operating income and expenditure to arrive at the after-tax profit (net income) for the year. Accounting standards require that certain gains or losses do not pass through the income statement but are taken directly to equity.

IAS 1 requires a statement of changes in equity (SOCE) to be presented to assist an understanding of the shareholders' investment in the company (equity) and how it has changed in the year. The SOCE is not the easiest statement to understand. However, if you are studying one, remember that its intention is to explain the movement in equity over the year. The opening and closing figures will match those appearing in the opening and closing balance sheets. Normally, the most significant item is the retained income for the year net of dividends. FRS 102 states that the intention of a SOCE is to present a full explanation of changes in the company's equity by setting out "an entity's profit or loss for a reporting period, other comprehensive income for the period, the effects of changes in accounting policies and corrections of material errors recognised in the period, and the amount of investments by, and dividends and other distributions to, equity investors in the period".

Starting with the opening balance, as shown in the balance sheet, the SOCE will show the gains or losses from transactions with shareholders as the owners of the company. It ends with the shareholders' total equity at the end of the year as shown in the balance sheet. If you have problems reading the statement, at least you have the two key anchor points readily visible: the opening and closing total equity figures shown in the balance sheets. For each heading within equity in the balance sheet, there should be a corresponding line in the SOCE to show any changes occurring during the year.

Total equity at beginning of the year
   +/– adjustments due to changes in accounting policy

= **restated balance**

Changes in equity during the year

> \+ issue of shares
> – dividends
> \+ retained earnings for the year
> +/– translation of foreign operation
> +/– available-for-sale financial assets
> +/– cash flow hedges
> +/– revaluation surplus
> +/– non-controlling interest

= **total equity at end of the year**

Total comprehensive income

When reading a SOCE the term comprehensive income (CI) will be seen. This excludes any new share issue or dividends paid to shareholders during the year and is defined in "Reporting Comprehensive Income" (FAS 130) as:

> *The change in equity [net assets] of a business enterprise during a period from transactions and other events and circumstances from non-owner sources. It includes all changes in equity during a period except those resulting from investments by owners and distributions to owners.*

Companies must report both net income (profit or loss) and CI in their financial statements. The difference between these is referred to as other comprehensive income (OCI). FRS 102 defines total CI as "the arithmetic difference between income and expenses". This will include unrealised gains or losses on available-for-sale marketable securities, foreign-currency transactions, pension liability adjustments and cash flow hedges. When the income or expense involved is realised – the transaction has been completed – they will be taken into the income statement. Until this time they are disclosed separately as being important in appreciating the change in equity during the year (see Chapter 3).

Retained profit

Under normal trading conditions a company retains some of the profit each year to assist growth and investment for its future development and success. In allowing the company to retain a part of the earnings made in the year rather than taking all the profit as dividends, shareholders are, in effect, lending this money to their company. Thus retained profit is a liability to the company and is shown as such in the statement of financial position. It is "owed" to the shareholders.

Share capital

Only shares or stock that have been issued and paid for by shareholders are shown in the balance sheet. These are referred to as the called-up or issued capital of the company. A company may have the ability to issue more shares from its authorised share capital. The number of authorised shares is the maximum that a company can issue. Most US companies disclose this information on the face of the balance sheet. In other countries, the authorised and issued share capital is usually set out in the notes to the accounts. The par, nominal or face value of the shares will also be disclosed. A company may issue shares that are only partly paid for with the balance due at some future date. Details will be provided in the notes.

Share price and the statement of financial position

Shares are always shown in the statement at their nominal or par value: for example, 25p, 10¢, or €10. The market price at which these shares change hands is irrelevant; there is no attempt in the statement to reflect the stock exchange value of shares. It is common practice for companies to issue shares of no-par value.

If a company is wound up or liquidated, it sells its assets, turning them into cash. This is used to repay short-term and long-term creditors (the liabilities of the company), and what is left (net worth or equity) is returned to the shareholders, who may receive more or less than the nominal value of their shares.

Ordinary shares

The ordinary shareholders or stockholders are a company's risk-takers. They may lose their investment completely if the company fails and there is insufficient money available to pay the creditors. They are the last group to receive any money from a company in liquidation. An ordinary share is classed as an "equity instrument". IAS 32 defines this as "any contract that evidences a residual interest in the assets of the entity after deducting all its liabilities".

Ordinary shareholders can lose only the nominal value of the shares they own, although they will normally have paid more than the nominal or par value of the shares on the stock exchange. They cannot be called upon to contribute any more funds to a company. Ordinary shareholders thus have a limited liability.

The bulk of most companies' share capital is provided by ordinary shares (called common stock in the US). In acquiring shares a shareholder obtains a stake or a share of the equity of a company. Legally, the owner of ordinary shares has a right to share the profits and assets of the company as well as certain rights and obligations connected with its management. Ordinary shareholders have no rights to dividends. Each year the directors decide whether or not to declare a dividend and the amount to be paid.

IAS 1 requires full details of share capital to be disclosed and divides shareholders' interest into three sections: issued capital, reserves and accumulated profit or loss. A company may have several different types or classes of ordinary shares. Shares may carry different voting rights, with some shares having more or less than one vote per share. There may be differences in their rights to participate in profits being preferred or deferred.

Treasury stock

A company can purchase (buy back) and cancel or hold its own shares. This has been possible in the UK since 2003. The shares are referred to as treasury shares or stock and form part of the company's equity. The result of share repurchase is to reduce the number of shares outstanding and increase the value of those remaining.

IAS 32 calls for the purchase of shares to be shown in the statement of changes in equity. To protect creditors there are legal limits to the proportion of shares a company may repurchase. A company cannot trade in its own shares, and if the shares are later sold at a profit this remains in equity and cannot be taken to the income statement. IAS 1 requires treasury stock to be deducted from equity. No gain or loss on the sale, purchase, issue or cancellation of a company's own shares is taken to the income statement.

Preference shares

Preference shares were introduced in the 19th century to allow investors to participate with less risk in companies. Preference shareholders normally receive their dividend payment before the ordinary shareholders receive anything, and if the company is wound up they get their capital back before the ordinary shareholders. In other words, they rank preferentially for dividend and capital repayment. In return for these benefits preference shares usually have a fixed rate of dividend and few, if any, rights regarding the management of the company. Issuing preference shares allows a company to raise long-term capital with a known cost: the dividend paid. However, the preference share dividends are not tax allowable as would be interest paid on a long-term loan.

A company may issue cumulative preference shares. If in one year there is insufficient profit to pay the preference share dividend, the obligation will be carried forward to the following year when the arrears will be paid before the ordinary shareholders receive anything. Preference shares may be offered with the right to share (participate) in profits beyond their fixed dividend. These are called participating preference shares.

Normally, preference shares are irredeemable. They form part of the permanent capital of the company and are not expected to be repaid. Sometimes a company issues redeemable preference shares. These may have a fixed date upon which they will be repurchased (redeemed), or the company may have the right to redeem then at any time. In rare circumstances, a company may issue participating redeemable preference shares.

Convertible shares

The term convertible can attach to either shares or loans. Convertible shares may be issued providing the owner with the right, at some time in the future, to convert them into ordinary shares.

A bank may be approached by a company for a loan. The company wants to pay as little interest as possible, and the bank wants the best security for both interest and capital. The bank may be persuaded to charge a lower than normal rate of interest in return for the right to convert the loan into ordinary shares at an agreed future date and price formula. The bank has security, as the money provided is not part of the company's equity but a loan. Also, if the company flourishes and its share price improves, the bank can make a profit by converting the loan into shares. Convertible redeemable preference shares may be issued, although they rarely are.

Reserves

A reserve is the setting aside of earnings in the statement of financial position and is shown as part of equity. There are two types of reserves: revenue and capital. The retained earnings accumulated over the life of the company will normally be the largest revenue reserve. Revenue reserves are considered free for distribution to shareholders as dividends. Capital reserves (legal or non-distributable reserves) are not considered distributable and so cannot normally be used for dividend payments. Examples of these are share premium account and revaluation reserves. When foreign operations are translated into the parent company's currency for inclusion in the balance sheet there will be differences in opening and closing carrying values. These differences are not taken to the income statement – they have not been realised – and so are shown within equity as a reserve.

Provisions

The term provision may appear within either non-current or current liabilities in a statement of financial position. IAS 37 defines a provision as "a liability of uncertain timing or amount". When a company has an obligation that is likely to require payment in the future, but the amount is uncertain, it is prudent to earmark resources for this event, that is, make a provision when:

- a company has a present legal or constructive obligation as a result of past events;
- it is probable that an outflow of resources embodying economic benefits will be required to settle the obligation;
- a reliable estimate can be made of the amount of the obligation.

IAS 37 recommends the use of present value calculations where this improves the quality of the information provided concerning a provision. An example is when a company sells a product to customers with a replacement warranty. Some products will have to be replaced, and the company should be ready to meet this obligation. However, the exact number of products that will have to be replaced cannot be precisely defined. The company considers that, based on previous experience, only 1% of products will require replacement within one year of sale. If it sells 10,000 units of the product and the replacement cost is $50 per unit, a provision of $5,000 could be created.

First-year replacement $50 $\times$ (10,000 $\times$ 0.01) = $ 5,000

The expected value of warranty costs of $5,000 will be shown as part of the year-end current liabilities. Where the liability extends for more than one year ahead, IAS 37 requires discounting techniques to be used to provide a present value (see below) and the provision would appear in non-current liabilities.

Provisions were originally developed to allow companies to show that they had prudently set aside resources to meet future expenses that were "either likely to be incurred, or certain to be incurred but uncertain as to amount or date". Companies soon realised that they could take advantage of provisions to massage their earnings. A company would make a provision for the anticipated losses on closing down a business or the costs of major restructuring following an acquisition. Significant amounts of one year's profit would be set aside – on the grounds that if it is going to make a loss, it might as well be a big one. Then the company would discover it had overprovided for the event and would bring the provision back to boost a future year's profit. These were called "big bath" or "kitchen sink" provisions. They proved a simple but effective tactic for an executive brought in to turn a company round. Investors expected to suffer in the first year and were delighted when "profit" returned in the second.

Big bath provisions have effectively been outlawed by IAS 37, which sets out clear rules for the creation of a provision. Management's intentions alone are not a sufficient reason to create a provision. There must be an unavoidable obligation on the company to incur the expense being provided for. A simple check is to apply the year-end test: if a company ceased to trade at the balance sheet date, would it still have to pay the amount involved? If not, there can be no provision made, as it relates to future, not past, business activity.

Contingent liability

Sometimes a company faces a possible future event that is uncertain and difficult to measure – a contingent liability or asset. It may be involved in a law action where the outcome is still unknown. IAS 37 defines a contingent liability as:

> A possible obligation that arises from past events whose existence will only be confirmed by the occurrence or non-occurrence of one or more uncertain future events not wholly within the control of the entity.

There is a problem of accurate measurement and so it cannot be recognised in the financial statements. However, users of the annual report should be made aware of its existence as it may well influence their view of the company. The information will be provided in the annual report notes. It is possible, but unusual, to find a contingent asset listed in the notes.

Share premium account

If a company issues shares to new or existing shareholders, it offers them shares of the existing nominal value. However, it will take full advantage of the fact that its shares are being traded on the stock exchange at a price above their nominal value. So a company with $1 nominal value shares, taking account of the current quoted share price, decides to offer new shares at a price of $4 and the issue is taken up. As each share is issued and paid for the company's balance sheet is adjusted.

$$Cash + \$4 = equity + \$4$$

For each share issued the company increases its share capital by $1. The remaining $3 is the extra amount above the nominal value, or the premium, that shareholders are willing to pay for a share. The share premium must be shown in a separate account as part of equity and is deemed a capital reserve.

$$Cash + \$4 = share\ capital + \$1\ and\ share\ premium + \$3$$

A capital reserve can be used only for legally determined purposes; for example, it cannot normally be used to pay dividends to shareholders, but it can be used to cover the expenses of share issues.

Retained earnings

As a company generates and retains profit, the shareholders' stake increases proportionately. The balance sheet figure for retained earnings shows the total amount of profit retained by the company over its life. Retained profit is a revenue reserve. It can be used to pay dividends to shareholders and for almost any other purpose a company wishes.

Revaluation reserve

A company may be allowed to revalue non-current assets. Where the fair value of non-current assets increases this may be reflected in an adjustment to the value of the assets shown in the statement of financial position. As far as possible, this should reflect the fair value of assets and liabilities. However, the increase in value of a non-current asset does not necessarily represent an immediate profit for the company. A profit is made or realised only when the asset is sold and the resulting profit is taken through the income statement. Until this event occurs prudence – supported by common sense – requires that the increase in asset value is retained in the balance sheet. Shareholders have the right to any profit on the sale of company assets, so the shareholders' stake (equity) is increased by the same amount as the increase in asset valuation. A revaluation reserve is created and the balance sheet still balances.

Non-current liabilities

Equity is a permanent source and current liabilities (creditors due for payment within one year) are a short-term source of finance to a company. Between these two extremes is the third building block on the liabilities side of the statement of financial position: non-current liabilities (long-term creditors and borrowing). These are sources of finance that do not have to be repaid within the coming year and are often called debt. In most companies debt consists of a mixture of long-term creditors and medium-term and long-term borrowings.

The notes supporting the statement should provide details of repayment dates of all loans and the rate of interest applying to them. Often a debenture appears as part of the long-term financing of a company. A debenture is a loan secured on the company's assets, normally with an agreed rate of interest and a fixed repayment date. It is possible for a company to issue a convertible debenture offering similar rights to those outlined for preference shares.

The time when major loans fall due for repayment is important in assessing the future viability of a company, because on the date of repayment the necessary cash must be available.

Another type of borrowing is through loan stock. This does not form part of equity (the ordinary shareholders' stake) and may or may not have the right of conversion into ordinary shares. It is often issued with warrants. The loan stock is not convertible, but the warrants allow the holder to purchase a fixed number of ordinary shares at an agreed future price and date. The advantage for the company is that the loan stock is repayable only on the set redemption date but new capital can be raised through the warrants.

Current liabilities

To an accountant, the term current means short-term, with short-term being taken as less than one year. A current liability – a creditor due for payment – is therefore an obligation that the company can be expected to fulfil within the 12 months following the date of the statement of financial position.

The current liabilities building block in the statement normally contains four main headings:

■ Trade and other payables

■ Short-term borrowings

■ Taxes payable

■ Provisions

The figure for trade payables comprises the money the company owes to its suppliers for goods and services delivered during the year. In most types of businesses suppliers are paid within 30–60 days, with the company taking 1–2 months from the delivery of the goods or services before making payment. Any creditors not due for payment within the 12 months necessary for them to be included as a current liability will be shown as a non-current liability in the balance sheet.

Until a company pays its creditors it has the use of the cash owed to them. Thus creditors act as a source of finance. Companies exceeding acceptable levels of use of short-term creditors to finance their business may be viewed as employing an aggressive financing strategy or they may be overtrading (see Chapter 3).

All borrowings due for repayment within 12 months of the balance sheet date will appear within current liabilities. In the UK, an overdraft, a form of short-term flexible borrowing, is technically repayable on demand so it is shown as a current liability. This will be the case even if there is an agreement with the bank to have the overdraft as a permanent source of finance.

The figure for tax shown in current liabilities can be taken as the amount owed by the company due for payment within the next financial year. Remember that there is no guaranteed match between the reported earnings for the year and the amount of tax actually paid. A heading of "deferred taxation" may be found. This represents the difference between the amount of tax owed and that recognised in the income statement (see Chapter 3).

Assets

The IASB Framework defines an asset as:

A resource controlled by the enterprise as a result of past events and from which future economic benefits are expected to flow to the enterprise.

Two building blocks appear on the assets side of the balance sheet: non-current or long-lived assets (these used to be called fixed assets) and current or short-term assets. Non-current assets are mainly tangible, such as the physical assets used to undertake the business of the company. They include land and buildings, plant and equipment, vehicles, and fixtures and fittings.

Non-current assets

Non-current assets are divided into two classes: tangible and intangible. Tangible assets are physical and have a finite useful working life. Investment in them ties up the company's available financial resources for a number of years.

Tangible assets are depreciated, amortised or written off over their useful life. They are shown in the balance sheet at their carrying value – normally cost less accumulated depreciation. IAS 16 and FRS 102 provide the basis for the provision of information on tangible assets. There is usually a single figure in the balance sheet for property, plant and equipment (PPE). These are assets used on a continuing basis in the company's business activities. The figure shown is their balance sheet value, net book value (NBV) or written down value (WDV), which represents their cost, or fair value, less the accumulated depreciation charged over their life.

To be recognised – included in the accounts – an asset must be owned by the company and have a clearly defined cost or value that can be reliably measured. Purchase price or historical cost is the most common basis for asset valuation, but there are several other options: replacement cost, net realisable value, present value (the discounted expected future cash flows) and fair value (market value). The initial cost of an asset may include all expenses necessary to get it into a working state – labour, materials and other costs are capitalised – as long as this does not result in a carrying value exceeding its fair value.

As with almost every figure appearing in the statement of financial position, it is to the notes in the accounts that you must turn to find useful details. At a minimum there should be, for each major component of tangible assets, details of:

- cost or fair value at the beginning of the year;
- accumulated depreciation charged at the beginning of the year;
- amount of depreciation charged during the year;
- any additions or disposals made during the year;
- net carrying amount (balance sheet) value at the end of the year;
- freehold and leasehold property.

Assets are shown at their "carrying value", which is often cost less depreciation. Ideally, the balance sheet would use the fair value of all assets and liabilities. Fair value represents the market value of each item: that is, the amount of cash for which an asset could be exchanged or a liability settled. This would offer a basis for assessing what the shareholders might receive if the company were sold or liquidated. In practice, the balance sheet contains a mixture of valuation methods (such as cost, replacement, present value) as well as fair values.

Government grants

Government grants or incentives are often available to encourage investment in PPE. IAS 20 allows the grant either to be deducted from the value of the asset or to be shown as "deferred income" in the balance sheet and written off over the life of the asset. Whichever method is adopted the reported earnings of the company are identical. For example, a company purchases an asset for $10,000 and receives a government grant of $2,000. The asset has an expected useful working life of four years. The asset may be shown in the statement of financial position at $8,000 and depreciated at $2,000 per year. The alternative is for the statement to show the asset valued at $10,000 and deferred income of $2,000. The asset is depreciated at $2,500 per year with deferred income of $500 per year set against this, providing a $2,000 per year net charge in the income statement.

Capitalisation of expenses

Companies used to have considerable flexibility in deciding whether or not to capitalise expenses. Rather than charging an expense in the income statement, it was taken to the balance sheet as an asset and profit was increased by reducing the amount of expenses charged against income. Now only the borrowing costs associated with a non-current asset, where it takes a considerable time to get it operational, may be capitalised. This treatment is governed by IAS 23, with the cost added to the carrying value of the asset and expensed (taken to the income statement) over its life as part of the depreciation charge.

Depreciation

IAS 16 defines depreciation as "the systematic allocation of the depreciable amount of an asset over its useful life". Depreciation is not an attempt to measure the change in value of an asset but a means, over its useful working life, of charging its cost to the income statement. Depreciation, or amortisation, can be viewed as representing the setting aside of income to provide for the future replacement of physical assets. It is to be expected that all assets, except land, are depreciated over their useful working life. As assets are used their value reduces. They become worn out, run-down or obsolete, and need replacing in order to maintain or improve the productive efficiency of the business.

Depreciation is a provision, a setting aside of current income to meet future eventualities, so it could be shown in the statement of financial position as part of equity in the same way as retained earnings.

Equity	$	Non-current assets	$
Depreciation provision	100	Tangible assets at cost	200

However, it has been traditional policy to deduct depreciation from the asset value in the balance sheet.

Non-current assets	$	$
Tangible assets at cost	200	
Less depreciation	100	100

Depreciation is charged as an expense in the income statement; this reduces reported profit. It is also deducted from the value of non-current assets set out in the balance sheet, thus reducing the value of the company's assets. The income statement is charged with the use of the assets and the balance sheet is adjusted to compensate. (See Chapter 3 for details of the depreciation charge.)

Inflation and non-current assets

Inflation can complicate the valuation of assets because $1 at the beginning of the year will purchase more than $1 at the end of the year. When inflation is low, it is reasonable to use historical cost – what the asset cost when acquired – as the basis for the valuation of a company's assets and depreciation.

A company that had not revalued property purchased in 1990 would face two problems in relation to its statement of financial position. First, the property would be undervalued because to replace it would cost significantly more than the 1990 figure. Undervaluing assets may improve the reported profit of the company, as a result of a lower than realistic depreciation charge, but it may prove dangerous by making the company an attractive target for takeover. If the published balance sheet value were used to set the acquisition price, it would be far below fair value (current market value). Second, if the property needs replacing or major investment to maintain it, the company may not have been setting aside sufficient profits, through depreciation, for this to be possible.

For example, an entrepreneur starts a company in 2008 with an investment of $10,000, which is used to purchase a non-current asset. The statement of financial position at this point is:

	$		$
Non-current assets	10,000		
Cash	0	Share capital	10,000

The asset has a useful working life of five years and, following IAS 16, is depreciated or written off in the income statement at the rate of $2,000 per year. Each year the company makes a profit of $2,000 (after depreciation). In 2013 the company's balance sheet would appear as:

	$			$
Non-current assets	10,000		Share capital	10,000
Less depreciation	10,000	0	Retained earnings	10,000
Cash		20,000		20,000

The $20,000 cash balance is the result of five years' retained profit ($2,000) and five years' depreciation ($2,000). The business has doubled in size between 2008 and 2013.

The entrepreneur decides to replace the asset and continue the business. However, at the end of 2013 an identical asset to that purchased in 2008 costs $20,000; the price has doubled because of inflation. The investment is completed and the balance sheet shows:

	$			$
Non-current asset	20,000			
Cash	0	20,000	Equity	20,000

The company is now in exactly the same position it was five years before; it has a new asset and no cash. Has the company really made the $10,000 profit shown in the balance sheet? Indeed, if it had been paying tax at 50%, it would be necessary to borrow money to replace the asset at the end of 2013. This example illustrates the problems of financial reporting under conditions of inflation and the benefits of fair value accounting – using the current market value of assets and liabilities.

The overriding rule of faithful presentation (incorporating prudence), supported by that of capital maintenance (see Chapter 6), requires that a company take account of the impact of inflation in the reporting process. There are many ways of countering or reflecting this in corporate reports. One approach is to take an appropriate index of inflation, such as the retail price index, and apply this to the assets and liabilities of a company to bring these to current values – current purchasing power (CPP) accounting. The simplest method is to use fair value (the current market value) as the basis for valuing assets and charging appropriate depreciation rates. IAS 29 deals with the issues of hyperinflation.

Asset revaluation and sale

The historical cost or a revaluation provides the basis for accounting for tangible non-current assets. Under conditions of inflation, using historical cost as the basis for depreciation will overstate real earnings. Revaluing assets will overcome this problem. IAS 16 requires that fair value (current value) be the basis of any asset revaluation. When an asset is revalued all other similar assets must also be revalued. This avoids the potential problem of having varying valuation methods within an asset class. The amount of any revaluation is taken to a revaluation reserve in equity.

Once a revaluation reserve is created it remains within equity. The increase in asset value cannot be taken into the income statement. If at some time after revaluation the fair value of the asset falls, the resulting loss of value is deducted from the revaluation reserve; it is not taken into the income statement.

If a company purchases an asset for $100,000 with an expected ten-year life, it will have a carrying value of $50,000 at the end of five years. If the asset is then revalued to $70,000 a revaluation reserve of $20,000 is created, and the balance sheet still balances. For the remaining five years the depreciation charge will be $14,000 per year ($70,000 ÷ 5). This is produced by charging the income statement with $10,000 (as in previous years) and reducing the revaluation reserve by $4,000.

Two years later the carrying value is $42,000, and the asset is sold for $50,000. IAS 16 requires the profit on the sale of $8,000 to be taken to the income statement, and the revaluation reserve of $12,000 ($20,000 less $8,000 depreciation) to be transferred to retained profit.

FRS 102 does not require annual valuations to be made. It is up to the company to ensure that the carrying values of its PPE do not materially shift from their fair values.

Foreign exchange

If a company trades or makes investments or acquisitions in another country, it usually has to deal in a foreign currency. A foreign subsidiary will keep its records in its own currency. For consolidation purposes these will have to be translated into the currency of the parent company. FRS 102 and IAS 21 provide the guidelines for foreign-currency transactions. You may find reference to three different definitions for currencies involved in foreign operations:

- Local currency – in which a subsidiary keeps its records.
- Functional currency – in which the parent company trades.
- Presentation currency – used in the group's financial statements.

   Reference may also be made to the following:
- Spot rate – the exchange rate at the date of the transaction.
- Closing rate – the spot rate at the balance sheet date.
- Average rate – the average exchange rate for the year.

If exchange rates remained constant, accountants would have few problems. Unfortunately, for both accountants and companies, exchange rates fluctuate, not only from year to year but also from minute to minute.

For example, if a company purchased a machine in France for $100,000 when the exchange rate was $1 = €1.25, it would appear in the balance sheet at $80,000 (100,000 ÷ 1.25). If the machine was purchased on credit and at the end of the year the amount was still owing and the exchange rate had moved to $1 = €1.10, the account payable (a monetary item) would be re-translated to $90,909 (100,000 ÷ 1.1) and the currency translation difference of $10,909 (loss) would be taken to the income statement.

If the $100,000 (at $1 = €1.25) represented the acquisition of a foreign subsidiary at the beginning or the year and at the end of the year the rate had moved to $1 = €1.10, the $10,909 currency difference would be taken not to the income statement but directly to equity (IAS 21).

If a UK company sells a machine for $10,000 to a US customer when the exchange rate is $1 = £0.63, the transaction is recorded as sale and receivable of £6,300. If, by the time payment is made, the pound has strengthened against the dollar to $1 = £0.57, only £5,700 will be received and an exchange rate loss of £600 will need to be recognised in the income statement.

If, rather than normal trading and investment activity, a company makes an acquisition in a foreign country, consolidated accounts will have to be prepared. To consolidate a subsidiary, some basic rules of procedure are required. There are several options available in choosing the exchange rate that best reflects trading during the year (for the income statement) and the year-end position (for the statement of financial position). The options are:

- average exchange rate for the year;
- exchange rate at the time of the transaction (spot rate);
- exchange rate at the end of the financial year (closing rate).

It is reasonable and practical to use the exchange rate applicable at the year end (the balance sheet date) for the consolidation of overseas assets and liabilities. It is most common for the net worth of a foreign subsidiary to be brought into the accounts at the exchange rate applicable at the balance sheet date. Any gain or loss does not reach the income statement but is retained in the parent company's equity. For trading transactions, either the exchange rate at the date of the transaction or an average rate is used with the profit or loss taken to the income statement.

Hedging

It is accepted that a prudent company will try to reduce or minimise its exposure to risk through exchange-rate fluctuations by covering the potential risks involved. For example, a company might borrow in the foreign currency a sum equivalent to the amount of the investment it is going to make in its foreign subsidiary. Or the company might take a put option to sell one of its long-term investments for an agreed sum in the future. This approach, which is called hedging, means that any change in exchange rates is automatically adjusted on both the asset and liability side of the statement of financial position. Hedge accounting adjusts the timing of the recognition of any gains or losses on either the hedged item or the hedging instrument so they appear in the same accounting period.

Do not mix up hedging with hedge funds. A hedge fund – the name comes from "hedging your bets" – is a private investment company that oversees the investment of its clients' money, not just in financial instruments, but in more or less anything, anywhere, as long as there is a profit to be made. Hedging is used not only for foreign exchange and foreign operations but also to protect companies against changes in interest rates, cash flow exposure, or specific asset values. IFRS 9 defines the objective of hedge accounting as:

> To represent, in the financial statements, the effect of an entity's risk management activities that use financial instruments to manage exposures arising from particular risks that could affect profit or loss (or other comprehensive income ...).

IFRS 9 recognises three types of hedging activity. A fair value hedge is to safeguard against changes in the value of the asset or liability involved. A cash flow hedge is to cover the company against variation in cash flows attributable to a specific risk or asset or liability. The third type of hedge is concerned with a company's net investment in a foreign operation.

Financial instruments

In 1998 the FASB issued FAS 133, "Accounting for Derivative Instruments and Hedging Activities", amended by FAS 161 in 2008, and the IASB released IAS 39, "Financial Instrument: Recognition and Measurement". These represented the first moves towards regulating the financial reporting of derivatives and other financial instruments. From 2005 the IASB worked with the FASB to further simplify and improve the reporting on financial instruments, gradually replacing IAS 39 with IFRS 9, applicable from 2015. FRS 102 defines a financial instrument as "a contract that gives rise to a financial asset of one entity and a financial liability or equity instrument of another entity".

An equity instrument is any contract having a residual interest – a share – in the net assets of the entity. The most common equity instrument is an ordinary share. During the 1980s there was widespread misuse of complex financial packages (compound financial instruments) or derivatives, mixing debt and equity, in order to disguise the true level of a company's borrowings. For example:

■ Convertible debt – carries the right to exchange for equity shares at some future date until which time interest is paid.

- Subordinated debt – in the event of liquidation it is repaid before the shareholders, but only after all other liabilities have been settled.
- Limited recourse debt – secured only on a particular asset.
- Deep discount bond – a loan with low interest issued at a substantial discount to its repayment value. A zero-coupon bond receives no interest.

IAS 39 provides two measures for financial instruments – fair value and amortised cost – and four different classifications of financial assets:

- Fair value through profit and loss – held for trading investments.
- Held-to-maturity – there is no intention to sell.
- Loans and receivables – not for short-term sale.
- Available-for-sale – any other financial asset.

Much of the debate has centred on the impairment in financial instrument value. IAS 39 was based on the incurred impairment – the realisation of the actual loss in value. There was considerable criticism following the 2008 crisis that this approach had delayed the exposure of the true extent of the losses incurred by financial institutions. It was claimed that the expected loss should have been the basis for impairment values. The incurred loss is an easily produced figure, as the loss has happened. An expected loss involves an estimate of the likelihood of an uncertain event occurring in the future.

As yet there is no single measurement, valuation method, or accounting treatment applied to all financial instruments. If you are lucky, the company you are studying will make things clear in its statement of accounting policies; but, unfortunately, there is no guarantee that the next company you look at will follow the same methods. This is a difficult subject, and all you really need to know when you see references to hedge accounting is that the company considers it has taken the necessary steps to counter the potential risks involved in the acquisition or holding of the assets concerned.

The statement of financial position will show the fair value of the financial instrument, and any gain or loss for the period will be shown as a separate entry in the income statement.

Risk

The annual report should provide information on a company's financial risk management objectives and policies with specific details of hedge transactions. IFRS 7, issued in 2005 and amended in 2010, complements IFRS 9 and IAS 32, requiring a company to provide sufficient information for the users of its financial statements to be able to assess the importance of financial instruments to its financial position and performance and to appreciate the nature and extent of the risks involved. Qualitative and quantitative information must also be provided on the nature and extent of risks from financial instruments, identifying credit risks, liquidity risks and market risks.

Two types of risk can be identified: financial and non-financial. Financial risk relates to the market, where changes may occur in exchange rates, interest rates and share prices. Non-financial risks relate to such matters as business operations and strategy as well as reputation.

Derivatives and risk

The term derivative is applied to many financial instruments, including futures, swaps, forwards and options. These can be difficult to understand, but all derive their value from an underlying item such as a share price, a foreign-exchange rate or an interest rate. They have a future settlement date and little or no initial cost, so the traditional historical cost value fails to reflect the true financial importance or potential impact of the contract. IFRS 9 defines a derivative as being a financial instrument with three characteristics:

- its value changes in response to the change in a specified item or event such as an interest rate, a commodity price or a foreign-exchange rate;
- it requires little or no initial investment;
- it is settled at a future date.

For example, a company using a commodity such as coffee beans, copper, or oil to generate revenue might insure against future price rises by agreeing to fix the future price paid for its raw materials with a forward contract. The raw material becomes the underlying item of a commodity futures derivative. The company is hedging the risk and uncertainties of the future market price and has certainty as to its future costs. The company offering the derivative is, in effect, betting that the future commodity price will be lower than the agreed contract price. If an adverse move in an exchange rate would be costly, it is reasonable for a company to insure against this event. Derivatives provide this safety net and are correctly used as part of a company's risk management activity.

Derivatives can be treated in the same way chips in a casino – a high-risk gamble on future outcomes – but such speculation should have no place in a normal company. Warren Buffett, an American investment guru, described them as "weapons of financial mass destruction". Nick Leeson gave an unhappy demonstration of the misuse of derivatives by gambling in the Japanese futures market in 1995 and bankrupting Barings Bank.

Option contracts

A common derivative is an option contract. For example, X buys from Z the option to purchase 1,000 shares in company A for \$3 per share at any time in the next six months. X is the holder of the option and has a financial asset. Z has a contractual obligation (financial liability) to sell the shares at \$3. If the shares rise above \$3, X will exercise the option and make a profit. If the shares rise to \$3.20, X makes a \$200 profit and Z makes a \$200 loss.

A premium is normally paid for an option. The shares in company A are the underlying financial instruments from which the option derives its value. \$3 is the exercise price of the option. If the option is not exercised and lapses, it has no value (it is out of the money) for X; if the price rises above \$3, it becomes in the money.

Intangible assets

Most of the assets shown as non-current assets in the statement of financial position are tangible, but there are often other long-term assets that are described as intangible. In general, accountants and auditors do not like intangible assets, which are fraught with potential danger. As their name implies, they are not physical items capable of normal identification and verification as are property, plant and equipment.

Intangibles are dealt with in FRS 102 and IAS 38 (revised in 2004), both of which use the same definition of "an identifiable non-monetary asset without physical substance". They are assets that the company owns. They are expected to be used to generate future income and are capable of separate identification and measurement. Examples of intangibles likely to be found within the non-current asset building block are as follows:

- **Marketing-related**
  - trade names or trade marks
  - internet domain names and newspaper titles
- **Customer-related**
  - customer lists and relationships
- **Artistic-related**
  - plays, operas, ballets, musical works and song lyrics
  - books, magazines, newspapers
  - audio-visual materials
- **Contract-based**
  - licences, royalties
  - advertising contracts
  - lease agreements
  - construction permits
  - employment contracts
- **Technology-based**
  - technology and trade secrets (processes, formulas)
  - computer software
  - databases

Brand names and know-how

Until recently it was not considered prudent for a company to include intangibles such as trade or brand names or knowledge-based assets such as intellectual property rights (IPRS) in its statement of financial position. Any knowledge a company has that may be converted into value may be considered an asset. Reference is sometimes made to intellectual capital as an intangible asset. This has been defined as: "The possession of knowledge and experience, professional knowledge and skill, good relationships, and technological capacities, which when applied will give organisations competitive advantage."

It includes marketing assets such as customer satisfaction and brand recognition. In the late 1980s in the UK, some companies, mainly in the food and drinks sector, began to include brand names they acquired – and in some cases developed – as an asset in their balance sheet. Their argument was that brands were a valuable commercial asset and that excluding their value from the balance sheet resulted in a potentially dangerous undervaluation of the company. It is reasonable to consider such assets as important for many companies. Brands such as Coca-Cola, McDonald's, KFC, Gucci, Prada, Google and Apple are worth many billions of dollars in their own right. Clearly, in attempting to place a value on some companies it is unwise to ignore intangibles such as brands or software programs.

IAS 38, when issued in 1998, was the first standard to tackle the treatment of intangible assets in financial reports. Brands, software programs, copyrights and similar intangibles create many problems for accountants. They have no real physical substance and are developed over a number of years with the cost being charged as an expense in the income statement. This development cost may bear no relationship to their market value. They have a useful life of more than one year, bring positive economic benefits to the company and can be sold. The only time their true value can be determined is when they are bought or sold. When a company purchases a brand name there is a clearly defined value or price, and this can be used to put the asset in the balance sheet.

It is possible to produce a simple, and rough, guide to the value of a company's intangibles based on its capitalisation: current share price multiplied by the number of shares in issue. Company capitalisation is regularly published in the financial media.

(Capitalisation + debt) – (net current assets + tangible assets) =
market value of intangible assets

If there are any intangible assets shown in the statement of financial position, deduct these from the market value of intangibles to discover the value being placed on assets not appearing in the financial statements. It is not unusual to discover that the market value of intangibles, as calculated here, represents a significant proportion of a company's total value. Do not forget that this figure includes the market's assessment of the future earnings of the company reflected in the current share price.

Treatment of intangibles

It is important to study the notes in a company's annual report on intangible assets, particularly if they are appearing for the first time. The notes to the financial statements should provide details of the basis of their valuation.

Tangible assets are depreciated; intangible assets are amortised. The amortisation charge for intangibles depends on whether they are seen as having a finite or an indefinite useful life. Normally, the straight line method of amortisation will be used to write off the asset over its useful life. As a simple common-sense safeguard, IAS 38 does not allow self-created intangibles, internally developed brands or similar intangibles into the statement of financial position.

In valuing a company or assessing its financial position, the treatment of intangibles can be crucial. It can be argued that intangibles are by their nature of debatable value and should be ignored in placing a value on assets employed in a company. Their inclusion can make it difficult to get an appreciation of the assets that might act as valid security to creditors and providers of funds to the company. Alternatively, if a company is being valued as a going concern on a continuing business basis, more often than not intangibles form an integral part and should not be ignored. Although difficult to value, they are essential to placing a realistic valuation on a company. In 2013 Diageo indicated that its brands, including Johnnie Walker, Smirnoff and Guinness, were valued at £9.48m, and represented 36% of the total assets of the company. These brands are assumed to have an infinite life and so are not amortised, but their value is reviewed each year. Prudence and caution may say remove intangibles, but commercial reality may say the opposite.

Goodwill

One intangible that has presented many difficulties for accountants is goodwill. Goodwill arises from business combinations, takeovers and mergers. FRS 102, IAS 27 (revised in 2008), IFRS 3 "Business Combinations" (revised in 2008) and IFRS 10 "Consolidated Financial Statements" (effective from 2013) have all made contributions to the accounting treatment of business combinations and the presentation of consolidated (group) financial statements. Goodwill is defined as the amount paid by one company for another over and above the fair value of the net assets appearing in its balance sheet – purchased goodwill. Brands and other intangibles therefore often form part of goodwill.

Goodwill is an important intangible and can arise only when dealing with a group of companies. It is produced when one company acquires another. On acquisition all the assets and liabilities of the subsidiary that can be separately identified are valued at their fair value. IFRS 3 defines goodwill as: "Future economic benefits arising from assets that are not capable of being individually identified and separately recognised."

The calculation of goodwill is straightforward: the purchase price less the fair value of the identifiable net assets acquired, referred to as the consideration. It is its treatment in the statement of financial position that is complex and has been the subject of considerable difference of opinion. IFRS 3 shows the calculation of goodwill as:

Goodwill = consideration transferred + amount of non-controlling interest +
fair value of equity interest − net assets recognised

For example, company A offers to purchase company B for $2,000 cash. Their statements of financial position are as follows.

$	A	B		A	B
Assets	5,000	2,000	Equity	4,000	1,500
			Payables	1,000	500
	5,000	2,000		5,000	2,000

Company B has net assets of $1,500 ($2,000 assets less $500 payables). Why might company A be prepared to pay $500 more than the balance sheet value of B? There could be many reasons. Company B may have intangible assets such as brands, patents, or valuable research and development, which, though of value, do not appear in the statement. Company A may wish to gain the benefit of B's management team with its flair, experience and expertise (management does not appear in either company's statement of financial position). Or A may be attracted by the potential future profit streams that it considers can be generated from B.

Goodwill can arise only as the result of a business combination: one company acquires another. It is not recalculated each year but will be covered in the impairment of asset values undertaken each year (see below). Goodwill is particularly significant in service or people-oriented businesses. If an advertising agency or an insurance broker is acquired, it is reasonable to assume that the principal assets will be the employees of the company and their client contacts, rather than the tangible assets. The net assets, or balance sheet value, of such companies might be minimal and the resultant goodwill high.

Company A decides that $2,000 represents the fair value of the net assets of B and so is an acceptable price to pay. Company B's shareholders agree and it becomes a subsidiary of A, and consolidated accounts are prepared. Everyone is happy, except the accountant of company A. There is a basic mismatch in the transaction. Company A has paid $2,000 for assets in B which are valued at $1,500. The books do not balance.

Cash paid out	$2,000	Assets acquired	$1,500

There is $2,000 cash going out and only $1,500 assets coming in. To solve this dilemma the accountant simply adds goodwill valued at $500 to the assets acquired in company B. The books now balance.

Cash paid out	$2,000	Assets acquired	$1,500 + goodwill $500

The amount paid for the acquisition is referred to as the consideration. However large or complex the statement of financial position of the company being acquired or however fierce and acrimonious the takeover battle, the calculation of goodwill is the same.

Goodwill = consideration paid − fair value of net assets acquired

Accounting for goodwill

The considerable conflict and debate generated by goodwill arise not so much from its calculation but from its treatment in the accounts of the acquiring company. The $500 of goodwill could be treated as an asset in company A's balance sheet and written off (amortised) over a reasonable number of years in the income statement or deducted from shareholders' funds in equity.

Until 1998 UK companies did not write off goodwill in the income statement but charged it directly against reserves in the balance sheet. Thus it was possible for the elimination of goodwill to have no impact on the reported profit appearing in the income statement. In 1998 the UK fell into line with the practice adopted by most other countries. Goodwill was shown as an asset in the balance sheet and written off over its estimated useful economic life − normally not more than 20 years − using the straight line method of amortisation. Under FRS 102 goodwill is given a finite life of not more than five years.

IAS 36 requires companies to allocate goodwill to the appropriate cash-generating units (CGUs) and to test this for impairment each year as a part of the preparation of their financial statements. If it is found that the value of goodwill has fallen, it is reduced in the balance sheet and a compensating adjustment is made to the carrying amount of the assets. This is the only way goodwill can be reduced in value.

Negative goodwill

It is possible for an acquisition to be made for less than the balance sheet value of net assets. The acquirer has made a good deal − referred to as a bargain purchase − or the acquisition is loss-making and seen as having poor future prospects. For example, BMW sold the Rover car division for £1. Rover did not last long under the new management. IFRS 3 requires that negative goodwill be recognised immediately and taken to the income statement as a gain.

Acquisitions and mergers

When one company acquires another, the acquiring company must bring the acquisition into its accounts as part of non-current assets – "investment in subsidiaries". IFRS 10 requires consolidated or group accounts to be prepared by the parent company.

A special purpose entity (SPE) or variable interest entity (VIE) may have been created for off-balance-sheet leasing or other activities, as in the case of Enron. Even though the parent company does not have legal control over such companies they are now, following the fair representation rule ("substance over form"), treated as a normal subsidiary and consolidated. The precise relationship between the parent company and the subsidiary should be made clear in the accompanying notes.

Continuing with the example used earlier, company A's balance sheet reflects the transaction, with cash being reduced by $2,000 and replaced by an investment in company B's shares valued at $2,000. When an acquisition is made all the assets and liabilities of the subsidiary must be recognised by the parent company at their fair value (IFRS 13). The fair value of A's assets is $1,500 and goodwill is $500. This is the "acquisition method" or "purchase method" required by IFRS 3 to be used with all business combinations.

$	A	B		A	B
Assets	3,000	2,000	Equity	4,000	1,500
Investment in B	2,000		Payables	1,000	500
	5,000	2,000		5,000	2,000

A consolidated statement of financial position would appear as:

Group AB ($)

Assets	5,000	Equity	4,000
Goodwill	500	Payables	1,500
	5,500		5,500

Non-controlling interests

In practice, often less than 100% of a company's shares are acquired. As a rule, when more than 50% of the shares of one company are acquired by another it is necessary to bring the new subsidiary into the parent company's consolidated accounts. If 80% of the shares are acquired the remaining 20% constitute what previously was termed a minority interest and is now called a non-controlling interest (NCI). IFRS 3 defines this as: "Equity in a subsidiary not attributable, directly or indirectly, to a parent." It allows NCIs to be measured as the proportion of the net identifiable assets at the date of acquisition or, as in US GAAP, at fair value.

If company A purchases only 80% of company B's shares for $2,000, A controls B. It owns the majority of B's shares and has so gained a subsidiary company which it will consolidate into its accounts. Goodwill is $800 as it has paid $2,000 for $1,200 of B's net assets (80% of $1,500). The NCI is 20% ($300) of B's shares that are owned by outside, non-company A shareholders. Company B is not a wholly owned subsidiary. The non-controlling interest will be shown separately in the consolidated balance sheet within equity. This is referred to as the equity concept of consolidation, with the NCI seen as having a share in the total equity of the group. The company's equity ($4,000) will be shown as part of the $4,300 (including the NCI) total equity appearing in the statement of financial position.

Group AB ($)

Assets	5,000	Equity	4,000
Goodwill	800	Non-controlling interest	300
		Liabilities	1,500
Total assets	5,800	Total liabilities and equity	5,800

The non-controlling interest ($300) is also entitled to 20% of the earnings of company B and this will be shown as a separate line in the consolidated income statement as an allocation of the group's net profit or loss for the year. Details of non-controlling interests will also be shown in the consolidated statement of changes in equity.

Shares rather than cash

Company A might consider issuing shares to acquire company B rather than using cash. If A's $1 nominal value shares are quoted at $2 on the stock exchange, it could issue 1,000 shares ($2,000) in exchange for company B. If B's shareholders agree, the acquisition can take place without any cash being involved. Company B is now a wholly owned subsidiary and the group statement of financial position is as follows:

Group AB (*$*)

Assets	7,000	Share capital	3,000
Goodwill	500	Share premium	1,000
		Reserves	2,000
		Liabilities	1,500
Total assets	7,500	Total liabilities and equity	7,500

The share premium arises from the issue of 1,000 $1 shares at $2 each.

Pooling of interests

Until the adoption of IFRS 3 in 2004 it was possible for acquisitions to be treated under the "merger accounting" or "pooling of interest" method. In 1998 the Daimler-Chrysler combination used this method, then allowable under US GAAP. It was assumed that two companies came together to run a joint business rather than one taking over another. Both companies shared equally in the management and earnings of the group. There is no goodwill created as the assets are taken into the consolidated balance sheet at their carrying value – not necessarily their fair value. IFRS 3 and FRS 102 banned the pooling of interest treatment of mergers and acquisitions.

Reverse takeover

It is sometimes the case that the acquirer becomes the subsidiary of the acquired company. This occurs when a small company takes over a larger one. The acquirer issues enough shares to exchange for shares in the acquiree for control to pass. For business combination accounting all that matters is which company has the controlling interest – the acquirer. Typically, a private company acquires a controlling interest in a dormant listed company where the share price is low. This company then acquires the assets of the private company. The private company has become a listed company without the hassle normally associated with such an event. This has proved an irritation to the SEC as several Chinese companies have, in recent years, managed to acquire a listing without being subjected to the normal stringent listing rules.

Associates, joint ventures and significant interest

There are several accounting standards dealing with the various issues of the investment by one company in another. IFRS 11 defines a joint venture as "a joint arrangement whereby the parties that have joint control of the arrangement have rights to the net assets of the arrangement".

FRS 102 defines a joint venture as "a contractual arrangement whereby two or more parties undertake an economic activity that is under joint control". The joint venture maintains its own accounting records and presents financial statements. There is normally a profit-sharing agreement between the parties involved.

An associate is a business where the investor has a financial interest or investment and some degree of control. IAS 28 and FRS 102 define an associate as "an entity ... over which the investor has significant influence and that is neither a subsidiary nor an interest in a joint venture".

Associates and joint ventures appear in the balance sheet as non-current assets. When one company owns or controls more than 50% of the shares of another that company is treated as a subsidiary, and it is consolidated into accounts of the parent company. If company A owns less than 50% of the shares of company B and is thus a non-controlling shareholder, it will show the investment as part of non-current assets in its statement of financial position, and the share of B's annual profit will be taken into A's income statement – "share of profits of associates".

A simple guideline has developed where 20% share ownership is taken as the defining level of control – the level used under US GAAP. If a company owns less than 20% of the shares of another, it is treated as an investment in an associate in the balance sheet and any income received is taken to the income statement.

It is often difficult to judge the degree of control one company has over another. This was a grey area well exploited in the 1990s when the use of associates and joint ventures was a popular means of creating SPEs or special purpose vehicles (SPVs), allowing companies to disguise the true nature of their involvement in an activity. It was possible for a company to disguise its true debt position and create fictitious revenue and profits. Enron claimed profits and hid enormous debt from investors through the creative use of a complex web of SPVs – some 3,000 at the time of its collapse. Remember the golden rule: beware if you cannot understand what a company is doing or where its profits are coming from.

Where between 20% and 50% of the shares are owned it is assumed there is some degree of control. IAS 28 provides a detailed list of factors that may define a significant interest or influence such as controlling the board or active participation in management decision-making. Even where an investor has no legal control over another company but can control that company, it must be consolidated in the investor's accounts – substance over form is required for fair representation.

Equity method

For both associates and joint ventures, fair representation is the ruling factor in presentation. The equity method of accounting is used to bring them into the financial statements. IAS 28 provides guidance for this approach, which is similar to that for accounting for subsidiaries. The broad aim is to show the investment in the associate as equal to the investor's share of the associate's equity, adjusting year by year for dividends and movements in reserves. The investor's statement of financial position initially shows the investment at its cost, within non-current assets, and adjusts each year for the investor's share of the profit or loss – which is taken to the income statement.

No goodwill can arise with an associate – it is not a subsidiary – but an annual impairment review must be completed and, if necessary, the carrying value of the investment reduced. Full details of associates should be found in the notes to the financial statements.

IFRS 11 matches US GAAP in requiring, from 2013 onwards, that the equity method be applied to joint-venture investments. The equity method is a simple means of providing information on an investment that does not necessarily provide full disclosure of the financial implications involved. For example, an associate may have heavy borrowings which are not fully disclosed, as only the investor's share of the net assets is shown in the statement of financial position.

The exact level and quality of the associate's profit is also not necessarily reported. Make sure you read all the information provided on associates and joint ventures carefully.

Current assets

A current asset is held for trading purposes. The three main headings found in this section of the balance sheet are inventory, receivables (debtors) and cash. Any item appearing within the current asset heading can be taken as either being cash or capable of being turned into cash within the company's normal business operating cycle – typically 12 months.

Inventory

Year-end inventory normally consists of a mixture of raw materials, work in progress and finished goods. In the UK it is sometimes referred to as stock. For retail companies, the year-end inventory consists almost entirely of finished goods in the shops or in the warehouse. IAS 2 defines inventory as: "Assets held for sale in the ordinary course of business; in the process of production for sale; or in the form of materials or supplies to be consumed in the production process or in the rendering of services."

The basic rule for inventory valuation is that it should be shown in the statement of financial position at the lower of cost or net realisable value – cost or fair value. The appropriate figure is the lower of what it cost to make or acquire and what someone might reasonably be expected to pay for it.

Receivables

Receivables (debtors, accounts receivable) represent the amount owed to a company by customers for goods or services that have been provided but at the end of the year have not yet been paid for. The amount due at the year end is shown as trade receivables.

If a company has experienced bad debts during the year, these should have been accounted for in the income statement. It is standard practice for a company to make a regular provision each year for bad or doubtful debts; a percentage of sales revenue is assumed to be non-recoverable. The figure for receivables appearing in the statement of financial position can be taken as good debts that the company realistically expects to collect under its normal terms and conditions of trade.

Most sales are paid for by customers within two or three months. Be cautious when the terms "long-term receivables" or "deferred" receivables or revenue appear. This indicates that the company has made sales but is shifting some or all of the income into future years, possibly as a means of smoothing volatile or uncertain earnings. Alternatively, the company may be suffering sales resistance and offering customers extremely generous and extended credit terms.

Debt factoring and securitisation

Companies sometimes enter factoring arrangements, whereby they "sell" their receivables or other debts to another company and have immediate cash available for use in the business. The receivables are sold at a discount to a factor, which then collects the full amount due. Receivables are usually factored "with recourse", allowing the factor to claim reimbursement from the company if the customer fails to pay. The alternative is "without recourse", where an appropriately higher discount to the factor will be required. Details of any significant factoring arrangements should be given in the notes to the annual report.

The term securitisation may be linked to trade receivables or other assets. It refers to the packaging of assets for sale to generate immediate cash flow, and was first developed by US banks in the 1970s to raise finance from the sale of mortgage loans. The 2008 global financial crisis was fuelled by somewhat excessive and casual trading in securitised mortgage loans. In 2000 Credit Suisse issued a collateralised debt obligation (CDO) of some $340m. By the end of 2006 it had lost $125m in value.

A simple definition of a subprime mortgage is where the property value was lower than the amount of the mortgage at the time of the loan (negative equity), surely not a sensible business activity to be involved in. Packages of highly suspect subprime mortgages were put together and traded by financial institutions in a reckless pass-the-parcel game. For several major companies and their CEOs it proved fatal to be left holding the parcel when the music stopped.

Cash and investments

Cash is defined as being the cash held by a company at the balance sheet date, including all deposits repayable on demand and net of any overdrafts. These are sometimes referred to as cash equivalents or liquid resources. Investments are included in current assets only if they are short-term. Any investments shown in this section of the statement of financial position can be taken as being liquid; that is, capable of being turned into cash within a reasonably short time – three months or less. FRS 102 defines cash equivalents as:

> *Short-term, highly liquid investments that are readily convertible to known amounts of cash and that are subject to insignificant risk of changes in value.*

Impairment of asset values

To assess a company's performance or financial position, it is essential to have a realistic figure for the value of assets employed – ideally their fair value. If the value of a company's assets falls and is unlikely to recover – a permanent diminution – the statement of financial position should reflect this and the income statement should take the loss. Assets should never knowingly be overvalued. IAS 36 deals with impairment with the overall objective of defining how the recoverable amount is determined and ensuring that assets are carried at no more than their recoverable amount – fair value – with regular impairment testing of both current and non-current assets.

FRS 102 requires an annual impairment test of all intangibles, including goodwill, because these assets are considered to have more uncertain value than others appearing in the balance sheet. At the end of the first year following an acquisition, companies must review the associated goodwill for impairment. For all other assets a test should be completed if the company has any indication that the asset is impaired. The value of an asset may fall because of adverse events or conditions, such as obsolescence or damage, or significant or permanent changes in the marketplace.

An impairment review consists of comparing the balance sheet carrying values of the assets against their recoverable amount. The recoverable amount is the higher of the asset's fair value less any disposal costs likely to be incurred or its value in use. Value in use is the net present value (NPV) of the future cash flows the asset is expected to generate. To arrive at the value in use of an asset, the future cash flows are estimated and then discounted using discount tables to produce the NPV.

Present value accounting

The use of present value accounting in the preparation of financial statements has become increasingly common. In the US, Concepts Statement 7 (CON 7) provides guidance for calculating fair values.

If a company sells a product to a customer for $10,000 with 12 months' interest-free credit, what figures should appear for revenue in the income statement and receivables in the statement of financial position? It is recommended that the present value (PV) of $10,000 be used – the value of $10,000 to be received in one year's time. If the appropriate interest rate is 10%, this is $9,091 ($10,000 × 0.9091). $9,091 represents the amount you would have to invest now at 10% interest to obtain $10,000 in one year's time – it is simple arithmetic to prove this for yourself. In the following year $909 "interest" will be recognised in the income statement.

To make the calculations discount tables are used, or, ideally, the inbuilt features of a spreadsheet such as Excel. If $10,000 is to be received in five years' time with an interest rate of 10%, the present value is $6,209 (discount factor 0.6209). This is the sum that would need to be invested now at 10% compound interest to accumulate to $10,000 after five years. Discounting is compounding in reverse. There are also annuity tables available to allow ease of calculation for regular streams of income or expense. The annuity present value for a five-year income stream at 10% interest is 3.7908. The present value of $1,000 per year for five years with 10% interest is therefore $3,791.

There are two possible approaches to the calculation of the present value of cash flows. The simplest is to use the discount rate adjustment method. This assumes a single interest rate can encompass all expectations, including risk, for future cash flows. The second is the expected cash flow method, where all expectations for future cash flows are considered with a range of possible outcomes and associated probabilities incorporated. The risks and uncertainties of future cash flows should, where possible, be taken into account. Probabilities can be applied to arrive at an expected value.

Possible cash flow ($)	10,000	40,000	60,000
Probability (%)	20	60	20
Expected value ($)	2,000	24,000	12,000	**38,000**

The expected value of the likely cash flows is $38,000. If an asset is being valued, the PV of the expected cash flow, using an appropriate discount rate, provides a fair value. Using a 10% discount rate for $38,000 receivable in one year would give a fair value of $34,546 ($38,000 × 0.9091) for the balance sheet.

NPVs can be quickly calculated using the inbuilt formulas in any spreadsheet. For example, a company owns an asset with a carrying value of $100,000. The asset could be sold for $70,000. It is expected to generate $15,000 per year for the next three years when it will have a disposal value of $50,000.

	Cash flow ($)	10% PV factor	PV ($)	$
Year 1	15,000	0.9091	13,636	
Year 2	15,000	0.8264	12,396	
Year 3	15,000	0.7513	11,269	
End value	50,000	0.7513	37,565	**74,866**

The carrying value is $100,000, the fair value is $70,000 and, using a 10% interest rate, the value in use is $74,866. The value in use figure is therefore used in the statement of financial position. An impairment of $25,134 ($100,000 − $74,866) is recorded in the income statement. In future, the value in use will provide the basis for the annual depreciation charge.

An impairment review may reduce the carrying value of an asset that has previously been revalued, with the reduction in value being charged against the revaluation reserve, not the income statement.

It is claimed that the 2008 financial crisis was not helped by financial institutions being coerced into using fair value accounting. If the balance sheet is required to reflect the current market value of an asset – a mortgage loan – this may be close to zero at the time the financial statements are prepared. There is no market for the asset – it is a toxic loan. The company reduces the carrying value of the asset in its balance sheet and takes the loss into the income statement, resulting in an even more gloomy and fragile picture being presented. This form of accounting treatment can cause volatility in earnings solely because of non-current asset valuation changes.

The impairment of asset values reduces shareholders' equity and can affect rates of return and gearing measures (see Chapter 6). Although impairment testing may appear to overcome many of the problems previously met in company valuation, it must be remembered that the only facts being offered are based on estimates and forecasts made by the reporting company.

3   The income statement

THE INCOME STATEMENT deals with the operating activities of a company and is intended to provide a report on its performance during the year. It was previously called the profit and loss account in the UK, and is sometimes referred to as the statement of earnings or operations in the US. The income statement gives details of a company's income and expenditure for the year. Where sales revenue is greater than expenses a profit is produced; the reverse results in a loss – hence profit and loss account. IAS 1 first issued in 2007 is the prime source for financial statement presentation. The IASB, working with the FASB to provide separate but convergent guidance, amended IAS 1 in 2010.

Income statement presentation format

Companies are allowed a free hand in their choice of title for the income statement, but IAS 1 uses "statement of profit or loss and other comprehensive income". Whatever the title the statement must show:

■ profit or loss for the period;
■ total other comprehensive income;
■ comprehensive income for the period.

The share of the profit or loss and comprehensive income due to a non-controlling interest (NCI) should also be disclosed. Profit or loss for the period is defined as "the total of income less expenses, excluding the components of other comprehensive income". All income and expenses recognised during the year are included in the profit or loss statement.

IAS 1 does not enforce a single form of presentation but offers a list of items that should appear on the face of the income statement. It also requires the disclosure of all material items of income and expense. Fair value is the basis of measurement. Companies may show expenses either by their function (for example, cost of sales, marketing, administration) or by their nature (for example, employee costs, depreciation). They may provide additional information to improve the usefulness of the statement.

Comprehensive income

In recent years the FASB and the IASB have increased the emphasis on comprehensive income to achieve their stated aim: "to improve the comparability, consistency and transparency of financial reporting". A statement of comprehensive income (SOCI) is intended to show both realised and unrealised gains and losses in the year that have had an impact on the equity of the company. Remember that most of the changes in financial presentation have been a reaction to the 2008 global financial crisis and so have focused very much on financial institutions. The FASB and IAS 1 define total comprehensive income as being:

> The change in equity during a period resulting from transactions and other events, other than those changes resulting from transactions with owners in their capacity as owners.

Previously, profits or losses that were seen as outside the normal operations of a company could be taken directly to shareholders' equity. Following the IAS 1 format, net income, as shown in a traditional income statement, is added to other comprehensive income (OCI). This provides comprehensive income (CI) and represents the overall result of a company's activities for the year. OCI will also be found in the statement of financial position as a single line within shareholders' equity. CI includes all gains and losses for the period both realised and unrealised.

If a non-current asset's value has increased during the year this will be included in CI. Dividends will not appear in CI as they represent a transaction with the company's owners.

Examples of OCI are:

- changes in a revaluation reserve (IAS 16 and 38);
- revaluation of actuarial net-benefit pension schemes (IAS19);
- foreign-exchange translation differences (IAS 21);
- changes in value of available-for-sale assets (IAS 39);
- changes in a cash flow hedge (IAS 39 and IFRS 9).

> Comprehensive income = profit or loss + other comprehensive income

IAS 1 requires other comprehensive income to be divided into two parts: items that may be reclassified (recycled) into profit or loss, such as foreign-exchange adjustments and cash flow hedges (gains or losses); and items that will never be reclassified, such as revaluation reserve movements, actuarial gains or losses on defined benefit pensions, and gains or losses on fair value equity instruments.

The comprehensive income figure also appears in the statement of changes in equity for the year. Companies may choose between providing a single statement of comprehensive income – adding the comprehensive income section at the end of the traditional income statement – or continuing with the traditional income statement and publishing a separate SOCI.

A typical IAS 1 comprehensive income statement showing expenses by function is as follows:

PROFIT AND LOSS	$
Revenue	**1,000**
Cost of sales	(550)
Gross profit	**450**
Other income	20
Distribution costs	(60)
Administrative expenses	(50)
Other expenses	(40)
Operating profit	**320**
Finance costs	(5)
Share of associate's profit	10
Profit before tax	**325**

Income tax expense		(110)
Profit from continuing operations		**215**
Loss from discontinued operations		(15)
PROFIT OR LOSS		**200**
OTHER COMPREHENSIVE INCOME		
Items that will not be reclassified subsequently to profit or loss		
Gain on property revaluation	15	
Actuarial gains on defined benefit plans	10	
Income tax	(5)	20
Items that may be reclassified subsequently to profit or loss		
Exchange differences	15	
Available-for-sale assets	(10)	
Cash flow hedges	15	
Share of associates other CI	5	25
OTHER COMPREHENSIVE INCOME		**45**
TOTAL COMPREHENSIVE INCOME		**245**
Total comprehensive income attributable to		
Owners of the company	220	
Non-controlling interests	25	
	245	

If the costs and expenses were to be shown by their nature, the profit for the year would not change but the headings used to arrive at it would. The statement of comprehensive income would follow as set out above.

	$
REVENUE	**1,000**
Other income	20
Changes in inventories	(200)
Materials consumed	(215)
Employee benefit expenses	(160)
Depreciation and amortisation	(90)
Other expenses	(40)
Share of associate's profit	10
PROFIT BEFORE TAX	**325**

Earnings per share	
Basic earnings per share	0.32
Diluted earnings per share	0.20

A key figure shown in the income statement, normally at the end, is that of earnings per share (EPS). This is calculated by dividing the after-tax profit by the number of equity shares in issue. Earnings per share will be shown from continuing and discontinued operations and as basic and diluted (see Chapter 6).

Profit considerations

Different profits for different purposes

A considerable amount of time could be spent discussing various definitions of profit. A starting point for an accountant might be that "a profit is produced when income is greater than costs"; for an economist it might be "what you can spend during the week and still be as well off at the end of the week as at the beginning". The accountant's definition necessitates the practical application of the principles of recognition, realisation and accrual. The economist's definition would probably include capital or financial maintenance as one of financial reporting's basic principles or rules.

Profit can be defined as the difference between a company's equity or net assets at the start and end of a period. Profit can arise only when equity has increased. For example, a company starts business with equity of $1,000 and uses this to purchase an asset that is later sold for $1,500. Inflation is 10% per year, and the replacement cost of the asset at the end of the period is $1,300. What profit has the company made? The simple answer, of course, is $500. Traditional historical cost accounting shows an opening equity of $1,000, closing equity of $1,500 and, ignoring inflation, a profit for the period of $500.

Profit	=	sales revenue	−	cost of sales
$500	=	$1,500	−	$1,000

If the purchasing power of the company is to be maintained, the impact of inflation must be taken into account. Financial capital maintenance calls for $100 (10% of the opening equity) to be set aside, resulting in a profit of $400.

If the intention is to maintain the physical operating capability of the company, sufficient funds must be available to replace the asset and continue the business. Operating capital maintenance requires $300 to be earmarked for the replacement of the asset and profit becomes $200.

What happens if an investment held by a company increases in value during the year? If the investment has not been sold (realised), should the increase in value be included in income for the year? Economists would argue yes. Accountants weighed down with prudence and realisation issues generally say no. Current financial reporting practice accepts the recognition of events or transactions that have not yet been fully realised.

One of the difficulties in reading an income statement is to decide what should be taken as "the" profit for the year. This depends on what is being looked for and why. There are different profits for different purposes. It is impossible to have a single profit figure for a company, let alone a single profit for all companies. That is why you will find several different profits appearing in the income statement. After following accounting standards and satisfying the auditor, companies must still be allowed some flexibility as to which figures they highlight in the financial report.

Matching and accrual

The income statement covers a company's financial year, which normally, but not always, consists of 12 months or 52 weeks. If the income statement's main purpose is to show the profit for the year, it is important that income and expenditure be matched to relate to the year in question. There is often a difference between when a transaction occurs (cash is paid or received) and when it should appear, or be recognised, in the income statement. For example, what happens when materials are used to produce products that are sold this year but the customer is not going to pay until the next financial year? Or when materials have been received and paid for this year but not yet used in production? In the income statement, the income produced during a financial year is set against the expenses associated with that income: income and expenditure are matched.

Profit is not cash

It must not be assumed that the profit displayed in the income statement is represented by cash at the end of the year. A company can show a profit for the year, but this does not mean it has cash available. Even if a company makes no investment in assets to sustain the business for the future, a profit in the income statement is no guarantee that adequate cash or liquid assets appear in the statement of financial position at the end of the year.

When preparing an income statement, an accountant includes the total sales revenue produced during the year. This figure includes both cash and credit sales. A company offering customers credit terms is, in effect, lending them its money until payment is made. A sale is made, and therefore included in the income for the year, but no cash may have been received.

Money owed by customers is referred to as either trade receivables or debtors. Credit sales are included in the figure for sales revenue in the income statement and appear in the statement of financial position as a heading within current assets. When customers pay the amount due, the figure for receivables is reduced and the cash balance increased by the same amount in the balance sheet.

A company taking advantage of credit terms offered by its suppliers for materials and services for use during the year may not pay for them by the end of the year. Until the suppliers are paid, the money owed (trade payables or creditors) is shown in the balance sheet within current liabilities. The timing difference between the recognition of a transaction or event and the associated cash movement can have important implications for a company. When the suppliers are paid, the figure for payables reduces and the cash balance is reduced by the same amount.

Overtrading

What happens when credit given exceeds credit taken? A company may be achieving a healthy profit margin on sales but, at the same time, offering its customers much better, longer, credit terms than it can obtain from its suppliers. The terms of credit given and taken have no impact on the profit disclosed in the income statement, but they can significantly affect the cash position or liquidity of a company.

For example, a company starts the year with $2,000 cash. With no credit given or taken, sales revenue is $10,000 and the cost of sales is $8,000. A profit of $2,000 is shown in the income statement and a cash balance of $4,000 in the year-end balance sheet.

$2,000 cash + ($10,000 sales revenue − $8,000 cost of sales) = $4,000 cash

If credit is given and taken, at the end of the year the company is owed $5,000 of the $10,000 sales revenue and owes its suppliers $1,000. The cash position then changes.

$2,000 cash + ($5,000 sales revenue − $7,000 cost of sales) = $0 cash

In both examples, the net current assets have moved from $2,000 at the start of the year to $4,000 at the end. However, with the credit policy adopted in the second example, the cash position has deteriorated from $2,000 at the beginning of the year to zero at the end. Although the company may be trading profitably, it is running down its liquid resources to possibly dangerous levels. This is often referred to as overtrading: profit being generated at the expense of liquidity.

If a company extended further credit or a major customer became a bad debt, it would be forced to borrow money to keep trading. Before such an event occurred, the company might be well advised to look for alternative forms of finance for its future operations and growth.

Since the dangers of overtrading are so clear, why do companies get into such positions? Overtrading is most commonly associated with growth. A traditional means of increasing sales revenue is to offer good credit terms to customers. If the financial implications of the sales policy are not taken into account, a company may show rapid growth in revenue and profit but run out of cash and be unable to continue trading.

Another reason for adopting a generous credit policy is because everyone else does. If a business has traditional terms of trade with customers or if the majority of companies in a sector decide to change their credit terms, it is difficult for one company, particularly a small one keen to gain market share, to act differently.

How long is a year?

The standard reporting period for all companies and all countries is 12 months and accounts are presented each year. Although this is logical and useful, the calendar year is not necessarily the best timescale for company reports. Annual reports may be suitable as a basis for assessing the performance and position of retail companies but not for companies involved in gold, oil or gas prospecting or planting oak trees.

In connection with a company's income statement, it is important to be aware that occasionally the year may consist of more or less than 52 weeks or 12 months. It is common for companies to have a trading year end on the last Friday of one month of the year or to be operating on internal reports covering 13 periods of 4 weeks in the year. As a result, some years may have 53 rather than 52 weeks. If this is the case, it must be taken into account before using the figures for analysis or drawing any conclusions from comparing one company with another. Though, in practice, this does not have much impact on the analysis of the company concerned.

More significant is where there is a major change in the financial year end. A company may wish to move its year-end reporting into line with other similar companies, or it may have become part of a group of companies having a different year end. This can cause problems for financial analysis, particularly if seasonality is involved, such as a retail company moving from an end-December to an end-March year end.

Continuing and discontinued businesses

The income statement will normally show revenue and profit divided into that produced from continuing operations, discontinued operations and any acquisitions made during the year. This makes it easier to analyse the company, with details of continuing operations providing the basis upon which to forecast likely future performance.

Any material events or items that will assist a user of the annual report should be disclosed. If a company acquires another during the year and the resulting revenue or profit is more than 10% of the total of the group, it would be reasonable to assume that this information will be disclosed separately, either on the face of the income statement or in the notes.

If a company disposes of or otherwise divests itself of a business this is called a discontinued operation (IFRS 5). When this occurs, the comparative figures are restated to highlight the revenue and profit or loss of that business. The division of operating profit between continuing and discontinued operations is shown in the same way. This makes it easier to assess revenue and profit trends and therefore what the company is likely to achieve in the forthcoming year from its continuing businesses. The FASB and the IASB are working towards providing guidance for better reporting of business disposals. Emphasis will be on presenting information only on the disposal of a major line of business or geographic area of operations representing a "significant strategic shift" in the business.

Associates and joint ventures

The company's share of the profit or loss of associates, or joint ventures or arrangements (Chapter 2), is shown separately in the statement of comprehensive income. In 2013, IFRS 11 replaced IAS 31, and together with IFRS 12 and IAS 28 now deals with the provision of information on associates and joint ventures. An associate is a business over which the company has a significant influence but not complete control. The investment in associated companies will be shown as part of non-current assets.

Nuts and bolts

Sales revenue and recognition

The first figure appearing in an income statement is normally that of sales revenue, turnover or income for the year – all intercompany sales will have been removed. IAS 18 deals with sales revenue and will be replaced by IFRS 15 from December 2017. In most cases sales revenue is shown net of any sales taxes. However, some companies quote gross revenue. Watch out for this when comparing companies within a sector for size, growth, or profitability; many of the ratios discussed in this book will be distorted if gross rather than net revenues are used as their base.

The income statement should provide a single figure for sales revenue. Do not assume, however, that there can be only one correct figure. A sale is not always easy to define. Is sales revenue to be recognised when the order is placed, when the customer's cash is received, or when the order is shipped? How should revenues flowing from a five-year service and rental contract or a three-year construction project be treated?

Deciding which figure to use for sales revenue is not as simple as it might seem. In 2001, in an attempt to make some sense of revenue recognition, the ASB published a discussion paper, *Revenue Recognition*, of over 150 pages, and in 2011, jointly with the FASB, *Revenue from Contracts with Customers*. This work forms the basis for IFRS 15. Businesses face a variety of problems in deciding at what point a sale should be recognised in the income statement. It may be assumed that when the right to or ownership of the goods or services has passed to the customer that is the point at which a sale is included in the income statement. FRS 102 states that this occurs when the company has "transferred to the buyer the significant risks and rewards of ownership of the goods".

Internet and software companies have caused problems for accountants as they try to devise rules for sales revenue recognition. There are B2C (business to end consumer) and B2B (business to intermediate consumer) transactions as well as barter deals to sort out. Is there revenue to recognise when two websites "swap" advertising space? The rule here is that if the value involved cannot be quantified – measured reliably – no revenue should be recognised. This is a good example of the accountants' rule: "If you can't measure it, don't use it". Another potentially fraught area is the treatment of customers' rights of return.

Revenue is used as the basis for assessing the past, current and likely future performance of a company. It is an important factor in profitability – normally, the higher the sales revenue the greater is the profit. Revenue recognition is a problematic area; more company restatements of financial statements result from this than from any other factor. Issues of consistency, comparability, prudence, accrual, realisation, recognition and substance over form have to be faced. A simple test is whether, following the transaction, a quantifiable asset – the right to receive income in the future – and a liability – the obligation to deliver – have been created. If this is the case, the revenue should be recognised in the income statement. IAS 1 states that income should be recognised when "an increase in future economic benefits related to an increase in an asset or a decrease in a liability has arisen and can be measured reliably".

IFRS 1 ensures that the income statement includes comparative and consistent figures for the previous year. Auditors have responsibility for the accuracy of the information provided. The US Securities and Exchange Commission (SEC) requires public companies to provide comparative figures for the current and previous two years. Figures for earlier years will be included in the company's five-year or ten-year historical performance table to be found elsewhere in the annual report.

Creating sales

In the 1990s there were numerous examples of creativity enabling companies to show substantial and consistent revenue growth, at that time mistakenly seen as a key indicator of performance and success. These included:

- goods on sale or return to customers treated as sales;
- secret "side agreements" giving customers the right to cancel a sale, but including it in the sales revenue for the year;
- all potential income from long-term contracts taken immediately rather than spread over the life of the agreement;
- taking a sale into income before the customer signs the contract;
- failing to make adequate provision for bad debts;
- sending invoices to customers for fictitious deliveries in the hope that, because of their poor internal control systems, they will pay;
- taking 100% of a sale as income even though the customer has paid only a 10% deposit;
- shipping goods early before the customer expected and including them as sales revenue for the current year – an extreme example was, when a customer refused delivery, to hire a warehouse, ship the goods to it and record the sales revenue immediately;

- grossing up sales, as when a travel agent sells a $1,000 ticket on which 10% commission is earned, but takes the full $1,000 as sales revenue;
- treating investment income and interest as operating sales revenue;
- lending money to customers to finance their purchases – the loan goes to the statement of financial position and the "sale" to the income statement;
- showing income from the sale of non-current assets as operating revenue.

More were added in the early 2000s, as the SEC brought to light:

- "channel-stuffing" – McAfee persuaded distributors of its computer-security software to hold excessive levels of inventory, using a special purpose entity (SPE) to repurchase unwanted inventory;
- making sure advertisers have funds to place adverts – Time Warner induced companies to place online adverts, which also enabled it to inflate its internet customer numbers to increase confidence in performance;
- HP Autonomy, a software company, appeared able to boost revenue by selling products at a loss to attract customers and calling this a marketing expense.

Moves by accounting bodies and stock exchanges have considerably reduced the scope for creativity in financial reports. Some of the analysis discussed later can help to highlight inconsistencies or blips in financial statements and at least signal that caution is required.

Segmental reporting

It is interesting to know a company's total sales revenue for the year, but it is much more useful to be able to see in which businesses and where in the world that revenue was generated. Foreign operations may be seen as being more risky than home-based businesses, and it is useful to know where a company is making sales and profit. Watch out for examples of the Pareto principle or the 80/20 rule. Vilfredo

Pareto, an Italian economist, found that 80% of wealth came from 20% of the population. Is a company generating 80% of income from 20% of its products or geographic areas? If so, is this likely to continue to be a practical and acceptable situation?

One of the most useful notes in a company's annual report to help you understand what it does, where and how well is the one on what is called segmental information or reporting, or disaggregated information. The segmental report analyses a company's turnover, profit and assets employed by major sector of activity and location. From this it is possible to study individual businesses within a group or conglomerate and to use the data to compare them with other, perhaps single business, companies. IFRS 8 provides guidelines for segmental reporting. In 2007 the EU endorsed IFRS 8 and its focus on the management information a company uses to assess its operating businesses.

The segment report should include at least 75% of a company's revenue and profit.

UK companies have been providing segmental details since 1967 and US companies since 1970. A segment can be defined using the materiality rule of 10%. If a business or operation represents more than 10% of a company's turnover, profit or assets, it should be shown separately in the segmental analysis report. IFRS 8 has provided guidance on segmental reporting since 2009. The aim is to show "information to enable users to evaluate the nature and financial effect of the business activities in which it engages and the economic environment in which it operates".

The information used by management to run the company should help define the segments for inclusion in the report, so the presentation will be completed from a management viewpoint. Basing the segment analysis on a company's internal management information is a positive step. But it means that no precise and detailed framework can be offered for the content and presentation of the report, as each company has its own methods. The information used regularly by the chief operational decision-maker (CODM) to assess performance and allocate resources should be considered a good starting point in framing the segmental report.

Generally, the three main areas of interest are revenue, profit and assets employed. Operating profit is commonly used in segmental reporting. Revenue is divided into that from external customers – as shown in the income statement – and that from other segments (internal customers). Where a single customer accounts for more than 10% of revenue the company must disclose this and identify the segment involved, but not necessarily provide any names or figures. The total assets and liabilities are shown together with depreciation and capital expenditure for each segment. Interest paid and received is also disclosed.

There is a choice to be made between the use of business or geographical segments as the basis for reporting to the company: "The dominant source and nature of the company's risks and returns should dictate whether its primary segment reporting format will be business segments or geographical segments."

These are normally referred to as operating segments. A 2012 survey by KPMG found that the majority of companies opted for a geographic-based segment report. A typical company will have around five segments in its segment report.

A business segment can be defined by reference to:

- nature of products or services;
- nature and technology of production;
- types of markets in which the company trades;
- major classes of customers;
- distribution channels.

A geographical segment can be defined by reference to:

- proximity of operations;
- similarity of economic and political conditions;
- relationship with operations in other geographical areas;
- special risks associated with a particular country.

There are often practical problems of allocating costs and expenses. For example, how can the total cost of a group's directors be allocated, by product or by market? Such costs are defined as common costs, and when they are not spread among the segments they appear as a single line in the segmental report. Intersegment trading may create some technical problems for accountants and directors and will be shown separately in the report.

Cost of sales

Cost of sales can be considered the cost of materials and employees and other direct and indirect costs incurred in generating sales revenue including:

- direct materials;
- direct labour;
- all direct production overheads including depreciation;
- inventory change;
- hire of property, plant and equipment;
- product development expenditure.

Companies do not normally provide any further analysis of the cost of sales, although additional information may be found in the notes on the income statement.

Often details of employee numbers, non-current asset depreciation, leasing, and research and development will be found in the notes.

Change in inventory

Cost of sales includes the change in inventory between the beginning and end of the financial year. This is part of the matching process. Sales revenue for the year should be charged only with the cost of goods used in producing that revenue. Any items remaining unsold at the end of the year should not be charged against the year's revenue.

Companies adopt either the perpetual method of inventory control where the records are updated each time a transaction occurs, or the periodic method where inventory is taken every now and again – including the year end. The statement of financial position value of a retail company's inventory is often calculated by taking the selling price of the goods on shelves at the end of the year and deducting the normal profit margin – the retail method.

The value placed on inventory can be an important factor

influencing the reported profit of a company. The basic accounting routine applied to arrive at the cost of sales charge in the income statement is as follows:

Opening inventory + purchases for the year = goods available for sale
goods available for sale – closing inventory = **cost of sales**

Inventory is often attractive not only to employees (shrinkage and wastage are euphemisms for theft) but also to those preparing a company's financial statements for the opportunities it may allow for creativity. For example, if a company, for whatever reason, were to increase the value of inventory at the end of the year by $1,000, there would be an automatic improvement of reported profit of $1,000. Cost of sales is reduced by $1,000 to bring about the profit increase. A simple form of creative accounting is where a company keeps old and obsolete items valued at their cost in year-end inventory.

$	Low inventory value		High inventory value	
Sales revenue		10,000		10,000
Opening inventory	1,000		1,000	
Purchases	8,500		8,500	
	9,500		9,500	
Closing inventory	3,500	6,000	4,500	5,000
Profit		4,000		5,000

Profit is improved and the statement of financial position value for inventory increased. Nothing physical has occurred to the inventory; only its value has been changed. For every $1 added to the value of closing inventory there is an extra $1 at the bottom line of the income statement. Inventory and its valuation is an area attracting close scrutiny from a company's auditor.

Valuing inventory

Although companies may be reluctant to admit that inventory is worth less than it cost to produce, the fair presentation requirement in financial reporting ensures that the simple rule of showing inventory at the lower of cost or net realisable value (NRV or fair value) is followed (FRS 102). The lower inventory figure shows caution in both the statement of financial position valuation and in defining the profit for the year.

IAS 2, originally issued in 1975 and revised in 2003, deals with inventories. The most common method of valuing inventory is called first in first out (FIFO). This assumes that the oldest inventory items are used first. As inventory is used or sold, it is charged to production or sales at the earliest cost price. Until it was banned in 2003, a method called last in first out (LIFO) – the reverse of FIFO – was commonly used by US companies.

The second means of inventory valuation is the weighted average cost method. The two methods are illustrated below using an example where 2,000 units of materials are purchased, 1,600 used in production, leaving 400 in the closing inventory.

Purchases	$	FIFO	$
1,000 units × $5	5,000	1,000 × $5	5,000
1,000 units × $7	7,000	600 × $7	4,200
2,000	12,000	1,600	9,200

The cost of sales charge in the income statement is $9,200 and the closing inventory (400 units) is valued at $2,800 (400 units × $7). If prices are rising, FIFO may be assumed to value inventory close to its replacement cost in the statement of financial position ($4,200), but the charge for cost of sales in the income statement ($9,200) will be comparatively low. With rising prices, FIFO provides a higher "profit" than LIFO. With falling prices, LIFO is best for profit.

Purchases	$	Weighted average
1,000 units × $5	5,000	
1,000 units × $7	7,000	
2,000	12,000	$12,000 ÷ 2,000 units = **$6 per unit**

The cost of sales is $9,600 (1,600 units × $6) and the closing inventory is valued at $2,400 (400 units × $6).

Always read the notes relating to inventory valuation. They should show that the company has taken the lower of cost or NRV to produce the balance sheet value of closing inventory.

When cost is the basis for valuing inventory this normally includes the costs of raw materials and supplies, wages and appropriate overheads (indirect expenses). Read the notes supplied in the annual report to see if there has been any change in the calculation of the cost of inventory. This may be done to adjust the reported profit for the year. Companies should be consistent in their valuation methods; if this is not the case, there should be a good reason for the change.

If only a single figure for inventory is provided in the statement of financial position, read the notes supplied to see the split between the three headings: raw materials, work in progress and finished goods. A substantial or continuing increase in the level of finished goods may point to trading problems.

Sometimes reference may be made to a "product financing arrangement" where the company has "sold" inventory to a finance institution, agreeing to repurchase this at a set price (including financing costs) and date in the future. The company gains immediate access to cash with the inventory acting as security for the loan. On the agreed date the company repurchases the inventory for delivery to customers. Details of any such arrangements should be included in the notes to the accounts.

Gross profit

Gross profit is the first profit shown in the statement of comprehensive income using the by nature classification of expenses. This is produced by deducting the cost of sales from sales revenue. Other operating costs and expenses are deducted from gross profit to provide the operating profit and profit before income tax for the year.

Auditors' fees

The fees paid to a company's auditors will be shown under administrative expenses in the income statement. This figure should clearly distinguish between fees for audit and fees paid to the same firm for other work such as consultancy assignments (unlikely nowadays) or special investigations. For UK FTSE 350 listed companies, total audit fees are around £1 billion per year. A company's audit committee has the responsibility of negotiating the audit fee and overseeing the work done. Details will be provided in their report.

Employee details

As part of the annual reporting process, companies disclose details of full-time and part-time staff, either the number at the end of the financial year or, more commonly, the average, by category, employed during the year. The total payment to employees is also shown. The employee or staff cost heading covers all wages and salaries, social security costs, pensions and other employment-related payments.

Anyone legally contracted to work for the company is an employee, including part-time workers and directors. Where a company has a contract with a self-employed person, who by definition is not an employee of the company, the money is normally included under the other costs and charges heading. Directors who have a service contract with the company are classed as employees. Thus the total cost of directors is included in the figure for staff or employee expenses. There will be separate notes that deal in some detail with directors' remuneration and rewards.

Pensions

The reward for long service with a company is normally a pension. In 1991 it was discovered that Robert Maxwell had misappropriated some £450m from his company's pension fund. This illustrated the importance of keeping the pension fund separate from the control of the company. Companies operating a defined pension plan had some control over the amount paid in and if the investments grew faster than expected, they could both reduce the charge and bring the profit into revenue. In 1992 the Cadbury Committee made recommendations on accountability and corporate governance. Pension funds now have assets that are legally separate from the company and cannot be touched even in the event of the company's bankruptcy. There are two types of pension scheme:

- Defined contribution. The employer pays a regular amount (normally a proportion of the wage or salary of the employee) into a pension fund. On retirement the employee receives a pension that is dependent on the size of the pension fund and its returns from investment. The company has no obligation to pay beyond its agreed contribution to the pension fund.

■ Defined benefit. The pension is linked to the employee's salary level or years of service. The company has an obligation to pay the pension whether or not the pension fund has sufficient assets or income. The company takes actuarial advice as to how much to put into the fund each year to allow future payment to retired employees. This will include the calculation of the average life expectancy of employees and the revaluation each year of the pension fund to produce a surplus or deficit.

The aim of accounting for pensions is to match the pension cost against income when it is paid. To defer any expense recognition until a pension is actually paid does not adequately match income and expense. In the early years there will be a low level of expense but it rises rapidly in later years. Matching the expected future cost against current income is crucial.

You may see reference to the "corridor approach", which was previously allowed under IAS 19 to set limits on the actuarial differences being taken to the income statement. From 2013 all actuarial gains or losses will be shown in the statement of other comprehensive income.

IAS 19, revised in 2011, deals with employee benefits, but not the financing of pension schemes. FRS 102 requires pension costs to be charged to the income statement with any actuarial gain or loss being recognised in full in the statement of comprehensive income. The statement of financial position will show the fair value of the pension obligation. The notes to the financial statements should offer full details of a company's post-employment benefits including a reconciliation of the movements during the year and the net asset or liability reported in the balance sheet.

Directors' rewards

Directors' service contracts

The Greenbury Code and the Hampel Committee (see Chapter 1) recommended that UK directors be given service contracts of no more than one year's duration. The 2006 Companies Act sets an upper limit of two years for directors' contracts, though shareholders can vote for a longer duration. The UK Corporate Governance Code, issued by the FRC in 2010, recommends that directors of large listed (FTSE 350) companies be subject to annual election by shareholders, and that all other company directors should serve no more than three years before re-election.

Directors' remuneration

The actions and activities of a company's directors form an important part of corporate reporting. In most countries there has been a flow of legislation, regulation or stock-exchange requirements covering disclosure of details of a company's financial dealings with its directors. The Cadbury Report stated:

> *The overriding principle in respect of board remuneration is that of openness. Shareholders are entitled to a full and clear statement of directors' present and future benefits, and of how they have been determined.*

The Combined Code requires that three or more non-executive directors form a remuneration committee. This committee is to develop and oversee the company's remuneration policy and the individual rewards of each executive director and the chairman. The committee will consider benefits in kind, share-based payments and any long-term incentive schemes. The intention is to provide a clear and transparent process for setting directors' remuneration, with no director being involved in his or her personal reward package. Normally, the terms of reference and other details concerning the remuneration committee will be found on the company's website.

In the UK, the Directors' Remuneration Report Regulations (published in 2002), the Combined Code on Corporate Governance, updated by the FRC in 2006, and stock-exchange Listing Rules govern the directors' report, which includes the remuneration committee report. This provides full details of the scope, membership and workings of the committee. Details of the individual directors' remuneration packages are normally shown here. There may also be details of the number of board meetings attended during the year by each director.

Included in the remuneration committee report will be details of each named director's:

- shareholding and options;
- salary and benefits (including increases during the year);
- bonuses and long-term incentives (cash and shares);
- key performance targets used in bonus schemes;
- service contracts;
- pension schemes.

The broad objective of a remuneration committee is seen as ensuring that:

> [The] levels of remuneration should be sufficient to attract, retain and motivate directors of the quality required to run the company successfully, but a company should avoid paying more than is necessary for this purpose. A significant proportion of executive directors' remuneration should be structured so as to link rewards to corporate and individual performance.

Best practice requires directors' rewards to be firmly based on appropriate objective performance-related measures. These are referred to as key performance indicators (KPIs), which are defined by the 2006 Companies Act as:

> Factors by reference to which the development, performance or position of the business of the company can be measured effectively.

The UK government became concerned that directors' remuneration was getting out of control, resulting in a failure of effective corporate governance. In 2012 measures were announced to provide for better oversight of directors' rewards through more detailed and structured directors' remuneration reports.

The directors' remuneration report is in two parts. The first sets out the company's remuneration policy and its development. Shareholders are offered the opportunity to vote on their directors' remuneration policy. The policy should be reviewed every three years. The second, published each year in the annual report (from 2014), explains how the policy was implemented during the year and the links between company performance and executive reward. A single figure for actual remuneration received by each director is shown.

Share options

Rather than being paid in cash employees may be given shares in their company. This is seen as an effective means of providing employees with the incentive to assist in the creation of a successful company. If the company performs well, the share price will rise and they will benefit. Share options may be offered as an alternative to pay or as part of an executive remuneration package. The current market share price can be taken as a simple guide to the benefits employees are receiving. Share options have long formed a part of directors' remuneration packages.

It can be argued that share options offer management rewards but no penalties, and that they focus attention on short-term gains that may not be in the long-term best interests of the company. Management does not have the same downside as shareholders if things go wrong.

Many companies operate share (stock) incentive plans (SIPs). These give all employees the opportunity of owning shares in their company. Other companies offer selected employees, as a reward for past or as an incentive for future performance, the right to purchase shares at a favourable price. Share options can be a more effective means of providing employees with net income than straightforward taxable remuneration. In the 1990s many e-companies offered share options. The cost to the company was negligible and no cash was involved. The potential reward for the individual could be significant, and this was expected to ensure loyalty and top performance. In 2000, when many of these companies joined the "99% Club" (their share price dropped to 1% of its previous level), the true value of the share options was revealed.

IFRS 2 (130 pages in length), IAS 26 and FASB Statement 123 deal with share-based payment schemes. A key issue is the timing: when does the benefit from the share option occur? When should it be recognised in the income statement? Is it on the granting of the option or when the option is exercised? Whether it is even appropriate to charge the income statement with the fair value of share options has been the subject of fierce debate between businessmen (anti) and accountants (pro). Both the FRC and the FASB were in favour of charging the fair value of the share option as an expense in the income statement, but they came under considerable corporate and political pressure not to follow this route. Eventually the accountants got their way.

Share options act to reduce shareholders' investment: when shares are issued their holding is worth less. There is a transfer from shareholders to management. IFRS 2 requires that the cost of the option be set at the time it is granted not when it is exercised. Share options are not revalued each year. The value of the option is set with reference to the fair value – normally the market price – of the shares when granted. If a comparable market price is not available, an option-pricing model – such as the Black-Scholes-Merton (BSM) formula, or the Cox, Ross and Rubinstein binomial model – may be used. The pricing model must take into account the:

- exercise price of the option;
- expected term of the option;
- current market price of the share;
- expected volatility of the share price;
- dividends expected to be paid;
- risk-free interest rate.

If a share option, expected to be taken up in five years' time, is offered when the current share price is $10, with a risk-free interest rate of 4%, the option value is $1.78 per share.

PV of $10 at 4% in 5 years = $ 8.22 $10 – $8.22 = **$1.78**

The time value of money (present value or PV) is used to calculate the value of $10 received at the end of five years with an interest rate of 4% as $8.22. If $8.22 is invested for five years at 4% interest, in the first year it would earn $0.33 interest, in the second year $0.34 and so on until the capital value at the end of the fifth year is $10. This calculation is completed using present value factor (in this case 0.8219) tables found in any spreadsheet application.

The risk-free interest rate is normally taken to be that of government treasury notes with a similar lifespan to that of the option. Any dividends that would have been received on the shares are similarly discounted and the total deducted from the option – they have been forgone – to produce the net value. The fair value of an option is charged to the income statement over its expected life – this is the period it is earned by the employees. A compensating adjustment is made to equity which will show the share options granted as a separate item.

The remuneration committee's report and notes should provide full details of each director's options awarded or exercised during the year and the number of shares involved at end of the year. There are some weighty notes in the annual report. Do not be put off as their study may well repay the effort of analysis. IFRS 2 ensures that as a minimum the following information will be available:

- the nature and extent of the scheme;
- how fair value was determined;
- the effect on the profit or loss for the period;
- the effect on the company's financial position.

Make a loss, take a profit

There have been many examples of directors receiving substantial sums – described by Vince Cable, a British politician, in 2012 as "rewards for failure" – in return for giving up their tenure of incompetence in managing loss-making companies. Charles Prince, CEO of Citigroup, left the company in some disarray. In 2007 it was expected that the bank might have to write off some $10 billion of subprime loans. Eventually, after a $45 billion government contribution, the figure was nearer $100 billion. Prince seems to have walked away with more than $40m, including pension, accumulated stock options and a final-year bonus of $12m. He did say "sorry", but he is likely to be remembered for his statement:

> When the music stops ... things will get complicated. But as long as the music is playing, you've got to get up and dance.

Other financial institutions were forced to make more than generous final payments to executives who had taken their company to the brink, and sometimes over the edge, of the precipice. Any payment in compensation for loss of office and any significant payments made to directors, including former directors, should be fully disclosed in the annual report.

The annual report gives details of the directors' aggregate remuneration or emoluments and identifies the total amount paid to each director for services in connection with the management of either the holding company or any subsidiary. Pensions paid to past directors are also shown. The disclosure should make it possible to identify all the payments made to directors during the year. For example, if a retired director is allowed to continue using a company car, the estimated value of this benefit should be shown separately within the disclosure on post-employment benefits.

Operating profit

An important measure and indicator of a company's performance is the profit made from running the business; that is, the profit generated from its operations. If gross profit is not shown, this is normally the first profit disclosed in the income statement. Operating profit is calculated by deducting the cost of sales plus other operating expenses from sales revenue. It is reasonable to assume that the operating profits of different companies trading in the same business sector can be compared on a common basis.

Depreciation and profit

Capital maintenance is an important factor in corporate reporting. To continue in business, a company is expected at least to maintain the current level of investment in operating assets and to replace these assets as they wear out or become obsolete. Capital employed is on one side of the statement of financial position and assets on the other. If assets are maintained, capital must also be maintained. One way of achieving this is through depreciation, the setting aside of current revenue for future reinvestment in the business. The cost of the asset is charged against income over its useful working life. IAS 16 requires all tangible assets, except land, to be depreciated, and defines depreciation as "the systematic allocation of the depreciable amount of an asset over its useful life".

It is possible to consider depreciation in at least three ways:

■ In the statement of financial position a company is expected to provide a reasonable representation of the fair value of its assets. In normal circumstances a new car is worth more than an old car. As an asset gets older and its value decreases, this change in value should be reflected in the statement of financial position.

■ As a company carries on its business, it uses resources. It incurs costs and expenses, uses labour and materials (direct costs), and uses up some of the value of the non-current assets, property, plant and equipment employed in the business. To produce a profit or loss in the income statement, all costs and expenses are deducted from revenue. The direct costs are charged and some allowance made for the cost of using the non-current assets during the year. Part of the value of property, plant and equipment has been used up during the year (indirect costs). To reflect this an amount is charged in the income statement. Thus depreciation may be considered to be the cost of the various non-current assets being used during the year.

■ If a company is to continue in business, at some stage it will have to replace its non-current assets as they wear out or become obsolete. To provide for this the company prudently sets aside funds. Depreciation is charged in the income statement but is not actually paid out to any third parties; it is retained in the company.

A company that fails to charge depreciation breaches not only the requirement of prudence in financial reporting but also the fundamental requirement of capital maintenance.

Calculating depreciation

The annual depreciation charge should reflect "the pattern in which the asset's future economic benefits are expected to be consumed".

There are many ways of calculating depreciation. For example, a company purchases an asset with an expected working life of four years for $10,000. The company makes a profit of $3,000 per year, 50% of which is distributed as a dividend to shareholders. At the end of the fourth year the replacement cost of the assets is $10,000.

If no depreciation were charged, the company would retain $6,000 profit ($1,500 for four years). If there were no other transactions, this would appear in the closing cash balance at the end of year four. There would not be sufficient funds available for replacement. Had the company charged $2,500 per year for depreciation (writing off the asset over the four-year working life), the net profit would have been only $500 each year. If 50% of this had been paid to shareholders as dividend, there would have been only $1,000 of retained profit at the end of year four. However, there would be $10,000 available in cash to replace the asset ($2,500 for four years). IAS 16 offers three methods of depreciation: straight line, diminishing balance and unit of production.

Straight line method

The simplest and most commonly used method of calculating depreciation is the straight line method. The cost or value of the asset is divided by its anticipated useful working life to produce the annual depreciation charge.

Cost of asset	$10,000
Estimated useful working life	4 years
Annual depreciation charge	$2,500

Diminishing balance method

A second method, often required by tax authorities, is the diminishing or reducing balance method. This is sometimes referred to as accelerated depreciation as the higher charges occur in the first few years of the asset's life.

Cost of asset	$10,000
Depreciation rate per year	50%

In the first year $5,000 depreciation is charged in the income statement. This reduces the carrying value of the asset to $5,000, and so in the second year the depreciation charge is $2,500. Under this method the asset is never written down to a zero value.

A variation on this approach is the sum of the digits method. The expected useful working life of the asset is four years. All the digits

– 1,2,3,4 – are added together, producing a total of 10. (If the asset life is ten years, the sum is 55.) In the first year the depreciation charge is four-tenths of the asset value ($4,000), in the second it is three-tenths, and so on, until in the final year one-tenth is charged to fully depreciate the asset.

Unit of production method

This is sometimes referred to as the unit of activity method. The total number of units that the asset is expected to produced is calculated. The cost of the asset is divided by this number to provide the depreciation charge per unit produced.

Cost of asset	$10,000
Expected units to be produced over asset's working life	100,000
Depreciation charge per unit of production	$0.10

If 30,000 units are produced in the first year, the depreciation charge will be $3,000. This depreciation method provides the most direct link between the use being made of the asset and the charge made against operating income. However, if the asset is not used during the year, there will be no charge against income even though, realistically, the asset can be assumed to have lost value.

The three methods of calculating depreciation will, each year, result in a different charge for the asset being made in the income statement and in its carrying value in the statement of financial position.

$	First-year charge	Year-end value
Straight line	2,500	7,500
Diminishing balance	5,000	5,000
Unit of production	3,000	7,000

Depreciation policy

Always read the notes on non-current assets and their depreciation carefully. A company's asset valuation and depreciation policies should be reasonable, prudent and consistent. If this is not the case, you need to satisfy yourself that income is not being manipulated. It is possible to boost reported profit if all expenses relating to an asset, including the interest charges for its finance, are capitalised rather than charged to the income statement. Compare the company's policy with that of others in the same sector to make sure there is conformity.

It is not difficult to imagine a situation in which a company would prefer not to operate a prudent depreciation policy. Low profitability might be bolstered by not charging any depreciation in the first year of a new asset being brought into operation. The company might argue that as the new investment – particularly if it is property – was operational for only part of the year, it is reasonable that it should not be subject to depreciation. Thus the new investment would generate revenue but not be burdened with the depreciation. Once such an approach is accepted, the consistency rule will ensure its application in future years.

Taxing matters

The profit before tax reported in a company's accounts is unlikely to be the profit used to calculate its eventual tax liability. A simple means of assessing this is to estimate the actual tax rate being paid on a company's reported profit. This can be done by using the pre-tax profit and income tax expense appearing in the income statement. The resulting figure can then be compared with the rate of company taxation for the country involved. A number of international companies have been criticised for managing their corporate structures to ensure they pay as little tax as possible in high-tax countries. This is tax avoidance and, though seen by some as unethical, is not illegal. Tax evasion is illegal.

Generally, the actual company tax rate will be found to be lower than the standard rate imposed by government. The rate of tax being paid should be disclosed, and the amount due at the end of the year shown in the statement of financial position as part of current liabilities. IAS 12 requires that the tax due on a company's ordinary operations should be shown in the statement of comprehensive income.

Tax allowable depreciation

If companies were allowed to set their own rates of depreciation in arriving at taxable profit without any external controls or guidance, no company would need to end up with a tax liability. The standard practice in most countries is to have two rates of depreciation, one that is allowed and accepted for tax purposes and one that is applied by companies in their financial reports. Inevitably, there is a difference between the profit a company declares to its shareholders and the profit it declares to the tax authorities. Accounting profit is defined under generally accepted accounting principles (GAAP); taxable profit is defined by IAS 12 as:

> *The profit for a period, determined in accordance with the rules established by the taxation authorities, upon which income taxes are payable.*

Deferred taxation

Depreciation is often the cause of a significant difference between a company's reported and taxable profit. A company has little option but to accept the tax rules prescribed by the country or countries in which it operates. If tax incentives are offered to encourage investment, any company can be expected to take full advantage of them. However, this can affect its reported after-tax profits. This is the result of what is called timing or temporary differences.

One explanation for the taxation differences is that a company may depreciate its non-current assets using the straight line method of depreciation but is required by the tax authority to use a different depreciation method – normally an accelerated rate method – in calculating its taxable profit. As an incentive to investment, companies may be allowed to charge 125% of the asset cost as tax allowable depreciation, or be allowed to charge the total cost against taxable income in the first year of operation. A difference arises in the amount charged in the income statement to arrive at the profit for the year and that used in the tax calculation. Some tax is deferred to future years.

A company may have interest income during the year of $5,000 which will be included in pre-tax profit. If tax is paid only when the interest is received in cash, and at the end of the year $1,000 is still due, the company's taxable profit will not be the same as its accounting profit. The impacts of investment and the associated tax implications may not occur in the same time period. This can distort the reported after-tax profits and is overcome by use of a deferred taxation account, sometimes referred to as a tax equalisation account.

IAS12 requires a company to show the amount of tax that relates to the pre-tax profit being reported. This is not the same as showing the actual amount of tax paid in the financial year. The income statement should show the amount of tax due to be paid in the current year (current tax expense). The statement of financial position should show the future tax liability (deferred tax liability). Deferred tax will be calculated using the expected future tax rates that will apply to the transaction involved. There may be both deferred tax liabilities and deferred tax assets. A deferred tax asset is where tax will be recoverable in future years including unused tax losses and credits.

Reconciling the books

Companies keep at least three sets of books. One is for management to enable them to run the company; the second is for the tax authorities to calculate the annual tax liability; and the third is presented to the shareholders at the AGM in the annual report. The three sets should, under normal sound accounting practices, be capable of reconciliation.

Capital or revenue

The decision on whether an item should be treated as capital (statement of financial position) or revenue (income statement) in the year reinforces the links between the statement of financial position and the income statement in connection with the treatment of non-current assets. Revenue expense is related to the normal business activity of the company or is concerned with maintaining the non-current assets. Capital transactions are normally intended to provide a long-lasting asset to the company.

The treatment of research and development (R&D) costs is a good example of the potential importance of the revenue or capital expense decision. The result of this decision can have a significant impact on both the income statement and the statement of financial position.

For example, a company invests $100,000 in R&D each year. It is expected that the new products and services delivered by the R&D will come on stream over the next ten years. The company's policy is to provide shareholders with a regular $25,000 dividend, as shown in year 1.

$	Year 1	Year 2a	Year 2b
Profit for the year	150,000	75,000	75,000
R&D expense	100,000	100,000	10,000
Profit	50,000	(25,000)	65,000
Dividend	25,000	0	25,000
Retained profit	25,000	(25,000)	40,000

The company experiences a downturn in business, profit is halved in year 2 and there is insufficient profit available to pay the dividend (year 2a). There is little the company can do in operational terms (generating additional revenue or reducing costs), but it might be tempted to consider a change in its policy for the treatment of R&D.

It could be argued that a better form of presentation and a more accurate reflection of the events would result from spreading the investment in R&D. That is, it would be better to spread the amount spent on R&D over the years when the new products and services result. It could be argued that it is unfair accounting treatment to burden one year's sales revenue with what is really ten years' investment in R&D.

The company opts to charge only one-tenth of the R&D spend against year 2 sales revenue, and to continue writing it off over the next nine years. The charge in the income statement is $10,000 (year 2b) and the balance, $90,000, is capitalised as a non-current asset in the statement of financial position.

The impact of this change in accounting presentation is that the company in year 2b shows a profit of $65,000, and so may pay the dividend to its shareholders. It also exhibits a new asset, R&D valued at $90,000, in the statement of financial position. Although it is not possible to fault the book-keeping involved in this exercise, it might be possible to raise questions about the validity of displaying R&D as an asset in the balance sheet.

There were many examples of companies capitalising R&D and then discovering that under pressure it was impossible for it to be translated quickly into positive cash flow. In response to this, and to avoid the potential misrepresentation or error in companies' financial reports, R&D became subject to an accounting standard which enforced the prudence rule and required companies to write it off as incurred.

IAS 38 defines research as "original and planned investigation undertaken with the prospect of gaining new scientific or technical knowledge and understanding". Development is defined as: "The application of research findings or other knowledge to a plan or design for the production of new or substantially improved ... products ... or services before the start of commercial production or use."

The future economic benefit likely to flow from research is uncertain. It is an intangible internally developed asset and, as with internally generated goodwill, it cannot be capitalised. IAS 38 provides a list of criteria which must be met for development expenses to be capitalised.

The example of R&D may now be only of historical interest, but many of the same issues face companies today regarding such intangibles as brand names (see Chapter 2). When a company is so desperate to show a profit that it throws the rulebook away, it is not unusual to see expenses capitalised. In the 1990s there were examples of companies:

- adding maintenance and repairs to non-current asset values;
- capitalising software that had dubious real value;
- capitalising internal software costs;
- capitalising marketing and advertising expenses.

Once this is done the cost is written off over a number of years or treated as a one-off non-recurring or special charge not affecting the current year's reported profit. With the CEO insisting "we have to hit our numbers", reducing real capital expenditure and capitalising operating expenses were crucial to WorldCom's creative accounting, contributing some $3.8 billion to the overall $11 billion fraud.

Interest

Interest paid by a company on borrowings and interest received on investments is shown either on the face of the income statement or in the notes. Often the income statement figure is for net interest payable, representing the interest payable less the interest received and any interest capitalised.

The total interest payable during the year should be divided into interest relating to short-term borrowings, such as bank loans, repayable on demand or within 12 months, and interest on loans falling due within five years.

Capitalising interest payments

If a company borrows money to complete a major project, such as building a new factory or hypermarket, it is possible, under IAS 23, to capitalise the interest payments and write them off following the company's normal depreciation policy. Although this is acceptable as the interest expense has been incurred to allow the asset to be built, it does increase the reported profit. The notes in the accounts should clearly indicate how much interest has been capitalised during the year.

When looking at the interest paid by a company, perhaps for use in an interest cover measure, it is best to use the total interest payable figure. That a company has capitalised a proportion of its interest payments does not affect how much interest it has to pay.

Effective interest method

When a company invests or borrows money for a number of years in return for interest payments, there are some issues of recognition and valuation to be tackled. A company sells a product for $50,000 with a down payment from the customer of $10,000 and five annual instalments of $10,000. If the current cash price for the product is $40,000, and the ruling interest rate is 5%, what should be shown in the accounts? It would not be correct to record a sale of $60,000 immediately in the income statement. IAS 18 requires the transaction to be shown as part sales revenue and part interest income spread over the life of the contract.

The effective interest rate must be calculated. This is the rate that discounts the expected future income or expense stream to equal the current carrying amount of the asset or liability. This is undertaken using discounting techniques.

Using the present value of an annuity table (regular amounts paid for a defined number of years), it can be seen that the 5% factor for five years is 4.3295. If $10,000 is to be received for the next five years, its present value is $43,295. If $43,295 were invested today at 5% interest, in five years' time it would be worth $50,000. Alternatively, if a loan was taken out for $43,295, it would be repaid (plus interest) with five annual payments of $10,000 according to the example below. The second column gives the 5% interest charge on the reducing balance and the third column the amount of principal that is being repaid.

Year	Payment, $	5%	Principal, $	Balance, $
				43,295
1	10,000	2,165	7,835	35,460
2	10,000	1,773	8,227	27,233
3	10,000	1,362	8,638	18,594
4	10,000	930	9,070	9,524
5	10,000	476	9,524	0

The present value can be used to calculate the amount to be brought into the income statement as recognised revenue. The company should recognise $53,295 ($10,000 down payment + PV $43,295) income in the first year. Each year the company would bring into the income statement the interest shown in column three of the example ($2,165 and so on).

Operating and finance leases

A further example of the distinction between capital and revenue items is found in the treatment of leases. FRS 102 and IAS 17 provide the guidelines for the treatment of lease agreements and define a lease as "an agreement whereby the lessor conveys to the lessee in return for a payment or series of payments the right to use an asset for an agreed period of time".

Should lease payments be treated as an operating expense (income statement) or as the acquisition of a non-current asset (statement of financial position)? The decision will affect reported profit for the year. The reporting of lease arrangements was manipulated by companies in the 1990s to bolster profits and disguise asset ownership.

The main criterion is whether the rights and associated risks and rewards of ownership of the asset pass to the lessee. If they do, the lease is capitalised and taken into the statement of financial position (a finance lease). If they do not, it is assumed that the asset is being rented and the lease payments are included as an operating expense in the income statement (an operating lease).

A finance lease is one "that transfers substantially all the risks and rewards incidental to ownership of an asset. Title may or may not be eventually transferred".

Substance over form – fair representation – requires that if the lease in effect transfers ownership to the lessee, it is treated as the acquisition of an asset. In 1974 Court Line, a UK package holiday company, collapsed. It leased its aircraft and kept them off-balance sheet. It had some £18m of shareholders' funds but more than £40m of lease obligations. Today the application of IAS 17 would ensure the substance of the lease agreements would show in the statement of financial position under the heading of finance leases.

Any other type of lease agreement is an operating lease. An operating lease shows the lease payments as an expense in the income statement and there are no entries in the statement of financial position.

A finance lease is recognised in the statement of financial position at the fair value of the leased asset or the present value of the minimum lease payments (MLP). If a lease is agreed for an asset with an immediate payment of $10,000 and three annual payments of $10,000, and an implicit interest rate of 10%, it has a discounted present value of $34,869 (down payment $10,000 × PV factor 2.4869). The present value of minimum lease payments is $34.869. An asset and a lease liability are recognised and depreciated over the lease period.

IAS 17 requires that leases be classified according to their life – within one year, 2–5 years and longer than five years – with the PV and MLP shown for each class of lease.

Dividends

The profit attributable to shareholders forms the potential source of dividend payments. A dividend can only be paid from profit. If a dividend were paid from capital, the capital maintenance rule would be breached. The dividends the company has paid (interim dividends) and the amount the directors have proposed for the year (final dividend) are normally shown as a single figure in the statement of changes in equity.

When a dividend is declared as 10% this relates to the nominal value of the shares involved, not their market value. A company with $1 or £1 shares paying a 10% dividend is offering shareholders 10¢ or 10p per share.

It is common for companies to offer shareholders, as an alternative to taking a cash dividend, a scrip or stock dividend. This has the advantage of not reducing the company's cash balances and of offering shareholders additional shares with the possibility of increased capital gains and future dividends.

No profit, no dividend

Basic good housekeeping would suggest that a company with little or no profit should not be expected to pay a dividend. Technically, it is possible for a company with a loss for the year to pay a dividend. As long as it has sufficient distributable reserves in the statement of financial position, and of course enough cash, a dividend can be declared.

Retained earnings

After all costs, expenses, and interest and dividend payments have been covered, what is left is retained earnings (net income or surplus). This is taken to the statement of financial position to add to the accumulating shareholders' interest (equity).

Pro forma profits

Always make sure the profit figures you are using are taken from the published income statement. A recent trend is for companies to offer "pro forma" financial information to investors. In 2002 the

International Organisation of Securities Commissions (IOSCO) recommended caution when using non-GAAP figures:

> *Investors should be aware that non-GAAP pro forma earnings measures are not prepared in accordance with the accounting standards applied to financial statements and may omit or reclassify significant expenses.*

In the US, the Sarbanes-Oxley Act of 2003 was supported by the SEC with firm rules covering all pro forma financial information released by listed companies

Interim reports

The annual report is not the only financial statement available to assist in the analysis of a company's performance and position. Listed companies are required to publish interim reports. These normally cover a period of three or six months. The objective is to keep investors aware of company performance. IAS 34 details the minimum content for an interim report. The report should assist in identifying any changes in the organisation, trends or volatility of company income, liquidity and cash flow generation. It should also bring investors up to date with new activities or circumstances arising since the last annual report. Comparative figures are provided.

There are two views of an interim report. US companies see it as part of the annual reporting process (integral view) and expenses are spread over the appropriate period. UK companies see it as a separate report (discrete view) to be prepared in exactly the same way as the annual report, and expenses are recognised as incurred with no spreading. A company can opt to present a complete set of financial statements rather than the condensed format, which includes a condensed:

- balance sheet;
- income statement;
- changes in equity statement;
- statement of cash flows.

Also disclosed are:

- earnings per share;
- dividends paid;
- segmental analysis;
- statement of accounting policies and methods;
- management discussion of events.

Companies generally publish their interim statements only online. Shareholders will not necessarily be mailed copies.

Preliminary announcements

Companies are expected to make a preliminary announcement of annual results and dividend within 120 days of the financial year end, with most companies complying within 90 days. The preliminary announcement contains information similar to that of an interim report, and, ideally, provides some linkage to the final quarter or second half of the year. It acts as a quick overview of the annual report and normally forms the basis of a company's press releases and media comments on its performance.

Receipt of a preliminary announcement used to be a major advantage for analysts as it was not mailed to shareholders. The internet now makes it possible for anyone using the company's website to have almost as speedy access to this information as the professionals.

4 The statement of cash flows

A COMPANY'S INCOME STATEMENT can show a healthy profit for the year, but this does not guarantee that it has the cash necessary to survive. Profit is not cash. Profit is an accounting measure; cash is a physical item. In the 1970s and 1980s many apparently profitable companies failed because of a lack of cash. This increased pressure for financial reports to give more emphasis to a company's cash flows, liquidity and borrowings. Thus the statement of cash flows became the third significant financial statement to be presented by companies in their annual reports. Cash flow statements were introduced in the US in the late 1970s and the UK in the early 1990s. Today the statement of cash flows is crucial in understanding the three elements of a company's underlying performance and position: operations, investment and finance.

No cash, no business

Profit is part fact, part opinion and occasionally part hope. Different assumptions, views and accounting treatment will produce different profits. Low profitability or loss-making operations may be distressing or embarrassing for management but not necessarily terminal for a company. Companies can survive without profit as long as they have cash available. Even a profitable company cannot survive without cash.

Every activity of a company is translated into cash at some time. Companies use it to pay employees and suppliers and customers use it to purchase products and services. It is necessary to allow investment in assets to support growth and to pay interest and dividends to providers of financial resources, and to pay taxes. At any time there is a single indisputable figure for cash, which can be physically counted and checked.

What is cash?

Cash is normally understood to be the notes and coins used in the day-to-day transactions of companies and individuals. For the purposes of accounting and financial analysis the definition of cash is slightly broader, including not only coins and notes but also money held in bank accounts and short-term investments. These cash or near-cash assets form part of a company's liquid assets and are referred to as cash equivalents. A starting point for assessing the strength of a company's cash position is to look at the changes in the amounts of cash held at the beginning and end of the year. All that is required is two consecutive statements of financial position. An increase in cash held could be taken to be a good sign, representing an improvement in liquidity. However, in making an assessment of a company's liquidity, any short-term borrowings, such as overdrafts in the UK, should be deducted from cash and bank balances to identify the net position.

Cash balances

For most purposes cash can be taken to include all cash and bank balances net of overdraft or other borrowings repayable on demand, and short-term investments readily turned into cash. In other words, the cash a company can readily find for immediate use. Although cash is essential in the running of any business, it is, except for any interest it may earn, a non-productive asset that can be used to increase productive resources or to repay debt, thus reducing interest charges and improving profitability. A company with a shortage of cash may be in trouble. A company with a lot of cash may not be operating as profitably as it could be. But you should be careful not to read too much into the cash balance given in the annual report. A large figure may simply reflect the setting aside of money to pay for items in the following financial year.

Cash equivalents

To understand the true liquid position of a company it is not sufficient to concentrate on cash in hand. Most companies make use of available cash balances, putting them to work to generate income. Short-term, even overnight, investments can earn interest. US GAAP and IFRS define investments that are less than three months to maturity, almost risk free and readily convertible into known amounts of cash, as cash equivalents. These are included with cash balances at the year end for the purposes of the statement of cash flows and the statement of financial position. FRS 102 defines cash equivalents as "short-term, highly liquid investments that are readily convertible to known amounts of cash and that are subject to an insignificant risk of change in value".

What matters

Working capital

To consider only the movement in cash and liquid assets over a period of time does not provide a sufficient basis for understanding the financial changes a business is experiencing. A better view of a company's financial position can be obtained if the scope of analysis is expanded to cover all current assets and current liabilities. Current assets are likely to be turned into cash, if they are not already in this form, within a fairly short period. Similarly, current liabilities will certainly have to be paid in cash within 12 months of the year end, if not much sooner. By deducting current liabilities from current assets to produce net current assets or liabilities, you get what is commonly called the working capital of a company. Changes seen to be occurring within the working capital of a business can be important indicators of its performance and position.

As a business is managed there is a continual movement of financial resources or funds including cash, as Figure 4.1 shows. In a typical business, inventory is produced or purchased, suppliers deliver raw materials, operating costs and expenses are incurred and customers buy the products. All these transactions are completed either in cash or on credit terms. Current assets and liabilities change to reflect the impact of transactions made to enable the business to operate.

FIG 4.1 **The working capital cycle**

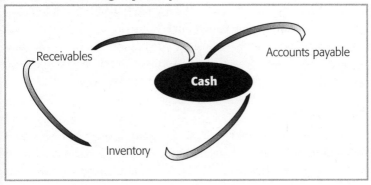

There are problems, however, in using working capital as a basis for analysing a business's financial changes. Concentrating on working capital movements alone ignores other sections of the statement of financial position, such as changes in non-current assets, shareholders' funds and long-term borrowings. Also it is possible for a company to control the level of current assets and liabilities at the time the statement of financial position is drafted. Immediately before the end of the financial year customers can be chased for payment so that there is an unrepresentative, low level of receivables; payment for plant and equipment can be delayed to allow a higher level of cash balances; and suppliers can be paid earlier or later than normal to adjust the level of credit.

Funds flow

For all businesses there are movements of cash resulting from transactions and events outside the area of working capital. There is more to a business than just the working capital cycle. Non-current assets may be bought or sold, dividends, interest and tax paid, loans raised or repaid, and shares issued or repurchased. When these items are included, a better foundation is provided for the analysis of movements in a company's financial resources. If all the changes between two consecutive statements of financial position are analysed, every financial movement will be covered. This is called funds flow analysis.

Funds can be defined as being any source of finance allowing a company to acquire assets. Cash raised from shareholders is a source of funds (finance) that can be used in the business. Additional credit taken from suppliers, although not cash, acts as a source of funds, enabling the level of inventory held to increase. Any liability increasing during the year acts as a source of funds available for use on the other side of the balance sheet to increase assets.

Sources and uses

The statement of financial position is the starting point for discovering what funds have been generated during the year and how these have been used in the business. The basic equation, assets = liabilities, ensures that in any year a company cannot use more funds than it generates or generate more than it uses; in other words, sources = uses. If more funds are generated than can be immediately used for operational purposes, paying interest and dividends or repaying borrowings, the surplus will appear in the year-end cash balances. Holding more cash is a use of funds.

Sources of funds

A company considering making an investment can fund it by:

- using existing cash balances;
- generating cash from operations;
- raising capital from shareholders;
- borrowing money;
- changing credit terms;
- selling assets.

Sources of funds fall into two categories: internal and external. Internal sources are largely under the company's control. A proportion of internal funds can be expected to be generated through the income statement. Shareholders can be an internal source of funds, but they also make demands on cash for payment of dividends. External sources comprise suppliers giving credit payment terms to the company and banks and other institutions providing short-, medium- or long-term finance.

In looking at the changes that have taken place between two balance sheets, a decrease in the value of an asset or an increase in a liability can be assumed to act as a source of funds to the business. However, common sense indicates that the revaluation of property during the year will show an increase in assets matched by an increase in liabilities (equity); since this does not indicate any actual movement in financial resources it should be ignored.

Sources = increases in liabilities and/or decreases in assets

Uses of funds

The funds available to a company during the year can be used for:

- increasing current assets;
- decreasing current liabilities;
- purchasing non-current assets;
- repaying borrowings;
- repurchasing shares;
- covering operating losses.

A change in customer credit policy resulting in an increase in receivables at the end of the year is a use of funds. Customers are, in effect, being allowed to borrow more of the company's money. Until they pay for the goods or services received they are tying up valuable financial resources that could be used elsewhere in the business. An increase in the value of an asset or a decrease in a liability, such as the purchase of a new machine, payments to suppliers or the repayment of a loan, can be assumed to have consumed funds.

Uses = increases in assets and/or decreases in liabilities

Funds flow statement

A statement displaying the changes in a company's financial position can be called a:

- funds flow statement;
- statement of changes in financial position;

- source and application statement;
- statement of cash flows.

A funds flow statement is produced by comparing two consecutive statements of financial position and identifying the changes that have occurred. This can be done by deducting, line by line, one statement from the other. The differences represent an increase or decrease in an asset or liability. All the changes that have occurred during the year are thus identified as representing either a source or a use of funds.

$	Year 1		Year 2		+/−
Non-current assets					
Plant and equipment	210		250		+40
Depreciation	(110)	100	(120)	130	+10
Current assets					
Inventory	60		75		+15
Receivables	30		40		+10
Investment	0		10		+10
Cash	10	100	15	140	+5
Total assets		**200**		**270**	
Equity					
Share capital	100		110		+10
Retained earnings	60	160	80	190	+20
Loan				20	+20
Current liabilities					
Accounts payable	30		40		+10
Taxation	10	40	20	60	+10
Total liabilities		**200**		**270**	

If the year 1 statement of financial position is deducted from that of year 2, the changes represent either a source or a use of funds during the year.

Sources	$	**Uses**	$
Retained earnings	20	Plant and equipment	40
Depreciation	10	Inventory	15

Share issue	10	Accounts receivable	10	
Loan	20	Investment	10	
Accounts payable	10	Cash	5	**80**
Tax	10 **80**			

The treatment of depreciation

In the example above, depreciation (amortisation) of $10 has been included as a source of funds. Although depreciation is charged in the income statement as an expense for the year, there is no cash movement. If the assets on which the depreciation charge is based are paid for in cash at the time of their acquisition, there will be no further cash movements associated with them until their disposal. Depreciation is a non-cash expense.

It is possible to show only the $30 net change in non-current assets after depreciation ($40 – $10) instead of showing the $40 investment in plant and machinery and the $10 depreciation charge separately. However, this could conceal the true financial movements associated with non-current assets. The depreciation charge of $10 has been generated by the company from its operations and is available for reinvestment in assets during the year. The company has not only maintained its productive resources but also increased them. It is better to view the changes that have taken place during the year as the company having spent $40 on additional plant and machinery.

It is important to understand that although it is common practice to refer to depreciation as a source of funds, this is technically incorrect. A change in depreciation policy has no impact on cash. A company cannot generate funds by changing its depreciation rates. If it decides to increase the depreciation charge from $10 to $20, this will reduce the reported profit by $10. The combined retained earnings ($10) and depreciation ($20) remain at $30, and there is no impact on the end of year 2 cash balance of $15.

From funds flow to cash flow

Until 1991 all UK companies had to include a statement of source and application of funds in their annual report. The accounting standard (SSAP 10) offered considerable flexibility on content presentation. With companies adopting slightly different reporting formats, however, it proved hard to compare their funds flow. Also the statement merely showed the changes taking place in the interval between two balance sheets. It did not provide the additional information necessary to assess a company's ability to meet its obligations, including payments to suppliers, shareholders and others as they fell due.

Pressure for change grew as users of financial statements made clear their dissatisfaction with the level of disclosure. They wanted to see clearly where financial resources were being generated, how they were being applied in the business, and the resultant changes in liquidity and borrowings. By 1990 most major UK companies were providing a cash flow statement which covered only the actual cash movements experienced during the year, rather than a funds flow statement.

Cash balance changes

It is sometimes helpful to adjust the presentation format of the funds flow statement to highlight the changes that have occurred in cash balances.

	$	
Opening cash balance		**10**
Sources		
Share issue	10	
Loan	20	
Retained earnings	20	
Depreciation	10	
Increase in payables	10	
Increase in tax payable	10	80
		90
Uses		
Increase in inventory	15	
Increase in receivables	10	
Investment	10	
Plant and equipment	40	75
Closing cash balance		**15**

Cash flow

The cash flow from sales revenue is not the same as the sales revenue figure appearing in the income statement. It is the actual cash received and does not, as under accrual accounting, include uncompleted credit transactions with customers. Cash inflows from customers and cash outflows to suppliers are produced by adjusting the total amounts of these by the credit element involved.

If sales revenue for the year is $150, the cash inflow can be calculated as:

$$\text{Cash inflow} = \text{sales revenue} + (\text{opening} - \text{closing receivables})$$
$$140 = 150 + (30 - 40)$$

The $30 owed by customers at the start of the year has been collected, and from the year's sales of $150 only $110 cash has been received ($150 less closing receivables of $40). The actual cash inflow from sales is $140 ($30 + $110).

Cash outflow to suppliers can be calculated in the same manner:

$$\text{Cash outflow} = \text{purchases} + (\text{opening} - \text{closing accounts payables})$$

Cash flow and profit

The management of profit and cash is the key to any successful business. There is little point in a company having profit but no cash – its long-term survival is likely to be difficult to manage. Equally, there is no advantage, apart from short-term survival, in having cash but no profit.

An appreciation of cash flow is essential to fully understanding the financial position of a company. Accrual accounting produces a cost of goods sold figure that does not match that of operating cash outflow. EBITDA (earnings before interest, taxation, depreciation and amortisation) does not equal net cash flow from operations as it ignores changes in the elements of working capital. There have been many examples of major companies disclosing a profit in their annual report, only to go into liquidation or receivership soon after because of a lack of liquid resources. A company could report an increase in working capital with inventory and receivables increasing during the year disguising the fact that cash was depleted to a dangerous level. The following example shows net current assets increasing from $25 to $30 but cash balances are run down to zero.

$	Year 1	Year 2
Inventory	20	30
Receivables	10	20
Cash	5	0
	35	50
Accounts payable	(10)	(20)
Working capital	**25**	**30**

A company may be creative in arriving at its reported revenue and profit for the year, but it is much more difficult, if not impossible without fraud, for it to create cash. Sales revenue may be increased by offering attractive credit terms to customers, but if the resulting receivables cannot be collected, cash balances will be run down and there may be difficulty in acquiring new inventory to service future business. Non-current assets may be revalued to produce an apparently healthier financial position, but there is no change in cash balances. In recent years there has been a shift in emphasis, with the statement of cash flows being seen as an integral and important part of the annual report.

The profit produced from operations (running the business) should be a major element of cash flow. If a loss is incurred, there is a positive internally generated cash flow only if the depreciation charge for the year exceeds the loss. Depreciation, a non-cash item, is added back to the profit for the year in the same way as in the funds flow statement.

A company may show a profit from making a credit sale to a customer but experience a reduction in cash balances. For example, a $150 sale to a customer and the associated materials and labour costs of $110 are recorded when the transaction is completed and included in the income statement for the year. However, there may be no increase in cash balances. If the suppliers have been paid $60 of the $110 cost of sales, but the customer has not paid the $150 owed, the income statement will show a gross profit of $40 and the balance sheet cash balances will be reduced by $60.

	$		$
Sales revenue	150	Cash inflow	0
Cost of sales	110	Cash outflow	60
Profit	40	Cash flow	(60)

Capitalising expenses and cash flow

By deciding to capitalise some of its expenses, interest payments or product development costs, a company can move the charge from the income statement into the statement of financial position, thereby improving the reported profit. However, the cash movements associated with the year's expenses remain unchanged. Following the capitalisation of an expense, it would be possible for the income statement to show a profit and the statement of cash flows to show a negative cash flow from operations.

Cash flow and dividends and tax

Operating cash flow is what remains after paying the direct costs and expenses of a business. Ideally, it is sufficient to cover interest on borrowing and income taxes, and then provide the source of dividends to shareholders. Where a company incurs a loss, it is still possible to declare a dividend as long as there are sufficient revenue reserves in the balance sheet and cash available to make the payment. But a company that continues to deplete reserves and cash resources in order to pay dividends will eventually run into trouble.

A simple rule of good housekeeping is that companies should pay shareholders dividends only from sound and positive cash flows. They should not have to rely on selling non-current assets or borrowings. A company making a dividend payment from declining operating cash flow may satisfy the short-term needs of shareholders but not have sufficient funds to reinvest in the business to provide for future growth and continuing profitability.

The statement of cash flows will show the cash outflows for dividends, interest and income tax during the year. The tax paid in one year is normally based on the previous year's profit – there is a delay between generating the profit and paying the tax. The income tax expense in the income statement will not match that appearing in the statement of cash flows. For reasons of clarity and simplicity, timing differences for payment of interest, dividends and non-current asset investment are ignored in the examples used in this chapter.

Working capital and cash flow

Any change in the amount of inventory held and the credit given to customers or taken from suppliers has an impact on both reported profit and cash flow. Increasing the amount of credit taken from suppliers acts as a source, and an increase in credit offered to customers is a use of available financial resources.

The relationship between current assets and current liabilities can be explored by looking at the movements that have taken place within working capital. Continuing with the example used earlier in this chapter, it can be seen that financial resources ($60) have been used to allow an increase in non-current assets ($40) and to increase working capital ($20).

$

Cash flow		
From operations	30	
Loan	20	
Share issue	10	
Investment in non-current assets	(40)	**20**
Increase in working capital		
Increase in inventory	15	
Increase in investment	10	
Increase in cash	5	
Increase in receivables	10	
Increase in accounts payable	(10)	
Increase in tax	(10)	**20**

Presenting a statement of financial movements in this way helps to explain the sources and uses of cash flow and separates the investing activity and capital structure changes from those of working capital and liquid assets.

Statement of cash flows

The statement of cash flows provides an essential link between the income statement and the statement of financial position. The detailed internal accounting records of a company are needed to prepare a statement of actual cash movements. It is not possible, as was the case with a funds flow statement, to prepare a statement of cash flows yourself from the annual report. The statement provides information on the changes in a company's opening and closing "cash and cash equivalents". That is the cash balances and bank balances available on demand and any other highly liquid investments, carrying no risk or uncertainty, that are capable of quick conversion into cash.

The aim of the statement of cash flows is to allow an assessment of a company's current and likely future capability to generate cash flows, and their timing and strength, and to allow direct comparison with other similar businesses. FRS 102 governs this statement and requires that cash flow be shown under three headings of business activity – operating, investing and financing – which when combined can explain the change in cash position over the year. This provides the basis for a meaningful assessment and prediction of cash flow and facilitates comparison with other companies.

The operating activities of a company can reasonably be expected to be the main source of its cash flows. The cash flow produced from running the business provides the basis for appreciating the quality of earnings and an assessment of the company's ability to continue to generate positive and strong future cash flows. Operating cash flow comes from:

Income from sales of goods and services, interest and dividends received –
payments to suppliers, employees, operating expenses and income taxes

Investing activities include the acquisition and disposal of non-current assets and other long-term investments. This is where a company invests for the future.

Financing activities relate to changes in the financial structure of the company. Changes in equity – the issue or repurchase of shares and dividends paid – and changes in borrowings are dealt with here. This is an important section in a statement of cash flows as it indicates the likely level of cash outflows required to service the providers of a company's capital.

Operating cash flow: direct and indirect methods

Companies can choose between two formats in presenting their operating cash flow: the direct and indirect methods (sometimes referred to as net or gross). Following US GAAP, companies using the direct method of presentation must also display the indirect method – FAS 95. The indirect method is the most popular presentation format, but it is not necessarily the most informative. It does not always make clear where the money came from or where it went.

The indirect method starts by adjusting the reported pre-tax profit figure for non-cash items that have been included in its calculation, such as depreciation or any investing or financing transactions.

When working capital increases the operating profit is greater than cash flow. When working capital decreases the cash flow from operations is less than operating profit. An increase in working capital is deducted from profit, and a decrease is added back to arrive at cash flow. The interest and tax are shown representing the actual amount of cash paid during the year, whether or not any interest was capitalised. The final adjustment is for tax to provide the net cash flows from operating activities. If appropriate, this final figure is divided between continuing and discontinued operations. The presentation of cash flow from operating activities using the indirect method is as follows:

Profit before income tax

Adjustments for:

Depreciation and amortisation

Foreign-exchange gain/loss

Profit/loss from sale of non-current assets

Interest paid/received

Increase/decrease in inventory

Increase/decrease in receivables

Increase/decrease in accounts payable

Income taxes paid

Net cash flow from operating activities

The direct method gives the same net cash flow from operating activities as the indirect method but in a different way. It shows gross cash in or out for each heading of operating cash flow. Presenting cash from operations using the direct method is:

Cash from sales revenue
Less:
>   cash paid to suppliers
>   cash paid to employees
>   cash paid for operating expenses

Cash generated from operations
>   interest paid
>   income taxes paid

Net cash flow from operating activities

Sales revenue can be assumed to be net of all sales taxes and after any bad debts. The cash flows for sales revenue and purchases are calculated in the same way as shown earlier in this chapter.

$$\text{Cash inflow from sales revenue} = \text{sales revenue} - \text{increase or} + \text{decrease in receivables}$$

$$\text{Cash outflow for purchases} = \text{purchases} - \text{increase or} + \text{decrease in accounts payable}$$

There may still be some allocation problems as it is impossible for any accounting standard to produce a set of rules tightly defining every possible event or transaction that a company might experience. There are still specific problems relating to financial institutions' presentation of cash flows. For several items in the statement of cash flows a decision has to be made on which heading they should appear under: are they operating expenses or investments? However, the statement will show the impact of the transaction in cash terms.

Always remember when using the cash flow from operations that there is no provision made for the use or replacement (depreciation) of non-current assets such as plant and machinery. Operating profit can be expected to be greater than operating cash flow.

Cash flow from investing activities

The next section of the statement of cash flows is that relating to the company's investing activities. Any increase in non-current assets resulting from their purchase will be shown here.

Inflows	*Outflows*
Sale of investments	Purchase of investments (not cash equivalents)
Sale of non-current assets	Purchase of non-current assets
Loans repaid	Loans made

Although a company may revalue some of its non-current assets, this has no impact on the statement of cash flows as there has been no cash movement. The acquisition and sale of subsidiaries, associates and joint ventures together with any dividends received from these will be detailed in this section. The acquisition or disposal of long-term investments will also be shown.

Receipts and payments for property, plant and equipment
Purchase or sale of subsidiary companies
Purchase or sale of associates and joint ventures
Dividends received from associates and joint ventures
Receipts and payments for intangibles

Net cash flow from or used in investing activities

There is a difference between the change in a non-current asset shown in the balance sheet and that appearing in the statement of cash flows. The statement identifies the actual amount of cash spent by a company during the year. The figures appearing in the balance sheet are subject to timing differences. An asset may have been purchased but not paid for at the end of the financial year, so an increase in assets is shown in the balance sheet but there is nothing in the statement of cash flows.

A crucial role of management is to make investment decisions allocating the available financial resources to appropriate parts of the business with a view to providing future profitable growth. The statement of cash flows shows the cash outflows associated with the investing activities of the company and the cash inflows when assets are sold. It indicates the total amount spent on assets during the year but does not necessarily disclose in any detail precisely where or on what the cash was spent. The statement of cash flows does not therefore provide a suitable basis for assessing the quality of the investments made.

Acquisitions and disposals

If a subsidiary is acquired or disposed of during the year, only the cash paid or received is included in the cash flow statement. A cash outflow is net of any cash gained from the subsidiary.

When an acquisition is made through the issue of shares, with no cash involved, the only impact on the statement of cash flows is the receipt of the subsidiary's cash balances. The price paid may be different from that appearing in the statement. Where an acquisition has been made there may be only a single figure shown in investing activities. IAS 7 requires that this should be supported by a summary of the cash flow impact of the acquisition showing the fair value of net assets acquired and details of how the deal was financed. This offers more scope to assess the true viability of acquisitions as the actual cash outflows and the impact on financing requirements are disclosed.

For example, a company uses a combination of shares and cash to acquire a subsidiary.

Consideration paid ($)			**Assets acquired** ($)		
Shares issued	80		Assets	50	
Cash	20	100	Goodwill	20	
			Cash	30	100

The subsidiary has been purchased and the net cash result is to increase group cash balances by $10: $20 has been paid out to acquire $30. It is only this net cash movement of $10 that is recorded in the statement of cash flows.

If possible, a view should be taken on whether the sale of a subsidiary or major business investment is part of a carefully planned strategy or merely the result of painful necessity. It is not always possible to be certain of the reason for a disposal through reading the management statements in the annual report. It is unlikely that a company will admit that a subsidiary was sold because it was running out of cash. More commonly, the terms "rationalisation", "refocusing", "re-engineering" and suchlike are used to explain and justify major business disposals.

Cash flow from financing activities

The third section of the statement of cash flows deals with the management of the financial structure of the company, showing any changes in borrowings and equity that have occurred during the year. From this section it is possible to track the flow of funds between the company and its owners, lenders and creditors.

Inflows	Outflows
Issue of shares	Repurchase of shares
Debentures issued	Debentures repaid
	Dividends paid

Dividends paid to shareholders are shown in this section. Interest payments may be shown here but are more likely to have been included in the operating activities section. Typically details will be provided for:

Equity dividends paid
Issue of shares
Share repurchases
Repayment of short- and long-term borrowings
Proceeds from short- and long-term borrowings
Capital and interest obligations under finance lease payments

Net cash flow from (used in) financing activities

The carrying value of assets held under finance leases is not normally separately identified in the statement of financial position but included in the figure for total non-current assets. Finance leases do not involve any cash outflow for capital. Where an asset is acquired under a finance lease during the year the actual cash outflows will be shown in the financing activities section.

Apart from internally generated sources of finance, a company has only two options: it can raise additional funds from new or existing shareholders through the issue of shares (a rights issue), or it can go outside the company and borrow money from a bank or other financial institution. If any equity shares are issued or repurchased, the cash movement will be shown here. Remember that any shares issued without cash payment affect the statement of financial position but not the statement of cash flows.

The statement of cash flows helps to identify how much money has been raised from shareholders and how much from short- and long-term external sources. Taken together with the internally generated cash flows, this gives a clear picture of the way in which the company has been financed during the year.

Management of liquid resources

For the purposes of the statement of cash flows, cash or cash equivalents is defined as cash and bank balances (less bank overdrafts) plus any current asset investment that is readily convertible into cash. As part of its financial or treasury management aimed at getting some positive benefit from idle cash balances, a company may make a short-term investment which will be shown within current assets. Surplus cash is used to earn interest, the investment having been planned to make sure that cash is available as and when required.

There will be a reconciliation linking the opening and closing cash and cash equivalents shown in the balance sheet with the cash flow for the year. This helps clarify the changes that have occurred. A typical cash flow statement will show:

Opening cash and cash equivalents	**XX**
Cash flows from operating activities	
Net cash inflow (outflow) from operating activities	**XX**
Cash flows from investing activities	
Net cash outflow (inflow) from investing activities	**XX**
Cash flows from financing activities	
Net cash inflow (outflow) from financing activities	**XX**
Closing cash and cash equivalents	**XX**

There will be comparative figures for the previous year supported by detailed notes for each major item.

Exceptional and extraordinary events

Every business is likely at some time to experience an exceptional or extraordinary event. When this occurs a company would rightly wish to draw analysts' attention to this item as not being part of the normal business activities. An exceptional item is part of the normal operating activities of the company but its size makes it necessary for it to be identified separately in the financial statements. Extraordinary items are one-off events that are material in size, not related to a company's normal activities and unlikely to re-occur.

Exceptional and extraordinary events were seen as being particularly relevant to the interpretation of earnings per share information. But there was criticism of the way in which some companies were creative in their decision on what to include under the heading "extraordinary" to disguise operational shortcomings. This option is no longer open to them. IFRS do not accept the term extraordinary, and in 2003 the IASB forbade references in companies' income statements to any income or expense as being extraordinary.

Foreign exchange and cash flow

Most companies transact business in foreign currencies and many have subsidiaries in other countries. To prepare the financial statements all transactions must be translated into the reporting company's currency. When foreign assets and liabilities are translated into a holding company's currency at the year-end date exchange-rate differences will occur. Foreign-exchange gains or losses on operating activities will be included in the section of the statement of cash flows dealing with the cash generated from operations – usually in the accompanying notes. The sections of the statement dealing with investing and financing activities will also have been adjusted for foreign-exchange gains or losses. The effects of foreign-exchange rates on the closing cash and cash equivalent figure will be shown as a separate item in the statement of cash flows.

The treatment of exchange-rate differences is complex. When looking at the statement of cash flows all you need to know is that it deals only with actual cash movements. Any exchange-rate differences that have not had a cash impact during the year are ignored.

Summary

- To complete a full analysis and assessment of a company the statement of cash flows must be used in conjunction with the income statement, which deals with the profit or loss made from running the business, and the statement of financial position.

- The statement of cash flows covers the same period as the income statement, setting out the changes in cash balances and borrowing that have taken place between the opening and closing balance sheets. It is useful in assessing a company's liquidity, viability and financial adaptability. An increase in reported profit need not be supported by positive cash flow.

- A reasonable starting point is to see if the company is showing a continuing and positive cash flow from its operations. Is there stability? Has the increase in cash flow over the previous year at least matched the rate of inflation?

- The statement of cash flows shows whether a company is generating or consuming cash. Has it proved capable of producing sufficient cash from the business or has it used up all available liquid resources and had to raise additional funds?

- A change in the relationship between operating cash flow (statement of cash flows) and net income (income statement) can act as a warning signal. If cash flow begins to lag behind income, ask why. One explanation may be that sales revenue is being massaged. Perhaps, to generate sales, customers are being given excessively generous credit terms. Net income increases in the year but, as receivables rise, cash flow does not follow.

- Remember that at any point in the statement of cash flows, a company can create a subtotal and highlight the figure. This does not mean that the figure is truly indicative of performance or position. Make sure your attention is not being distracted from more important evidence contained in the statement.

- If a business is absorbing large amounts of cash, this will be evident in the statement of cash flows. A forecast can be made of how long the company could support the cash outflow.

- The quality of a company's cash flow depends partly on management's competence and partly upon the nature of the business and its areas of operation. Even exceptional management may achieve only low profitability and poor cash flows in a declining business sector. Its quality must also be judged on the basis of how much cash comes from continuing operations: the more the better.

■ Study changes in cash balances and in each element of working capital. If, for example, inventory and customer credit levels are increasing, the company may be in trouble; the inducement of extra credit is not leading to additional sales. The company may be in danger of overtrading.

■ Where is the cash flow coming from? In most groups, individual companies and business sectors have different cash flow patterns, but there should be at least one business capable of generating positive cash flows to help finance others with negative cash flows develop and survive. Showing cash flows as part of a company's segmental reporting would be useful.

■ Other useful indicators of company performance are whether more or less cash is being held at the end of the year than at the beginning, or whether the company's borrowings have increased or decreased during the year.

■ The statement of cash flows can show whether a company has the necessary liquid resources to pay a cash dividend, and whether it is likely to generate sufficient cash to meet its obligations, including loan repayments, as they fall due.

■ The current year's statement of cash flows can be used as a basis for forecasting future years' cash flow. Depreciation is simple to calculate and forecast for future years. Rates are known and assumptions about future investment in additional assets can be allowed for to provide a fairly accurate estimate for future years' depreciation charges.

■ The profit contribution to cash flow is less easy to predict accurately. For most businesses, it is the least certain element in a cash flow forecast. However, an estimate can be made based on the trend shown for previous years.

PART 2

Assessing the facts

5 Guidelines for financial analysis

THIS CHAPTER gives some general guidelines on the calculation and interpretation of the ratios covered later. Perhaps the most important rule to remember is to keep it simple.

Comparability and consistency

The figures used in the analysis of a company or for the comparison of a number of companies must as far as possible be truly comparable. In calculating rates of return there is no point in taking the pre-tax profit of one company and comparing it with the post-tax profit of another. A company that capitalises interest may appear to have a better profit performance than one that does not. If, rather than the interest figure appearing in the income statement, the total interest payment for the year is used for both companies, there may be no difference in their profitability.

It is essential to make sure that consistent figures are used in the ratios being developed. Companies may change the ways in which they present their financial data and define individual items in the financial statements. Always check that the analysis has been adjusted to take account of such changes; the notes to the financial statements should give details of these as well as other crucial matters.

Never rely on a single ratio

It is inadvisable to judge a company on the basis of a single ratio. Either the previous year's ratio should be calculated to gain an impression of how what is being considered is changing and what is the trend, or the ratio of one company should be compared with that of companies operating in the same business or of a comparable size. The ratios in Appendix 1 offer some benchmarks for the sector and country against which individual companies may be assessed.

The more years the better

Do not judge a company on the basis of a single year's figures. Three or, ideally, five years' figures should be analysed to get a clear view of the consistency of a company's performance and to highlight any movements in the ratios that require explanation or investigation.

The annual report should contain a five-year or ten-year history of the company. This can provide a useful start point in analysis. All the figures appearing in the history should be consistent and comparable. Any changes in the company's structure, operations or accounting policies will have been taken into account and all previous years adjusted as necessary.

The company history is a good source of financial statistics: employee numbers, dividend payments, earnings per share and share price. Sometimes companies present useful information on R&D or capital expenditure. Before starting an analysis check with the history to see what is immediately available – this may avoid some duplication of effort.

Year ends

One problem in comparing companies is that they are unlikely to have the same financial year end. In most countries there are three popular dates: March/April, September/October and December/January. A company's choice of year end depends on such things as the date it was founded, fiscal legislation, or the nature of its business. Companies involved in seasonal businesses are unlikely to want to prepare year-end accounts at the peak of their trading cycle, so few retailers have December 31st as their financial year end.

Differences in year ends and the timing of the publication of results often create problems in producing tables for cross-country and cross-company comparison. The best that can normally be done is to bring together companies reporting within the 12-month period, although this may span two calendar years. This may result in some distortions because of seasonality, but at least it provides an acceptable common time base.

How many weeks in the year?

Care should also be taken to make sure that the income statement is for a standard 52-week year. A company may have adjusted its year end and so have more or less than 12 months' trading contained in the accounts. For example, a change may follow a merger or acquisition where one company moves to bring its year end into line with the other. In such cases, the data used in the analysis can be adjusted back to 52 weeks or 12 months by dividing the data by the actual number of weeks or months covered in the income statement and then multiplying by either 52 or 12. However, bear in mind that such an adjustment may result in a distortion.

Average, median or mode?

It is often advisable to top and tail league tables of companies operating in a selected sector to provide some guidelines on average performance or position. Extremes of performance or position, although of considerable importance to the companies concerned, are best ignored when trying to determine averages or standards for a set of companies or a business sector. Otherwise an extreme case can distort any average being calculated.

In many cases, it is preferable to use the median rather than the average as the benchmark. If ten companies are being compared and the indicator being used gives a figure of 10 for nine companies and 100 for one company, the average (190/10) is 19. This results in nine out of the ten companies being below average.

A better guide may be the median or the middle or mid-point figure in a table showing the ranking of companies or ratios. Where there are odd numbers of items the median is the middle figure. In the example below, the median of the first line is 7.

2	5	7	9	12
	6	8	10	11

The median can be calculated from the formula $(n + 1) \div 2$, where n is the number of items in the group. With five items this provides $(5 + 1) \div 2 = 3$, the third item in the list. With an even number of items the formula identifies the position of the median between the two mid-point figures $(4 + 1) \div 2 = 2.5$. The median is halfway between 8 and 10 = 9.

An alternative measure is to take the mode, that is, the figure that occurs most often in the table. The mode is best identified by eye rather than by calculation, and of course it is possible for a table to be bimodal (with two modes).

Investigate variations

When the ratios of a company cause it to stand out among others in the same sector it is important to try to discover the reasons for the variation. It may be that the company is unique and setting standards of performance or financial structure for the rest of the sector. However, care should be taken that its uniqueness is not merely the result of the application of accounting practices different from those of other companies.

Similarly, any sudden and dramatic shift in a company's performance or position should be investigated. A significant improvement in reported profit may be the result of a one-off sale of an asset or changes in the accounting treatment of items in the financial statements. It does not require a great intellect to use creative accounting methods to produce a one-off high level of profitability for a company. The real art is in maintaining such an illusion. Once accounts are being manipulated a company is walking a tightrope, and each year more oscillations are generated, guaranteeing that at some time in the near future it is going to cry for help or fall off. Be on the lookout for any inconsistencies in the figures being presented.

In financial analysis it is safest and usually most productive not to give the benefit of the doubt. When a company displays markedly different characteristics from others in the same sector, it is best to assume that this is not a positive signal until further investigation proves otherwise.

Graphs and charts

For many people a graph offers the best means of displaying a series of financial data and information. Setting out five years' turnover and profit or profit margin and the return on total assets in a graph provides an ideal way of identifying trends and annual movement, and is certainly more effective than a table packed with figures containing the same data. Standard spreadsheet software packages make it easy to turn a set of figures into a graph, bar chart or pie chart.

Check the integrity

Companies have been making increasing use of graphic displays on their websites and in their reports. But what kind of picture is being presented? It is a simple matter to disguise or distort a trend in, for example, profit growth by picking a scale for a graph that delivers the message you want to give. The two bar charts in Figure 5.1 display exactly the same annual profits. If you take the trouble to measure the bars with a ruler, both charts show the final year profit is four times that of the first year. However, for most people the one on the right appears to indicate the better performance.

Never rely on someone else's analysis

It is safest never to rely entirely on someone else's analysis, particularly if this is offered by the company being studied. Always base the company assessment and calculations on the original financial data available in the financial statements.

Percentage rules

A useful aid to interpreting a financial statement is to express the figures in percentage terms, particularly when studying one company's data for a number of years or data for several companies. Percentages simplify things wonderfully, reducing figures that may be presented in billions, millions or thousands to a single comparable measure. Furthermore, they make it easier to spot trends or differences, as the following example of a statement of cash flows shows:

FIG 5.1 **Two ways of telling the same story**

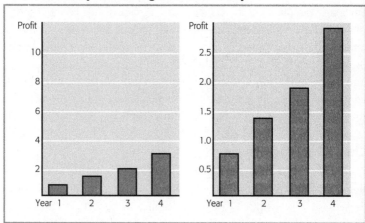

	$m	$m	%	%
Cash inflows				
Operating activities	885.2		90	
Financing activities	94.4	979.6	10	100
Cash outflows				
Investment and finance	197.6		20	
Tax	231.8		24	
Investing activities	279.6	709.0	28	72
Increase in cash		**270.6**		**28**

Common size presentation

Similarly, a percentage-like presentation approach, known as common size presentation, makes it easier to analyse and compare the contribution each source of finance makes towards the financing of the total assets employed by companies. Often it is useful to present all the important items in an income statement as percentages of sales revenue. An added advantage to the application of common size presentation is that where companies are reporting in different currencies, all currency differences are automatically removed.

If total assets are expressed as 100, sources of finance can be shown in relation to this, as the following example shows:

	Year 1	Year 2	Year 3	Year 1	Year 2	Year 3
	$	$	$	%	%	%
Non-current assets	1,515	1,580	1,729			
Current assets	1,573	1,704	1,692			
Total assets	3,088	3,284	3,421	100	100	100
Equity	926	1,314	1,711	30	40	50
Non-current liabilities	618	656	343	20	20	10
Current liabilities	1,544	1,314	1,367	50	40	40
Total liabilities	3,088	3,284	3,421	100	100	100

The process is simple. Each source of finance is divided by total assets and multiplied by 100. For example, in year 3, capital and reserves (equity) of $1,711 divided by total assets of $3,421 and multiplied by 100 gives 50%. The three sources of finance can be clearly seen, and it is much easier to identify changes and trends from this form of presentation than from the three years' balance sheets.

Any changes in leverage (gearing) can quickly be spotted when the common size presentation is used and debt/equity ratios can easily be calculated. This offers an alternative means of both calculating and interpreting gearing. From the first year's balance sheet, total debt of $2,162 divided by equity of $926 gives a debt/equity ratio of 2.3:1. The same calculation can be completed directly from the common size presentation. In year 1, total debt (70) divided by equity (30) produces the ratio 2.3:1 or 233%. By year 3 this can be seen to have reduced to 1:1 or 100%. The long-term debt ratio could be calculated in the same way, with long-term debt (20) divided by long-term debt and equity (20 + 30) giving a ratio of 0.4:1 or 40% in year 1 moving to 0.33:1 or 33% in year 3.

This presentation format can be used to explain how one side of the balance sheet, total assets, is being financed. For every $1 of assets employed in year 1 shareholders contributed 30¢, and by year 3 this had become 50¢. What remains of each $1 has been provided from external sources, debt and current liabilities; in year 1 this was 70¢ and in year 3 it was 50¢.

$m	Turnover		Operating profit		Net assets	
	Year 1	Year 2	Year 1	Year 2	Year 1	Year 2
Class of business						
Consumer goods	956	998	65	71	408	421
Office equipment	488	532	15	22	188	201
Medical equipment	694	725	72	84	484	526
Electronic systems	355	501	−6	9	125	201
	2,493	**2,756**	**146**	**186**	**1,205**	**1,349**
Geographic analysis						
UK	860	877	61	63	451	434
Rest of Europe	485	498	32	34	274	255
North America	484	508	39	42	185	287
South America	307	486	−6	19	159	196
Asia/Australasia	259	333	19	26	136	177
Others	98	54	1	2	0	0
	2,493	**2,756**	**146**	**186**	**1,205**	**1,349**

%	Turnover		Operating profit		Net assets	
	Year 1	Year 2	Year 1	Year 2	Year 1	Year 2
Class of business						
Consumer goods	38	36	45	38	34	31
Office equipment	20	19	10	12	16	15
Medical equipment	28	26	49	45	40	39
Electronic systems	14	18	−4	5	10	15
	100	**100**	**100**	**100**	**100**	**100**
Geographic analysis						
UK	35	32	42	34	37	32
Rest of Europe	20	18	22	18	23	19
North America	19	18	27	23	15	21
South America	12	18	−4	10	13	15
Asia/Australasia	10	12	13	14	11	13
Others	4	2	1	1	0	0
	100	**100**	**100**	**100**	**100**	**100**

This approach can also be used to analyse a five-year record, segmental report or one of a company's financial statements, as in the example.

Index numbers

The use of index numbers is another way of shedding light on the performance of a company. The result – a trend statement – offers a more reliable means of identifying trends in performance or position than a common size statement, as the following example of a company's five-year financial record shows:

$	Year 1	Year 2	Year 3	Year 4	Year 5
Turnover	5,200	5,500	6,100	6,300	6,600
Pre-tax profit	350	400	475	490	520

If the figure for each year is divided by that of the base year and the result multiplied by 100, a series of index numbers is produced. The year 2 turnover ($5,500) divided by that of year 1 ($5,200) and multiplied by 100 gives 106.

	Year 1	Year 2	Year 3	Year 4	Year 5
Turnover	100	106	117	121	127
Pre-tax profit	100	114	136	140	149

In interpreting index numbers it must be remembered that they relate directly to the first year. Turnover in year 2 increased by $300 ($5,500 – 5,200), which was a 6% increase and was reflected in the index number movement from 100 to 106. However, it is incorrect to assume that the turnover increase in year 5 was also 6% (127 – 121). Turnover in year 5 increased by $300, which was less than a 5% increase on the $6,300 of year 4. The turnover in year 5 represents a 27% increase on that in year 1. Of course, if year 2 was used as the base (100), a different picture would be presented.

Growth rates and trends

Assessing the rate at which change is occurring can be useful in financial analysis. To measure the percentage change from one year to the next the calculation is:

$$100 \times [(\text{year 2} - \text{year 1}) \div \text{year 1}]$$

Turnover and profit growth for the second and the last year are:

	Year 1 to year 2	**Year 4 to year 5**
Turnover	$(5,500 - 5,200) \div 5,200 = 5.8\%$	$(6,600 - 6,300) \div 6,300 = 4.8\%$
Pre-tax profit	$(400 - 350) \div 350 = 14.3\%$	$(520 - 490) \div 490 = 6.1\%$

The company has an apparently steady growth in turnover. Where there is a significant level of inflation, growth patterns can be distorted. To overcome this problem an appropriate measure of inflation, such as the retail price index, can be used to adjust turnover. To express turnover for any year in year 5 dollars, that year's turnover is multiplied by the year 5 index divided by that year's index. For example, to express year 1 turnover in year 5 dollars the calculation is:

$$\$5,200 \times (140 \div 100) = \$5,200 \times 1.4 = \$7,280$$

The adjusted figures provide a better basis for interpreting the real underlying growth patterns. Based on the adjusted figures for the five-year period, profit increased by 6% and turnover decreased by 9%.

	Year 1	**Year 2**	**Year 3**	**Year 4**	**Year 5**
Turnover ($)	5,200	5,500	6,100	6,300	6,600
Inflation index	100	110	120	130	140
Adjusted turnover ($)	7,280	7,000	7,117	6,785	6,600

Compound growth rates

To assess the growth trend over a number of years the compound growth rate can be calculated. There are statistical formulas for calculating it, but as in most cases all that is required is a broad indicator of the rate, the table below can be used for most situations.

From the five-year financial record table appearing in an annual report it is possible to calculate growth over four years. If, using the figures in the example above, the final year figure is divided by that of the first year, the resultant factor can be read from the table to discover the approximate compound growth rate over the four-year period:

Turnover $6,600 \div \$5,200 = 1.27$ Pre-tax profit $520 \div \$350 = 1.49$

Looking at the four-year column in the table, the closest figure to 1.27 is 6% and to 1.49 is 10%. Thus over the period turnover has grown at the rate of just over 6% per year and pre-tax profit at just over 10% per year.

	2 years	**3 years**	**4 years**	**9 years**
1%	1.02	1.03	1.04	1.09
2%	1.04	1.06	1.08	1.19
3%	1.06	1.09	1.13	1.30
4%	1.08	1.12	1.17	1.42
5%	1.11	1.16	1.22	1.55
6%	1.12	1.19	1.26	1.69
8%	1.17	1.26	1.36	2.00
10%	1.21	1.33	1.46	2.36
12%	1.25	1.40	1.57	
14%	1.30	1.48	1.69	
16%	1.35	1.56	1.81	
18%	1.39	1.64	1.94	
20%	1.44	1.73	2.07	
25%	1.56	1.95	2.44	
30%	1.69	2.20	2.86	
40%	1.96	2.74	3.82	
50%	2.25	3.37	5.06	
60%	2.56	4.10	6.55	
70%	2.89	4.91	8.35	
80%	3.24	5.83	10.00	
90%	3.61	6.86	13.00	
100%	4.00	8.00	16.00	

If the growth for the last three years is required, the calculations would be:

$$\$6,600 \div \$5,500 = 1.2 \text{ and } \$520 \div \$400 = 1.3$$

Moving down the three-year column, this indicates a turnover growth of just over 6% and profit growth of just under 10% over the last three years. It should be noted that a compound growth rate is based only on the first and last years. The company providing the five-year record could have made a $600 profit or loss in year 3 and the compound growth rate would not be affected.

Foreign currencies

Analysing a number of companies based in the same country avoids any problems associated with currency. Making an international comparison is inevitably more difficult. There is little point in trying to compare a US company's $96,000 profit per employee with a French company's €90,000 and a UK company's £60,000. The best way to deal with this problem is to translate all the figures involved into one currency. However, there are potential difficulties in doing this, the most obvious being which exchange rate to use. Two options are the exchange rate ruling at the balance sheet date of each company or the average exchange rate for the year. The simplest method, although by no means the most accurate or representative, is to take all the currencies involved and use the exchange rates of the day the analysis is being completed to translate the figures into a single currency base.

If the three example companies are being compared from a UK base, the figures can be adjusted to show the ratio in sterling equivalents.

	Rate	£
$96,000	1.6	60,000
€90,000	1.5	60,000
£60,000	1.0	60,000

The three companies can now be directly compared in a currency you are used to working with. Thus international comparisons can be made of the size, efficiency and performance of companies. However, care must be taken in adopting this approach, particularly when the analysis is looking back over a number of years. The revaluation of one country's currency against those of others would almost certainly result in a dramatic shift in the translated values for any ratios being used in the year in which this took place.

Using databases

In 1997 a six-digit NAICS (North American Industry Classification System) began to be used. In 2011 Companies House in the UK adopted a five-digit SIC (standard industrial classification) for filing company information. It may be useful to find out which SIC or equivalent code best fits the company being studied. This will help you find similar or competing companies to enhance the analysis and may prove useful when using a database.

If a commercial database is available as the source of company data and information, this will allow ease of access to the financial statements with the advantage that each one is set out in a standard format. This is particularly helpful when comparing companies operating in several countries. The figures will be in a consistent form and the accompanying text translated into a common language, considerably reducing the stress of analysis. Note, however, that commercial databases take the figures provided by companies in their financial statements at face value when producing ratios. If you suspect creative accounting has been employed, you will need to use the information in the annual report.

It should be accepted that databases occasionally change the format of their financial data presentation. Adding or removing a line in the income statement or statement of financial position can throw out any spreadsheet calculations if the raw data are imported directly into the spreadsheet. Always check to ensure that the data input is consistent before completing or using in any form of analysis (see Chapter 10).

6 Measuring profitability

THIS CHAPTER IS CONCERNED with the analysis of company profitability. It starts by concentrating on the data contained within the income statement (profit and loss account) and then broadens out to include the statement of financial position and other sources of financial data and relevant information.

What is profit?

One definition of profit is that it represents the surplus of income over expenditure. In accounting, where income is greater than expenditure a profit is produced, and where expenditure is greater than income a loss results. Hence in the UK the statement dealing with revenue and expenditure was termed the profit and loss account. The term income statement, or statement of comprehensive income, is now more commonly used.

Defining and measuring profit provides one of several areas of argument between accountants and economists. Economists direct their attention to what may happen in the future: the present value of future income. Accountants are more concerned with what has happened in the past: revenue less expenses. An economist may prove to be accurate in forecasting what will actually happen but is less likely to be able to state precisely when it will happen. An accountant, however, might argue that in most cases an economist only has to define profit whereas an accountant has to quantify it each year as a single figure in a set of accounts.

Different perspectives

The term profit may mean different things, not only to economists and accountants but also to a company's various interest groups, each of which views the profit a company makes from a different perspective.

■ **Shareholders** may be most concerned about the ability of a company to maintain or improve the value of their investment and future income stream. They look to the company to generate sufficient profit to provide for dividend payments and an increase in the market value of the shares they own. In most annual reports the company's shareholders are provided with a detailed statement of the changes that have taken place during the year in their investment in the company (see Chapter 2).

■ **Lenders** of money may be expected to be most interested in evidence to support the company's ability to continue to pay the interest on borrowed funds as this falls due.

■ **Customers** may be concerned to assess how much profit is being made, particularly if there is regulation of the business sector intended to offer some level of customer protection. Now that increasing emphasis is put on high standards of customer service and satisfaction, there is little advantage in making excessive short-term profits at the long-term expense of the customer.

■ **Competitors** are most interested in comparing their own performance and efficiency with that of other companies operating in the same business sector.

■ **Management and other employees** are usually most interested in the profit being generated from their section of the business and in assessing their personal employment prospects. Senior managers are expected to focus on the overall levels of profitability being provided by the company's main operating units, its strategic business units (SBUs). Their interest should be focused on the future potential rather than the historical performance of the company.

■ **Business and investment analysts** may be expected by their clients or employers to provide an indication of whether a particular company's shares are worth holding or buying for future gain, or are best sold immediately. They will study the current year's profit and compare it with previous years and that of other companies, and set this against their assessment for the future of the business sector to forecast profit trends.

The fundamentals of capital maintenance

Profit can be defined as the difference between the capital (net assets) shown in a statement of financial position at the start of an accounting period and that shown at the end. If this profit were distributed to shareholders as dividend, the financial capital of the company would be unchanged (financial capital maintenance). All companies are required to maintain their financial capital. It is also reasonable to expect a company to maintain its ability to produce the goods or services upon which its business depends by providing for necessary non-current assets replacement (operating capital maintenance).

Economists and accountants agree that in arriving at a figure for profit, note must be taken of the assets being used or capital employed by the company to generate that profit. Before a profit can be declared, the "using up" of part of the assets or capital employed in the business must be charged as part of the overall costs and expenses for the year. This, as discussed in Chapter 3, is fundamental to accounting theory and company law, and is normally achieved through the charging of depreciation. It can be seen as the setting aside of funds for the eventual replacement of the company's assets when this becomes necessary.

A company that did not charge depreciation but paid dividends to shareholders might not be retaining sufficient funds to maintain the asset base of its operations. This would be reflected on the other side of the balance sheet in a reduction in the shareholders' stake in the business. As a result, the capital employed and potentially the ability to pay its creditors and repay borrowings would be eroded.

In short, a company that fails to make consistent and reasonable or prudent provision each year for depreciation will overstate its real profitability and store up trouble for the future. It is therefore important to make sure that in arriving at its stated profit, a company not only fulfils the requirement of capital maintenance but also follows all the basic principles of income statement preparation (see Chapter 3).

Starting considerations

The starting point for analysing and assessing profitability is most likely to be the annual report, which provides on a regular basis data on a company's activities. The income statement sets out the company's income and expenditure. The result will be a profit where total income is greater than total expenditure and a loss where the reverse is the case.

$$\textbf{Profit} = \text{total income} - \text{total cost}$$

This equation appears to offer a simple definition of profit. But how is cost calculated? It is worth remembering the story of the executive who, exasperated at never receiving a clear answer to any question he asked his accountant, demanded, "What is one plus one?" The accountant smiled and replied, "Are you buying or selling?" Because it is rarely possible to provide a clear and unambiguous definition of the cost of any product or service, it is difficult to define profit and therefore to interpret the figure a company declares as its profit.

For the purposes of the ratios and analysis covered in this chapter, it is assumed that the income or sales revenue figures used exclude all sales taxes or equivalents. In the UK it is normal to give sales revenue exclusive or net of value-added tax (VAT).

Sales revenue during the year is often divided into income generated from continuing and from discontinued business operations. This division continues in the statement of profit for the year. The intention is to show consistently each year where the company has been generating income and profit, and to make it easy to see how much the businesses that will contribute subsequent profits (or losses) have generated in the year being reported. A company that has disposed of a profit source and not reinvested in another may be giving up the income that would have contributed to future profits.

Measuring sticks

It is possible to prepare a table listing companies operating within a business sector by the monetary value of their profit for the year. This list, with the largest numerical profit at the top and the smallest at the bottom, shows which of the chosen companies was making the largest profit. It might also be useful in revealing the total profit made by the selected companies. However, such a list would not necessarily tell you which of the companies was the most profitable. To discover this, a number of ratios can help.

Profit margin ratios

The income statement can provide the basis for calculating the profit margin as a start to the analysis of a company's profitability. It is calculated by dividing profit by sales revenue and expressing the result as a percentage.

$$\textbf{\% profit margin} = 100 \times (\text{profit} \div \text{sales revenue})$$

Gross profit margin

Working down the income statement, the first profit normally displayed is the gross profit, which is produced by deducting the cost of sales from sales revenue for the year. It is normally safe to assume that the cost of sales includes all the direct materials and services provided by suppliers, direct employee remuneration and all direct overheads. However, it is essential to read the notes providing additional details of the figures appearing in the income statement.

Unfortunately there is, as yet, little real consistency in how different companies present crucial information. For example, some companies deduct the remuneration of all shop-floor employees in arriving at gross profit and some do not. When several companies are being analysed, it will probably be necessary to make some adjustments to the figures provided in the accounts before you can be confident that profitability ratios are truly comparable.

$$\textbf{\% gross profit margin} = 100 \times (\text{gross profit} \div \text{sales revenue})$$

The gross profit margin, often simply referred to as the gross margin, offers a reasonable indication of the basic profitability of a business and is useful when comparing the performance of companies operating within the same sector. When one company has a totally different level of gross margin, it is worth trying to discover why. Is this due to more efficient management of operations, a different cost structure or definition of sales revenue?

Movements in the level of profit margins may be caused by many factors. For example, gross margin is influenced by changes in the mix of products or services being marketed by a company and is directly affected by price increases or decreases. Similarly, changes in production efficiency or materials purchasing affect the cost of sales, which in turn have an impact on gross margin. The potential for incorrect inventory valuation to distort profit, and thereby gross margin, was discussed in Chapter 2.

Operating profit margin

Operating profit usually follows gross profit in the income statement. It will include any other income and allow for all a company's expenses of distribution, administration, research and development and general overheads.

Care must be taken to make sure there is consistent treatment of any turnover and profit relating to joint ventures and associates. If the total turnover figure is being used, the total operating profit – including the share of joint ventures' and associates' profit – should be matched with this.

The operating profit margin offers an assessment of the profitability of a company after taking into account all the normal costs of producing and supplying goods or services and the income from selling them. Financing costs, such as interest payments on bank loans, or investment income, and interest earned on bank deposits are not included.

% operating margin = 100 × (operating profit ÷ sales revenue)

If a company has a consistent level of gross margin but a declining operating profit margin, it is worth investigating why. One explanation could be efficient purchasing and basic cost control but poor control of general overheads, which are increasing without any compensating improvement in sales revenue.

At this stage you should turn to the notes that accompany the figures for sales revenue and operating profit in the income statement. As described in Chapter 3, these notes offer a valuable source of information on exactly where a company is generating revenue and, linked to this, the level of profit being made in each business sector and geographic area of operation (segment analysis).

Because comparative figures are given for the previous year in the notes, it is possible to identify movements not only within a sector but also among the various geographic areas where a company has an interest. With some additional historical data any significant trends can be identified. Often it is possible to make comparisons with other companies operating in the same sector and location.

Pre-tax profit margin

Moving down the income statement, the next step is to deduct the remaining expenses and charges from operating profit to produce the profit before tax (pre-tax profit or PTP) for the year. In arriving at the profit before tax, finance costs and income and share of profit or loss of associates will be deducted. The pre-tax profit margin shows the level of profitability of a company after all operating costs and expenses except tax and dividends to shareholders have been allowed for.

% pre-tax profit margin = 100 × (pre-tax profit ÷ sales revenue)

A company maintaining a stable operating profit margin but a declining pre-tax profit margin may have raised finance for investment upon which it pays interest, but the investment has yet to be translated into either reduced costs or increased revenue. The interest charge is deducted in arriving at the pre-tax profit for the year, but no income has yet been generated from the investment of the finance raised.

After-tax profit and retained profit margins

It is possible to calculate both the after-tax profit margin and the retained profit margin from the income statement, but such ratios do not offer any significant additional help in the overall appreciation of a company's profitability. Income tax expense is deducted from pre-tax profit to give profit for the year from continuing operations. Any profit or loss from discontinued operations is added or subtracted to arrive at the final profit in the income statement, the profit or loss for the year. The total profit or loss will be divided between the owners of the company and any non-controlling interests.

The efficiency ratios

The next step in analysing a company's profitability is to combine information from the income statement and the statement of financial position in ways that enable you to measure how efficiently a company is using its assets or capital employed.

$	A	B	C
Revenue	100	100	100
Profit	20	20	27
Assets	100	125	150

For example, companies A and B have a 20% profit margin and C has a 27% profit margin. On the basis of this measure, C appears to be the most profitable company and it is impossible to distinguish between A and B. The following ratios can be used as part of a more detailed analysis of profitability.

Rate of return on assets or capital employed

The overall rate of return on capital or assets can be calculated by dividing profit, taken from the income statement, by assets or capital employed, as shown in the statement of financial position, and expressing the result as a percentage.

% rate of return on assets = 100 × (profit ÷ assets)

% rate of return on capital = 100 × (profit ÷ capital)

If this ratio is calculated for the three companies, their rates of return on assets are seen to be:

A	B	C
20%	16%	18%

Company C has the highest profit margin (27%), but it has a greater investment in assets than A or B. Company A has the same profit margin (20%) as B, but it has a lower asset base and so shows a higher rate of return. Linking the assets employed in the business to the profit being generated by them offers a more realistic measure of profitability than the use of profit margin ratios alone. Company A with a 20% return on assets is now identified as the most profitable of the three.

Which profit? What assets?

When dealing with profitability ratios it is important to recognise that there is no single method of calculating rates of return and that the same term may be used to refer to quite different things. A rate of return on assets (ROA) may be produced using the gross, operating, pre-tax or after-tax profit. It is not usual to use gross profit in a rate of return measure, but there is no reason why this should not be done for a number of companies to provide the basis for performance comparisons and the analysis of a business sector.

Which profit measure to use?

As with any art, financial analysis is subject to fad and fashion. A ratio is adopted, rises in repute, declines and is replaced. One measure of profit currently enjoying favour is that of earnings before interest, taxation, depreciation and amortisation (EBITDA). It is argued that this measure strips out all the incidentals to highlight the real profitability of a business and is not biased by capital structure, tax systems or depreciation policies. It can be used to produce an EBITDA earnings per share figure.

The holy grail of financial analysis is the discovery of a single foolproof measure of company performance. EBITDA can be useful as part of a detailed analysis of a company, but there are flaws in its claimed perfection. EBITDA ignores the cost of non-current assets employed in a business, yet surely these are as much an operating cost as anything else. As a measure of profitability it is a long way from the bottom line of the income statement, and so ignores not only depreciation but also interest and tax. A company delivering an after-tax loss from a huge investment in non-current assets financed by equally substantial borrowings could look quite healthy on an EBITDA basis. A variation on EBITDA is EBITDAR where R is for rental and operating lease expenses. This is sometimes used by retailers as it removes store occupancy expenses to provide a more comparable trading margin.

Whichever profit is selected, the end result will be the return on assets, but each of the possible profits will produce a different level of return. For each ratio the denominator has remained constant but a different numerator has been used. Before making use of a pre-calculated rate of return figure always check which profit has been used to produce the ratio.

Similar problems can arise in selecting the denominator for the ROA ratio. This could equally well be the total, operating or net assets employed. Whichever figures are used, the end ratio is correctly described as a ROA for the company in question. If the three companies in the example above had used different definitions of profit and of assets, it would not be of any practical benefit to try to draw any conclusions by comparing their rates of return. For this reason, rate of return ratios given in annual reports or by analysts should not be taken at their face value.

In short, in calculating comparative rates of return it is essential that there is consistency in both the numerator and the denominator in the equation. In other words, you should ensure that each company's ROA is calculated in the same way.

Averaging assets

As soon as a figure for assets or capital is taken from the balance sheet for use in the development of a performance measure there is a problem. The balance sheet provides the financial picture of a company on the final day of its financial year. The income statement is a statement of the company's ability to generate revenue and profit throughout the financial year. The income statement is dynamic, covering the whole year; the balance sheet is static, showing the position only at the end of the year. The year-end balance sheet incorporates the retained profit appearing at the foot of the current year's income statement. Any finance raised during the year for investment in operating assets, even in the last few days of the year, appears in the balance sheet as a source of finance and an asset. For the purposes of rate of return ratios, there is a mismatch between the income statement and the balance sheet.

To overcome this, an average figure for assets or capital is often used in calculating rates of return. This clearly should produce a more accurate ratio, but, for most purposes, it is probably not worth the time and effort involved. Moreover, it may be difficult to get the necessary data for earlier years.

One instance where more detailed analysis is required, with perhaps an average asset or capital figure or other appropriate adjustment, is when a company has experienced major changes during the year. For example, it may have raised capital or made a major acquisition or disposal.

Rate of return on total assets

A useful ratio in analysing company profitability is the rate of return on total assets (ROTA). Total assets, as set out on one side of the balance sheet, represent the total of non-current and current assets employed in the business. The other side of the balance sheet shows the total of equity and liabilities used to finance these assets.

Irrespective of the way in which assets are financed (by using shareholders' funds, debt or short-term borrowing), or of how the total capital and debt are employed (in non-current assets, investments, intangibles or current assets), total assets represent the total resources available to a company to conduct its business. It is therefore appropriate to look at a company's ability to generate a profit on the basis of the total assets it has employed. Using an alternative to total assets as the denominator can make true comparisons difficult, as companies use different means of financing their business.

% return on total assets = 100 × (pre-interest and tax profit ÷ total assets)

When total assets are used, the numerator should be the pre-interest and tax profit (PITP) or, more commonly, earnings before interest and tax (EBIT). This identifies the true return on assets before any financing costs are deducted. By the same logic, interest or income received from financial investments, which form a part of total assets, is included in this profit figure.

Return on total tangible assets

As intangible assets are often considered of less certain value than tangible assets, it is possible to argue that only the tangible assets employed in a company should be taken into account when measuring its rate of return. To arrive at a figure for tangible assets that can be used to determine the return on total tangible assets (ROTTA), deduct any intangibles set out in the non-current assets section of the balance sheet from total assets.

Return on (net) operating assets

To make further practical use of the segment details provided in the annual report, it is worth calculating the rate of return on operating assets (ROOA) or the return on net operating assets (RONOA). The figure for operating profit can be taken straight from the income statement or, for each business sector, from the segment notes. It represents the profit made by the company after allowing for all normal business costs and expenses but before interest and taxation.

Net operating assets

Net operating assets are the assets employed to support the running of a business, assuming that short-term creditors are used to finance short-term assets.

Some companies' balance sheets contain a separately identified figure for total assets less current liabilities (see Chapter 2). This presentation assumes that current liabilities have been used to finance current assets. The net current assets (or liabilities) when added to (subtracted from) non-current assets provide an indication of the total long-term capital and debt employed in the business. This figure can be used as the denominator for measuring the return on net operating assets.

Net operating assets =
operating non-current assets − net current operating assets

Net current operating assets

In arriving at the figure for net current operating assets, cash and short-term investments within current assets are excluded, as are any short-term borrowings or debt repayments appearing within current liabilities. These items are financial rather than physical operating assets. The intention is to show the profitability of the business excluding any financial asset or liability and allied income or expense.

Operating non-current assets

Within the non-current asset section of the balance sheet the tangible assets are shown at their fair carrying value – normally cost less accumulated depreciation. Intangibles and investments are separately valued and displayed. Intangible assets are included in this definition of operating non-current assets. However, because operating profit is before any interest or other non-operational items, any investments shown within the non-current asset heading should, in theory, be deducted. In practice, making such adjustments normally introduces as many problems as it solves. When in doubt keep the analysis simple and consistent.

NOA equals NOCE

The net operating assets (NOA) equal the net operating capital employed (NOCE) of a company.

Operating non-current assets		Equity
Plus inventory + receivables		*Plus* long-term borrowings and creditors
Less accounts payable		*Less* non-current asset investments
		+/− net cash balances
Net operating assets	=	**Net operating capital employed**

Breaking down RONOA

If the RONOA is calculated using at least two years' figures, this may be linked with the information provided on operating assets set out in the segment notes quantifying the investment in each sector and geographic area. This analysis will give an indication of how effective a company is in using its available operating assets in each sector. Comparison can be made with other companies and some benchmarks of performance developed.

The shareholders' return

So far the analysis of rates of return has concentrated on the operational side of a business in measuring the level of profit generated on the assets of a company. Shareholders are the principal stakeholders in a company; they own the company, and can be presumed to have invested their money with a view to receiving some benefits or returns. They want to profit from their investment.

Shareholders may use the profitability ratios described so far in this chapter to monitor a company's performance and to compare it with others in their portfolios or against business sector averages.

The after-tax profit should be used in developing measures of shareholders' return. After a company has covered all costs, expenses and tax, and provided for any non-controlling interests in the profit, what remains, often called profit attributable to shareholders, is available for dividends. The after-tax profit can be paid out in dividends to shareholders or retained to finance future growth and development.

It is possible to develop an after-tax rate of return on assets, which can be useful when considering the track record of one company but is of less value for comparing companies. As each company has its unique tax position – for example, one may own freehold property and another leasehold property, or they may be operating in different countries – it is difficult to draw any firm conclusions on performance in addition to those provided by the pre-tax profit ratios. But although after-tax profit may be of less interest as a basis for comparing companies' performance, it is crucial to every company's shareholders. It represents the end result of management's activities in running the company on their behalf throughout the year.

Which figure to take from the balance sheet to represent the shareholders' stake or investment in the business is more problematic. In most balance sheets the shareholders' total funds are defined as equity. Preference shares or other non-voting capital are often found within the figure for equity. Strictly, these should be removed in the calculation of shareholders' returns, because it is only the ordinary shareholders, the owners of the company, that are being considered here, not other providers of long-term finance and capital.

The figure for shareholders' funds may have several different labels attached to it:

Net assets = total assets − (current liabilities + debt)
Capital employed = net assets
Equity = capital employed
Equity = capital employed = net assets

Once the shareholders' investment has been identified it is possible, using the after-tax profit, to calculate an appropriate rate of return. This rate of return may be defined as:

■ return on capital (ROC);

■ return on capital employed (ROCE);

■ return on shareholders' funds (ROSF);

■ return on equity (ROE);

■ return on investment (ROI);

■ return on net assets (RONA).

Earnings per share

Investors often make use of earnings per share (EPS) as a measure of the overall profitability of a company. EPS is normally to be found in the income statement (see Chapter 3). As with any pre-calculated ratio appearing in an annual report, care should be taken to discover precisely how it has been derived. Also remember EPS is backward looking as it is based on historical profitability. The basis of an EPS calculation is:

EPS = after-tax profit ÷ the number of shares in issue

This effectively links profit with a single share. If you owned one company share, how much profit did the company earn – but not necessarily pay out – for you in the year? Inevitably problems can arise in defining what income was really available to shareholders and how to define a share. IAS 33 (similar to FAS 128) deals with the calculation and presentation of EPS figures. Earnings is defined as the after-tax profit (less any minority interests and preference dividends) for the year – the profit attributable to ordinary shareholders.

> **EPS** = profit attributable to ordinary shareholders ÷
> weighted average number of shares

The weighted average of shares may be calculated by taking the number of equity shares in issue at the beginning of the year, adding this to the number at the end of the year and dividing by two. However, a more accurate timing weight may be called for. For example, a company has 1,000 ordinary shares in issue at January 1st. On June 1st it issues 250 fully paid shares. On December 31st there are 1,250 shares in issue.

> **Weighted average** = $1{,}000 + (250 \times 7/12) = 1{,}146$ shares

Where partly paid shares have been issued the equivalent number of fully paid shares is used in the EPS calculation. Where a company has treasury stock this is deducted from the denominator in arriving at the EPS figure.

A useful variation on the normal EPS calculation is to replace the after-tax profit with that of operating cash flow for the year, to be found in the statement of cash flows.

> **Operating cash flow EPS** = operating cash flow ÷ number of shares

The dilution factor

Two EPS figures are likely to be provided: basic and diluted. Basic EPS is calculated as above. Diluted EPS is calculated using the same net profit but assuming all convertible securities have been converted into shares. This will include any:

- convertible debt and preference shares;
- share warrants and options;
- employee stock purchase plans.

For listed companies reference can be made to their 10-Q or 10-K reports to check the denominator being used in the diluted

EPS calculation. When a loan is converted into shares there will be a saving in interest payments. Profit after tax increases, as does the number of shares used in the diluted EPS calculation. Diluted EPS will always be lower than basic EPS. The numerator and denominator for both will be shown in the notes to the financial statements.

Options and warrants

A share option gives the holder the right, but not the obligation, to acquire shares at an agreed price for a specified time period. Options may be offered to employees (see Chapter 3). If the share price rises above that of the option, it is beneficial to the employees to exercise their option (in the money). If it does not (out of the money), they have no obligation to part with any cash. IFRS 2, revised in 2008, deals with share-based payment schemes.

Sometimes a company raises finance and as an incentive it attaches a warrant to the debt to allow the future purchase of shares at an agreed price. Warrants are either detachable (they can be traded separately) or non-detachable (they cannot be traded).

A company with $500 after-tax profit has 1,000 shares in issue with a current market value of $5 each. It offers employees the option to purchase 200 shares at $4 – the exercise price. If the option is taken up, the company will receive $800. If it had sold shares on the market, it would have needed to issue only 160 shares ($800 ÷ $5). In effect it has issued 40 shares for free (the dilutive element in the EPS calculation) if the option is taken up. This is taken into account in calculating the diluted EPS.

Basic EPS	$500 ÷ 1,000	= **$0.50**
Diluted EPS	$500 ÷ (1,000 + 40)	= **$0.48**

Employee options are taken into account from the date of issue (grant date) in calculating the diluted EPS. Often these will form an important factor in arriving at the fully diluted EPS.

A put option is where the holder has the right to have the company repurchase shares at a specified price.

Comparing earnings per share

It is a mistake to assume you can compare profitability based on EPS. A difference in EPS can be brought about simply by differences in share capital structure. Two companies could have an identical EPS but one company has twice as many issued shares as the other. Two companies could have an identical after-tax profit of $100 and share capital of $1,000. But if one company had issued 25¢ shares and the other $1 shares, the earnings per share would be very different: 2.5¢ and 10¢.

A rights issue

When a bonus or rights issue is made all previous EPS figures are recalculated to allow comparison over time. A bonus issue provides shareholders with, for no payment, additional shares in proportion to their existing holding. A rights issue is an offer to existing shareholders to subscribe for additional shares. Following the 2008 financial crisis, several companies made – or tried to make – rights issues to improve their debt/equity ratios. A company can communicate easily with existing shareholders and it is assumed that they will be positive towards the company and so provide a less costly means of raising additional capital.

How do shareholders know whether the offer is worthwhile? A value must be placed on the shares involved. A company with 1,000 shares in issue with a current market value of $5 offers shareholders the right to acquire one new share for every four held (250 shares) for $3.50 per share.

$$(1,000 \times \$5) + (250 \times \$3.50) = \$5,875 \div 1,250 = \mathbf{\$4.70}$$

The theoretical value of the rights issue shares is $4.70. With more shares in issue the price may drop, but this is potentially an attractive offer to shareholders when compared with the current market share price of $5.

False conclusions

It is important to recognise that it is not possible to compare two companies' earnings per share and draw any useful conclusions.

	A	**B**
After-tax profit($)	100	100
Share capital ($)	100	100
Number of shares	1,000	200
EPS	0.10	0.50

The two companies have an identical after-tax profit for the year and value of issued share capital. Company A has 1,000 shares of 10¢ each in issue and company B has 200 shares of 50¢ each in issue. It is wrong to assume by looking at the EPS that company B is more profitable or a better performer than company A. A difference in EPS may be simply be the result of companies having different share capital structures.

Useful conclusions

The most effective way to compare companies' earnings per share is to use the compound growth rate. Looking at the rate at which earnings have been growing over a number of years allows comparison of the ability of companies to improve their earnings.

Dividend cover

Having arrived at the after-tax profit for the year, the next step for the directors is to decide what dividend they intend to pay to their shareholders. The final dividend will not be paid until after the AGM at which the shareholders vote on the directors' proposal; it is unusual for the dividend to be rejected. Every major company should have a clear policy on dividend payments and dividend cover. The directors may explain this in their report.

To gain some appreciation of the safety of a company's dividend policy the dividend cover ratio can be calculated.

Dividend cover = after-tax profit ÷ dividend paid

A company paying a $10,000 dividend from $20,000 after-tax profit has a dividend cover of 2. It has $2 of after-tax profit available for every $1 of dividend distributed to shareholders; 50% of earnings is paid out in dividend. It can be useful to replace the figure for after-tax profit with that of the year's operating cash flow – to be found in the statement of cash flows – as the nominator in this ratio.

Cash flow dividend cover = operating cash flow ÷ dividend paid

The cash paid in dividends to shareholders will be found in the financing activities section of the statement of cash flows. Using this ratio answers the question of how well operating cash flow covers any dividends paid. It can provide a much more acute appreciation of the safety of dividend payments to shareholders. The lower the dividend cover the more concern there is for the shareholders' future income stream.

Mind the gap

If the dividend per share is deducted from the earnings per share, what remains is the per share retained earnings for the year. The cash flow statement can provide a similar measure:

Earnings per share – dividend per share = **retained earnings per share**

or

Net operating cash flow per share – dividend per share
= **retained cash flow per share**

The retained earnings per share is an important element in the assessment of the financial performance and position of a company. For any company it is to be expected that a continuing and significant source of funds is its current operations (the income and cash flow statements). A healthy and consistent level of retained earnings reinvested in the business is an indication that rather than relying on borrowed money, a company is generating a good proportion of the required financial resources internally.

The annual report will contain a typical five-year or ten-year history, where a company may show both the earnings and dividend per share for each year. It is worth bringing these two together to see the relationship. The gap – the difference between earnings and dividend per share – indicates how much each year the company is generating from its operations to plough back into the business for future growth. The larger this figure the better it is for the company. Net operating cash flow can also be used in the analysis. A company that is retaining little or no profit (operating cash flow) must inevitably be looking to its shareholders or outside sources of capital to finance any major investment programme or activity.

Smoothing earnings

Earnings per share is a popular means of measuring company performance. It is also a ratio often used as a performance target as part of management incentive schemes.

There is an understandable tendency among directors to prefer to show smooth profit growth over a number of years rather than a series of volatile shifts. It makes it appear they are in control of the business. The achievement of such a trend can also calm investors. In extreme cases directors may allow their enthusiasm to edge them into creative accounting. Read the small-print notes to see if there is any mention of excessive inventory write-offs. If the current year is showing high profit, some unsold inventory may be written off as a loss. Next year the company can sell this for 100% margin. The profit has been time-shifted (see Figure 6.1).

Companies X and Y might have achieved the same level of profit. Company X shows a steady profit growth whereas Y has a volatile pattern of earnings. Investors will prefer company X. Although

FIG 6.1 **Different ways of making the same profit**

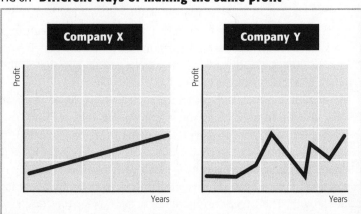

profitability may be identical, there appears to be more certainty (less risk) with an investment in X. This is often said to be because of the "quality of earnings" of one company compared with another.

It is generally accepted that a smooth upward profit trend is better than a track record similar to the skyline of the Swiss Alps. Given the choice, most companies would prefer to see their profits increase gradually over a number of years. Smoothing profits is attractive. A smooth profit trend indicates that management has firm and effective control of the business.

Creative profits

Directors may be tempted to become creative in their financial statement presentation. This is particularly true if they have a personal interest in their company's performance – share options, commission, or bonuses for achieving performance targets.

Profits can be smoothed in many creative ways, for example by changing depreciation policy or capitalising expenses. The time at which a transaction is recognised in the financial statements can be an important consideration. If a major event producing large profits is not brought into this year's accounts but moved to the following year, reported profit can be effectively smoothed; this is not uncommon for German companies.

It is much more difficult to produce a profit immediately than to shift profit from this year to next. There is a temptation for a highly profitable company, uncertain of the future, to set aside some of its current profit for a rainy day. A reserve might be created. A cash sale of $100 is not taken into the income statement but placed in the balance sheet as "deferred revenue". Next year the $100 revenue is brought into the income statement and the reserve disappears. A variation is to pre-pay expenses: pay some of next year's expenses in cash and include them in the current year's cost of sales.

It is to be hoped that auditors will catch any such tricks. As yet the most extreme example of manipulating reserves was WorldCom, resulting in an overstatement of profit in 2000 of some $3 billion.

Pension fund accounting, off-balance-sheet financing, the manipulation of reserves and provisions, year-end inventory valuations and the treatment of bad debts have all, in their time, helped to smooth profits and influence balance sheet valuations. The steady flow of IFRS and various watchdog organisations have improved matters considerably, but always be on your guard.

Use your own analysis of a company as the basis for assessment. Do not rely on ready-made analysis provided in the annual report. Many commercial databases that offer financial analysis take all the figures in the financial statements at their face value. The arithmetic may be good but the quality rotten.

Dividend politics

In most countries, when a company's profit declines it is expected that the dividend will be reduced; this is common-sense housekeeping. In the UK in the 1990s this rule did not appear to hold. The dividend cover for many companies declined rapidly as profits fell during the recession, but dividends were maintained.

There are at least two possible explanations for this. It could be claimed that company directors were taking a long-term view in deciding what dividend it was appropriate for their shareholders to receive, allowing for the inevitable fact of business life that as years passed there would be peaks and troughs in the actual profit generated. The possibility of short-term fluctuations in dividend cover was accepted to provide long-term regularity and security of dividend payment to shareholders. Alternatively, it could be that company directors, particularly chairmen and CEOs, were worried that if they did not deliver the level of dividend their major shareholders, the institutional investors, were relying on, the share price of the company might fall and they might be faced with personal job insecurity. Institutional shareholders rely on the dividend streams from their investments to support their own businesses.

The management of a company failing to perform with respect to dividend is likely, at least, to be open to criticism, and possibly the target for direct attention and action. Directors of family owned or controlled companies may find themselves under pressure to continue paying dividends that allow shareholders to maintain their lifestyle but may not necessarily be in the best long-term interests of the company. In the 2008 financial crisis, many companies reduced or ceased their dividend payments. This of course compounded the problems for the financial institutions that normally relied on the dividends as a regular and reasonably secure source of income.

Dividend cover ratio

Companies usually pay dividends from after-tax profit for the year; otherwise the capital maintenance requirement discussed at the beginning of this chapter would be breached. Thus a dividend cover ratio of 1:1 showing that a company is distributing all of its profit to shareholders and retaining nothing to support the future development of the business can be taken as being the uppermost limit of prudent dividend policy. It would certainly be unusual, if not unacceptable, for a company consistently to operate on less than 1:1 dividend cover.

$$\textbf{Dividend cover} \quad = \quad \text{after-tax profit} \div \text{dividends}$$
$$= \quad \text{earnings per share} \div \text{dividend per share}$$

The Du Pont pyramid of ratios

The use of the rate of return ratio as a measure of company profitability and performance is widespread and effective. If only one measure of a company's performance were allowed, most would choose the rate of return. Yet simply to take the profit for the year and express it as a percentage of the assets or capital employed in a business is a fairly blunt approach to measuring profitability. A single figure from the income statement is linked to a single figure from the statement of financial position. If this exercise is completed for two companies and the returns of both are similar, what conclusions can be drawn?

	A	B
Sales revenue ($)	300	100
Profit ($)	25	40
Assets ($)	125	200
ROA (%)	**20**	**20**

Both companies have a 20% rate of return on assets. To gain a clearer understanding of the level of a company's profitability and how the profit is being made, there is much to recommend the use of the Du Pont approach, named after the US company credited with pioneering work in this area. Sometimes this is referred to as the construction of a pyramid of ratios, because all the ratios can be presented as a pyramid with the rate of return as the summit (see Figure 7.1).

Profit and cash flow measures in rate of return

In assessing the rate of return for a company, two separate questions are being addressed. First, the ability to make a profit from its operations; second, the efficiency with which it is utilising its available assets and capital to produce that profit.

In all the following ratios, the net operating cash flow – from the cash flow statement – could be substituted for the profit figure. This provides the basis for assessing the cash generating capability of a company, and makes a useful supplement to the profitability analysis.

Take the profit margin

To answer the first question – the level of profitability of a company's operations – the profit margin offers an appropriate and easily identifiable measure. If the profit margin is calculated for the two companies in the above example, for company A it is 8.3% and for B it is 40%. On this basis company B is the more profitable with a profit margin almost five times greater than that of company A.

Introduce the asset or capital turn

A new measure – the asset or capital turn – must be identified to answer the second question and obtain a view of a company's efficiency in the use of its assets or capital. The only reason for a company to maintain assets is to support the conduct of its business and to assist the generation of current and future profits. The success of this intention, in accounting terms, can be measured through the level of sales revenue. The greater the level of sales revenue being generated from the use of the assets employed in the business, the greater is the level of effective utilisation of those assets.

$$\textbf{Asset turn} = \text{sales revenue} \div \text{assets}$$
$$\textbf{Capital turn} = \text{sales revenue} \div \text{capital}$$

If this ratio is calculated for the two example companies, it can be seen that they have quite different levels of ability to generate sales revenues from their assets.

A $300 \div $125 = **2.4**
B $100 \div $200 = **0.5**

Company A is turning over the assets employed 2.4 times each year, whereas company B manages to turn its assets over only once every two years. Company A has proved capable of generating $2.40 of sales revenue for each $1 of assets employed while company B has managed only $0.50. If one company is a retailer and the other a heavy goods manufacturer, there is little point in pursuing the comparison. However, if both the companies are operating in the same business sector, the conclusions of comparative performance and profitability will be justified and explanations for the differences sought through further analysis.

Bring the two together

It is now possible to take these two companies and examine the differing means by which they have achieved an identical 20% rate of return. Company A has the lower profit margin but the higher asset turn. If the two ratios are brought together, it can be seen clearly how the rate of return is being produced.

% rate of return on assets = % profit margin $\times$ asset turn

A 8.3% $\times$ 2.4 = **20%**
B 40% $\times$ 0.5 = **20%**

Draw a chart

The combination of the profit margin and asset turn ratios to give the return on assets may be displayed in a chart, or pyramid of ratios. The use of the supporting ratios to those of a company's profit margin and asset turn is discussed in Chapter 7.

The presentation in Figure 6.2 of the rate of return as the combining of the two component ratios is a useful basis for the assessment and comparison of companies' performance. It is essential to calculate

FIG 6.2 **Return on assets**

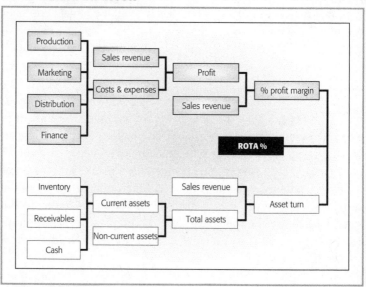

the overall rate of return of a company, ideally completing this for a number of years to see the trend and allow direct comparison with other companies. It is also important to try to discover precisely how a company is achieving its level of profitability. What is the relationship between the profit margin and the asset turn? Is it consistent, and if not, why is it changing?

Using the ratios

The relationship between the two component ratios can be visualised as a seesaw with profit margin at one end and asset turn at the other (see Figure 6.3). Company B in the example has a higher profit margin but a lower asset turn than company A.

Although both companies have an identical 20% rate of return, it is the result of a different balancing act between the two ratios. A company trying to improve its rate of return can do so only by adjusting either or both of the two component ratios. Can it improve the profit margin through improved cost efficiency or increased prices or a combination of the two? Is it possible to improve the ability to

FIG 6.3 **The asset turn/profit margin seesaw**

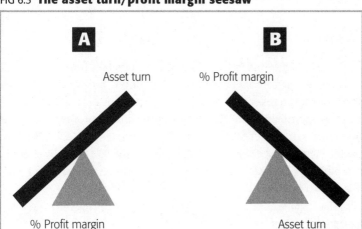

generate sales revenue from the same or fewer assets – for example, through lower inventory levels – or can investment be made to provide additional sales revenue at lower cost without harming the asset turn?

A company concentrating on only one of the two component ratios in an attempt to improve its rate of return is likely to run into difficulties. An example, based on a real-life situation, can illustrate the issues involved. The average return on assets for the sector is 20% (10% profit margin and 2.0 asset turn). Company X, at the bottom of the league table for profitability for the sector, recognises that performance must be improved. A small investment is made to increase capacity and, with a view to improving sales volume, the profit margin is reduced.

$	Average	Year 1	Year 2	Year 3	Year 4
Sales revenue	1,000	800	825	850	850
Operating profit	100	60	52	48	44
Total assets	500	600	650	650	650

Profit margin (%)	10.0	7.5	6.3	6.6	5.2
Asset turn	2.0	1.3	1.3	1.3	1.3
ROTA (%)	**20.0**	**10.0**	**8.0**	**7.4**	**6.8**

Prices are cut – the easy bit – and the margin falls from 7.5% to 5.2%. One end of the seesaw has been pushed down, but what happens if the other end refuses to come up and there is not as great an increase in sales as anticipated? The result is a decline in profitability. If the asset turn remains at 1.3, with a profit margin of 5.2%, ROTA drops to under 7% in year 4. Maintaining the original 10% ROTA requires either a profit margin of 7.6% (7.6% $\times$ 1.3 = 10%), or an asset turn of 1.9 (5.2% $\times$ 1.9 = 10%).

League tables

Having calculated the profit margin, asset turn and overall rate of return for a selection of companies, a league table can be prepared. First, the companies can be ranked according to their rate of return. In most cases ROTA is as effective a measure as any for this purpose. This ranking highlights the most profitable companies within the chosen business sector.

Benchmarking

A ROTA table can help determine what should be taken as an acceptable or expected rate of return for a company operating within a particular business sector. The mid-point in the table provides an indication of the average or median rate of return for the sector. A benchmark for comparison is now available. Companies producing higher than the average rate of return can be identified, as can those that are trailing in the league. If at least three years' figures are used in the table, the trend whereby each company arrived at its current place in the ranking can be observed.

Deeper understanding

Separate tables can be prepared ranking the selected companies by profit margin and asset turn. These will help in interpreting the ROTA ranking. The two component ratios will also contribute to a deeper understanding of the way in which each company has generated its overall rate of return. Is the seesaw tipping the right way?

A food retailer can be expected to have a comparatively low profit margin but higher asset turn than most other types of retail companies. Discount retailers operate on the basis that low prices (low profit margins) result in more sales and produce a high asset turn: "pile it high and sell it cheap". In the ROTA listings the discount retailers, as is to be expected, are towards the top end of the asset turn ranking but lower down for profit margin. Similarly, a company manufacturing a simple unchanging product, for example nuts and bolts, may be able to edge its prices up in return for excellent customer service and quality, but as any other form of product differentiation is difficult it is likely to be operating on low profit margins.

A quality department store may be able to charge high prices to achieve a good profit margin, but it will also find it necessary to provide a pleasing environment for its customers (such as carpets, wide aisles and escalators) which requires capital investment and reduces the asset turn. A manufacturer of a premium product may be able to generate high profit margins but be forced to invest in expensive machinery and facilities necessary for its production.

The rate of return of a company may be viewed as resulting from its pricing policy as much as from internal efficiencies or levels of asset utilisation. Equally, it could be argued that rate of return is directly dependent on the quality of a company's financial management. If major assets are not purchased but rented, or just-in-time inventory control is introduced, the asset turn will be improved. Although a single factor may, at one time, be more significant than others, it is dangerous to take this in isolation as "explaining" rate of return. The two ends of the seesaw should be examined independently, but they should also be recognised as being directly and inseparably linked in the rate of return measure.

Like-for-like sales

Business sectors often use their own indices to prepare league tables, and these can be mistaken for profitability measures. The retail sector places considerable emphasis on like-for-like sales growth as an indicator of performance. The aim is to present a measure of year-on-year sales growth that is not distorted by sales from stores opened in the current year – these being excluded from the calculation. The assumption is that this truly indicates the underlying revenue growth, and so provides a comparative performance measure. A well-known retail saying is that "sales are vanity, profit is sanity".

When interpreting companies' sales growth, always check to see whether there have been any acquisitions during the year or substantial exchange-rate movements. These will affect the apparent growth of sales but are not within the control of the company. Food retailers can be expected to include store extensions in their like-for-like comparison. This means they will be able to compare the sales from the old 10,000 square metre store with the newly extended 20,000 square metre one.

Immediately after the peak selling season like-for-like sales are given considerable emphasis in retail performance analysis: the higher the figure the better is the company rating. It is unwise to take too much notice of such analysis, and it is certainly a mistake to assume it has anything to do with profitability. A company selling at a loss is more likely to generate higher like-for-like sales growth than one striving to maintain or increase profit margins.

Internally, the like-for-like sales ratio can be of great benefit to management. If calculated in a consistent manner it can indicate, period by period, how the business and its individual units are performing. It can prove a good key performance indicator.

It is unlikely that any two companies will calculate their like-for-like sales in exactly the same manner, so be careful in using this as the basis for comparison. There is no accounting standard or even firm guidance on presenting like-for-like figures. Companies may not even use the same time period for their calculations and have the option of excluding stores subject to refit or resizing. Bear in mind that, as yet, there is no independent audit of like-for-like figures. As soon as companies realised the importance analysts attach to a particular measure they did their best to deliver the right figures.

Value added

Market value added

One way of calculating value added is to use market value added (MVA). This measures the net value of the company to shareholders – the "price to book" ratio. The total shareholders' equity (to which the market value of debt may be added) is deducted from the current market value (capitalisation) of the company (to which debt may be added). A positive figure means that value has been added to the shareholders' investment and a negative one means the investors have lost out. For example, if the capitalisation of a company is $100 and the shareholders' equity in the balance sheet is $50, for every $1 of shareholders' equity the company has added $1.

Economic value added

A popular approach to assessing corporate performance is to use economic value added (EVA), which measures after-tax profit against the estimated cost of capital – normally taken as the weighted average cost of capital (WACC, see Chapter 9). Companies should be expected to produce not only an accounting profit but also one that more than covers their cost of capital. It is argued that EVA is better than earnings per share or price/earnings ratios as these do not take account of the real cost of capital.

A simple example of the calculation of EVA is shown below. After the charge of $10 ($100 × 10%) representing the estimated cost of capital, the company shows an EVA of $30 for the period.

			$
After-tax profit	$40	After-tax profit	40
Capital employed	$100	Cost of capital	10
Cost of capital	10%	**Economic value added**	**30**

A positive EVA indicates that a company is providing investors with added value. A company with a consistent EVA should have an increasing MVA; it will be generating a rate of return above the cost of capital so the share price should rise. For example, the three companies in the following example are all generating a positive return on capital employed.

$	A	B	C
After-tax profit	50	60	50
Capital employed	200	400	600
Cost of capital (10%)	20	40	60
ROCE (%)	**25**	**15**	**8**
EVA ($)	**30**	**20**	**−10**

Although company C produces a positive 8% return on capital employed, it is actually destroying shareholder value with a negative $10 EVA. In practice, the calculation of EVA requires several adjustments – to allow for the treatment of R&D, goodwill and brand values, leases and depreciation – to be made to the after-tax profit figure. It is claimed that EVA, as a single monetary figure, is better at concentrating management attention on the 'real' results of running the business than are standard performance ratios such as ROTA. EVA is often used as a basis for managers' performance-related incentives.

Value-added statement

Value added is an effective means of both measuring company performance and identifying the way in which the various interest groups involved share in the resources generated. If a value-added statement is not provided in the annual report, it is easy to develop one based on the income statement. Retained earnings can be defined as:

$$R = S - (B + Dp + W + I + Dd + T)$$

R = retained earnings
S = sales revenue
B = bought in materials and services
Dp = depreciation
W = wages
I = interest
Dd = dividends
T = tax

Value added is the difference between sales revenue and the amounts paid to external suppliers of goods and services. This can be derived from the following equation:

$$S - B = W + I + Dd + T + Dp + R$$

Some companies provide a statement of value added in their annual report. Value added is produced by deducting from sales revenue or income all costs and expenses due to a company's suppliers of goods and services. The difference is the value the company has added to the goods and services it received.

Value added = sales revenue − purchases and services

If the annual report contains sufficient data, you can prepare a simple value-added statement, which can be used to reinforce the ratio analysis discussed earlier in this chapter. Having arrived at the total of the value added for the year, the next step is to see how this was divided up among the company's internal and external interest groups. If sales revenue is expressed as 100, representing 100 pence or cents or 100%, the proportion of revenue being allotted to each interest group can be shown.

$		
Sales revenue		100
Suppliers	50	
Employees	20	
Interest	5	
Tax	5	
Shareholders	5	85
Retained profit		**15**

Presenting income and expenditure in this way is popular with many companies. The value-added statement has proved to be a useful and practical means of communicating financial information to employees who find the annual report somewhat impenetrable.

A value-added statement can be displayed as a bar chart or pie chart. A pie chart can effectively represent $1 or £1 and show how each unit of income or sales revenue received by the company in the year was shared out: how much went to suppliers, employees, shareholders and government, and how much was left as retained profit for reinvestment into the business at the end of the year.

Dispensing with profit

All the figures set out in the income statement can be incorporated in a value-added statement. For example, a single figure for profit for the year is sufficient in a value-added statement rather than the five or six years that appear in a typical published income statement. Companies often found that if they provided employees with the published income statement, one of the first questions that arose was which of the numerous profits shown should be used as a measure of profitability, and therefore as a basis for wage negotiations. Indeed, the word "profit" need not appear in a value-added statement. What is left after all interest groups have received their share of the value added (the retained profit of $15) may simply be referred to as "amount retained for investment".

If a value-added statement is prepared for a number of companies operating in the same business sector, it may be used for comparison and the development of benchmarks.

Value added and shareholders

It can be argued that the prime objective of any company is to create value for its shareholders. Whether this should focus on maximising shareholder value or producing a balance between the interested parties (stakeholders) active in the company is open for discussion. During the 1990s companies increasingly focused on shareholder value, so much so that it almost became a mantra. Shareholder value is often mentioned in annual reports, but it is not so often or easily quantified.

Shareholders can gain value from two sources: an increase in share price or receipt of dividends. A company with high value added can decide either to reinvest funds in the business to provide continued growth or to give increased dividends to its shareholders. One simple measure of shareholder value is:

(Sale price of shares + dividends received) – purchase price of shares

Shareholder return can be calculated as:

(Dividend + (current share price – purchase share price)) ÷ purchase share price

If the dividend for the year is 10¢, the shares cost 100¢ to buy and the current price is 105¢, if the shares were sold, the shareholder return would be 15%.

$$(10 + (105 - 100)) \div 100 = 0.15 \ (15\%)$$

Such value measures can be readily understood by investors, but are not normally immediately available from the financial figures found in the annual report.

Business drivers

Value-based management (VBM) is concerned with all aspects of a business, but particularly with the five "business drivers" from which shareholder value can be created:

- initial capital invested;
- rate of return on capital;
- rate of return required by investors;
- growth in capital invested;
- number of years involved.

Shareholder value analysis

Another means of quantifying shareholder value is through shareholder value analysis (SVA). This concentrates on seven value drivers:

- sales growth rate;
- operating profit margin;
- cash tax rate;
- fixed capital investment;
- working capital investment;
- the planning horizon;
- the cost of capital.

Free cash flow

An important factor in SVA analysis is the free cash flow (FCF) generating capability of a company. This is the cash flow available after allowing for capital maintenance and interest payments. FCF is calculated as follows:

> Operating profit
> *Plus* depreciation
> *Less* cash tax paid
> = Cash profits
> *Less* investment in non-current assets and
>   investment in working capital
> **= Free cash flow**

FCF is useful in providing an indication of the level of a company's cash flow generation. It also measures the amount of cash potentially available to cover the financing costs of the business after all necessary investment has been made. Can the company safely consider raising more finance or making a major capital investment? Companies often provide figures for their FCF, but there is no standard definition of the term so be cautious in using them.

If all interest payments are deducted, the resultant "levered free cash flow" indicates the amount of cash potentially available for dividends and future growth. It is useful to compare the growth in free cash flow with that of earnings. If the trends are significantly different, is it possible to find the reason?

Summary

- Profit is not the same thing as profitability.

- Profitability can only be measured using a ratio that combines profit with at least one other figure from the income statement, the statement of financial position, or somewhere else in the annual report.

- The preparation of profitability league tables comparing companies operating in the same sector makes it easy to see how they are performing against the median benchmark.

- Never rely solely on one year's figures; 3–5 years' figures should be compared and an explanation sought for any big changes between one year and another.

- The most effective starting point in comparing the performance of a set of companies operating in the same business sector is to use the gross profit margin. This shows the level of a company's profitability after covering all the direct costs and expenses of running the business. For companies undertaking the same type of business, some common levels of gross profit margin are to be expected.

- Whichever profit figure is used, make sure that any "one-off" profits or losses are removed. It is a company's continuing and sustainable operating profit that should form the basis of any profitability assessment.

- Avoid using a company's own profitability indices, such as EBITDA. A company is free to be selective as to how a ratio is calculated and presented. Where a company uses non-GAAP measures this should be fully explained.

- To provide a comprehensive measure of profitability, you must determine how efficiently a company is using its assets to generate its profit. If only one measure of profitability is used, it should be that of rate of return. The rate of return on total assets (ROTA) ratio (profit before interest and tax expressed as a percentage of total assets) is the best to use. The figures needed to calculate it are easy to gather from a typical annual report. It can be used to make direct comparisons between companies as it is not subject to distortion resulting from differing forms of financial structures, the profit is before any financial charges and the denominator is not affected by the way in which the assets have been financed. The use of ROTA is particularly recommended when companies operating in different countries are being compared because it overcomes many of the problems of obtaining comparable figures.

- To understand a company better, see how it is achieving its rate of return by looking at the asset turn as well as the gross margin.

- Remember that RONA and ROTA measures are not affected by the financial structure of a company (leverage or gearing). Two companies with different capital structure can be directly compared as to their ability to generate profit from their assets.

- The segment notes in the annual report offer a valuable additional source of data to help assess a company's profit performance, as well as providing an appreciation of trends and shifts in the balance of its activities. Segment data are normally shown on an operating profit and operating asset basis. This allows the calculation of the return on operating assets for each business and geographic sector.

- Shareholders are obviously interested in the profitability of their company but can be expected to focus on the after-tax profit and the dividend they receive. A key measure for shareholders is earnings per share (EPS). This is calculated using the after-tax profit, with a few adjustments, as the numerator and the weighted average number of shares in issue as the denominator.

- Shareholders and analysts are interested in what remains after the dividends have been paid out of the after-tax profit (the retained profit available for investment). This is an important indicator of the ability of a company to self-finance its operations. The more profit a company can reinvest in the business, after satisfying shareholder dividend requirements, the better.

- Also of interest is the dividend cover ratio, that is, what proportion of the profit is paid out in dividends. When the ratio is calculated for several years it gives a useful insight into a company's dividend policy and also how well a company has done in any particular year.

7 Measuring efficiency

THE THREE "E"S – efficiency, effectiveness and economy – provide the basis of value for money. The efficiency of a company can be defined as the relationship between the output of products or services and the input of resources necessary for their delivery. Quantified as a ratio of output to input, the efficiency of one company can be measured over time and compared with that of others. One of the main responsibilities of management is to make efficient use of the human, physical and financial resources available to a company. This chapter considers various means of measuring, assessing and comparing companies' efficiency of utilisation of each of these three categories of resources.

Practical control of efficiency in companies must be carried out internally. It is the focus of management accounting rather than financial accounting and external reporting. In most cases information about the internal control systems of companies is not available to outsiders.

Human resource management

The total employee cost and number of people employed for the current and previous year will normally be found in the notes in a company's annual report. A company's website is probably the easiest to access source of any available employment statistics.

Problems of definition

It may seem unlikely that it should be difficult to define the number of employees of a company, but unfortunately it is true. In the annual report a company may define the number of employees as being any of the following:

- the average number employed during the year;
- the number employed at the end of the year;
- the total number of full-time and part-time employees;
- the number of full-time equivalent employees.

A full-time equivalent (FTE) is produced by dividing the total number of hours worked by all employees by the standard number of hours in the selected working period: a week, a month or a year. This definition is popular in the retail, hotel and catering sectors and in other organisations where large numbers of part-time workers are employed. If the standard contract is to work 35 hours per week for 47 weeks per year (5 weeks allowed as holiday), the FTE is 1,645 hours per year. An employee working 4 hours per day for the 47 weeks counts as 0.57 FTE.

$$20 \text{ hours} \times 47 \text{ weeks} = 940 \text{ hours per year}$$

$$940 \div 1,645 = 0.57$$

When a number of companies are being studied in order to assess the comparative efficiency in the use of human resources, it is important as far as possible to use a common basis for the definition of the number of employees. In most cases, the figure for employees given in the annual report will be either the average number employed during the year or the number employed at the year end. A straight comparison between two companies based on an analysis where one provides a figure for average employees during the year and the other for year-end total employees is potentially misleading. However, when comparing a number of companies, particularly if they are located in different countries, there is often no other option.

Average remuneration per employee

Most companies provide a figure for the total wages and salaries paid during the year – employee benefit expense. If total remuneration is divided by the number of employees, the result is the average remuneration per employee.

Average remuneration = total wages and salaries ÷ number of employees

Where there are significant variations in average remuneration between companies in the same sector, first check (and this applies to all the ratios of efficiency in this section) to see if there is a difference in the definition of the number of employees. If this is not the explanation, further investigation is required to discover the reasons for the variation. One company may be operating in a different segment of the market or be based in a higher- or lower-cost employment area than another. It is not appropriate to use this ratio as a measure of efficiency to compare companies in different countries, but it may be of use in deciding where to locate a business.

The figure given for the total employee costs can be assumed to include the remuneration of a company's directors since they are employees. Directors normally receive above-average pay, but it is unusual for this to result in the distortion of the average remuneration ratio for a major company; and, if necessary, you can subtract directors' remuneration as it is given separately (see below).

Interpreting the figures

A company seen to be offering its employees well below what appears to be the norm for the sector or the national average wage for the country in which it is based may be efficient in the control of employee cost; but whether such a policy will prove to be in the best long-term interests of all concerned is questionable. In recent years, many companies defending their executive remuneration packages have reaffirmed their belief that "if you pay peanuts, you get monkeys". There is no reason to assume that this is not equally true for the shop or factory floor.

When a business sector is being investigated, it may be useful to have some indication of the total numbers employed in it and the position of companies as employers. This can be achieved by preparing a table ranking the companies according to numbers of employees and calculating the total. From this the importance of an individual company as an employer within a sector, or of a sector as a source of employment within a country, can be highlighted. If employee figures for a number of years are available, then any employment trends by company or by sector can be identified.

The long-term view

Companies often choose to provide employee statistics as part of their five-year or ten-year record of financial performance. Where this information is available it can be used to study a company's record as an employer. Over a number of years a company can be expected to show some consistency in its number of employees. If a company increases the number one year and reduces it the next, it may be exhibiting weakness. Management may not be in control of the business and may be unable to plot and follow a medium-term, let alone a long-term, action plan. In a company that relies on highly skilled employees to deliver its products or services, a hire-and-fire employment policy usually has a negative impact not only on employee loyalty and productivity but also, eventually, on the company's financial performance.

Other sources of information

In addition to a company's annual report, newspapers, magazines and journals can be useful sources of information. Large changes, either up or down, in a company's employee numbers are often the subject of informed comment. Trade journals that cater for the business sector a company is in can also be helpful.

Sales revenue per employee

Having looked at the number of employees and their average remuneration, the next step is to consider employees' contribution to the generation of sales revenue and profit. If sales revenue is divided by the number of employees, the ratio of sales revenue per employee is produced. This is a measure of the ability of a company to generate sales revenue on the basis of its employees.

Revenue per employee = sales revenue ÷ number of employees

This ratio should be calculated for a number of years to see the trend for the selected company. It is particularly useful when used to compare a number of companies operating in the same business sector. Companies can be ranked in order of their sales per employee, and, if data are available for a number of years, their relative and changing positions in the league table can be assessed.

Interpreting the figures

Differences between companies in the sales per employee ratio can often be explained by differences in their focus within a sector. A discount food retailer is likely to have higher sales per employee than a department store, and the rate for a fashionable boutique may be even higher. A labour-intensive goods manufacturer will have lower sales per employee than one with a highly automated plant. A construction company that subcontracts much of its work to other companies rather than undertaking this itself will have a much higher sales per employee ratio than one that does not subcontract. When studying a business sector, it is important to look at variations among companies in the level of this and other ratios and to try to explain any trends exhibited, both for individual companies and for the sector as a whole. A company may then be seen in the context of its business sector to be setting, following or matching the general standards of performance and trends.

Compare the ratios of sales and remuneration per employee. A company only just managing to earn enough revenue to cover its wage bill and associated employment costs will not be producing exciting rates of return. A company that cannot generate sales revenue per employee of at least double the average wage applying in its country of operation can be assumed to be if not already in trouble then certainly heading for it.

Profit per employee

Most businesses can be expected to strive to produce the highest level of revenue per employee possible, but it is profit rather than revenue that may be seen as the only true measure of efficiency. There is little point in generating revenue if this does not in turn produce profit. The ratio of profit per employee is a measure of the ability of a company to produce profit based on employees.

Profit per employee = profit ÷ number of employees

Chapter 6 discussed the importance of the selection of an appropriate profit from the income statement to produce a meaningful profit margin. The same issues are involved in the decision about which profit to use in the ratio of profit per employee. It is probably most effective to concentrate on the gross and operating profits per employee as measures of how efficiently a company is using its employees and the employees' contribution to its overall performance and success.

Interpreting the figures

As with the ratio of sales per employee, the trends for both individual companies and the business sector should be studied. Individual company performance in profit per employee can be compared with the average or standard for the sector and year-by-year movements assessed. Significant one-off shifts in this ratio should be investigated to discover if they are the result of a change in the efficiency of a company or some other action or event, such as an acquisition or disposal of a labour-intensive subsidiary. Where possible, it is most effective to concentrate on the continuing business operations of a company and to ignore any exceptional profits.

Value added per employee

Chapter 6 dealt with using a value-added statement to investigate a company's cost and expense structure and the way in which the corporate cake is divided among various interest groups. Value added can be defined as the difference between the revenue received by a company and the amount it paid for goods and services. It is easy to produce a figure for the value added per employee, and, as with profit per employee, the higher the ratio the better is a company's performance.

Value added per employee = value added ÷ number of employees

Employee cost per unit of revenue or unit of value added

A third measure relevant to efficiency in the utilisation of employees can be produced by dividing the total employee cost by sales revenue and presenting it as a percentage. This produces the employee cost per unit of sales revenue.

Employee cost per unit of revenue = 100 × (employee costs ÷ sales revenue)

Value added may be used in place of sales revenue to produce a ratio of employee cost per unit of value added to indicate the proportion of value added of a company being devoted to employees.

The employee cost to sales ratio shows what proportion of each unit of sales revenue generated during the year was taken up by employee remuneration and allied expenses. Broadly, the lower the ratio the better it is for the company. If less of each unit of revenue is devoted to employee remuneration, there will be more available for other purposes.

$	A	B
Sales revenue	100	100
Employee costs	30	20
Employee cost per $1 sales revenue	**0.30**	**0.20**

Interpreting the figures

For every $1 of sales revenue generated during the year, company A puts 30¢ and company B puts 20¢ towards employee remuneration and associated expenses. If the amount set aside for employment expenses is taken as a measure of efficiency, company B appears to be performing better than company A. There may be a number of reasons for the variation between the two. Company B may employ fewer people or pay a lower rate to its employees, or it may be operating in a different segment of the market and be able to charge a higher price for its products or services.

Relating employee cost to revenue is a useful way of comparing companies operating in the same business. If the ratio is calculated for a representative number of companies, an average or median can be found for the sector against which individual companies can be measured and compared over time.

Where the ratio of employee cost to sales revenue is used for international comparison, major variations can be expected because wage levels differ and social security and other benefit charges may be included in the total employee cost. It is therefore not recommended that too much weight be placed on this ratio for comparison of companies operating in different countries.

Tangible non-current assets per employee

In many businesses the investment in tangible non-current assets provided to assist employees is an important factor in gaining an overview of the efficiency of a company's activities. If heavy engineering companies or car manufacturers are being analysed, it is useful to assess their ability to generate sales revenue and profit per employee and to maintain control over total employment costs; but measurement of investment in assets used in the production process to support employees' activities is equally important in assessing each company's efficiency in human resource management.

If the total of tangible non-current assets shown in the balance sheet is divided by the number of employees, the ratio of tangible non-current assets per employee is produced.

Tangible non-current assets per employee =
tangible non-current assets ÷ number of employees

Interpreting the figures

This ratio provides a basis for comparing companies with respect to the investment they have made in assets necessary for their production activities. For example, a car manufacturer can be expected to require continued and substantial investment in robotics to maintain the quality and level of output and, perhaps, to allow a reduction in employee numbers. This will be reflected in the asset per employee ratio. A company undertaking the necessary investment can be expected to display a higher figure for the ratio than one that is not.

The use of this ratio may also be appropriate when analysing some service organisations. For example, when studying the passenger transport sector the amount of non-current assets per employee may be used to compare one company with another to assess the supporting investment in trains, planes, ships, buses or coaches. The ratio can also be employed to highlight for further investigation the variation between companies operating in the same line of business but in different countries.

Inevitably there will be problems of comparison, as some companies may own their factories and plant and machinery and others may rent or lease these assets. However, when the non-current asset per employee ratio is prepared for a number of companies operating in the same business, it provides a useful measure of the comparative levels of investment in assets used in the production process. The average or median ratio for all of the companies being studied gives a base against which to assess individual companies and, over a number of years, to observe any trends that are developing in a business sector.

Operating or net assets per employee

If a company provides detailed segmental information that includes the allocation of employees between sectors and geographic locations, the ratios described above can be adapted to provide measures for each unit. It should also be possible to calculate the operating assets or net assets per employee from the segmental information provided. If it is possible to prepare these ratios for a number of years, movements in the allocation of a company's employees between businesses and countries, as well as the supporting investment in productive assets, can be observed.

Directors' remuneration

Included in the employee's remuneration figure is that for the company's directors. The annual report will contain a report from the remuneration committee providing information on the company's remuneration policy.

In a KPMG report, *Directors Remuneration 2012*, it was shown that the CEO of a FTSE 100 company had a median base salary of £800,000 and more than £3m total earnings. For a FTSE 250 company the figures were £450,000 and £1m. For several years there has been widespread criticism of what have been described as "fat cat" remuneration packages given to some directors. The annual report contains details of the remuneration or emoluments of all a company's directors. The figure for directors' remuneration or emoluments can be taken to cover their salary, profit share, bonus payments and other benefits. It should include not only bonuses for good performance but also any one-off payments for redundancy, contract severance or "golden goodbyes". Whether a board member gets the money as a result of competence or incompetence, it is an expense to the shareholders. Shareholders have become increasingly irritated by payments made to directors that bear no relationship – except inverse – to company performance or investor returns.

The fact that the UK and US governments had to use taxpayers' money to ease the shock created by the 2008 banking crisis revitalised calls for curbs on executive pay. Even when their companies failed, or shareholders lost their investment when they were taken over, some executives walked away with multimillion-dollar pay-offs. In the UK the collapse of Northern Rock and several other banks in 2008 required government intervention; and in 2012 the Co-operative Bank, having discovered a £1.5 billion "black hole" in its balance sheet, saw no reason to change its directors' remuneration policy. Exactly how many trillions of dollars the US government used to support its problem companies is still being calculated. There can be no doubt that the 2008 global financial crisis created the stimulus for much tighter oversight of executive remuneration packages.

In 2013 the UK government amended the 2006 Companies Act to enforce much stricter reporting of directors' remuneration. From 2014, listed companies must publish an annual directors' remuneration report. Information is provided for each named director showing for the current and previous year:

- a single figure for the total remuneration received;
- salary and fees received;
- all taxable benefits;
- performance achievement payments;
- pensions benefits;
- share options.

It is now possible to make direct comparisons between companies of directors' rewards for similar functions, such as marketing or IT. A graph and table will show the performance of the company's market share price and an appropriate comparative index. All major decisions on directors' remuneration will be stated and comment made on any substantial changes from the previous year. The future remuneration policy will be described and shareholders will be invited to vote on it.

Plus dividends

It is important to remember that the figure for directors' remuneration in the annual report does not necessarily include any dividends received by directors on shares they own in the company. To gain a fuller picture of the total income that flows to directors from the company, the number of shares they own should be multiplied by the dividend paid. This is easy to do, as the annual report will contain a table listing directors' names and the number of shares owned or in which they have a beneficial interest. The dividend per share is often displayed at the foot of the income statement.

Share options

Directors and other employees of a company are often given share options. Share option schemes are considered a standard means of motivating and rewarding a company's workforce. An individual is offered the right to purchase a company's shares at some time in the future at a predetermined price. For example, a director may be offered the right to purchase 1,000 shares in two years' time at $2 each. If in two years the share price reaches $4 and the director exercises the right to purchase, a profit of $2,000 is made (although if shares are then sold there may be a capital gains tax liability).

IFRS 2 – similar to FAS 123 – provides guidance on the treatment of share option schemes. Employee stock options (ESO) and incentive stock options (ISO) are common in the US. In the UK you may see reference made to government-approved schemes, such as:

- EMI – enterprise management incentives;
- CSOP – approved company share option plans;

- SIP – share incentive plans;
- SAYE – save as you earn option schemes.

These schemes set limits on the level of individual employee's participation and define any tax implications.

The treatment of share options (IFRS 2) requires the fair value of the option to be shown as an expense in the income statement and a compensating increase to be made in the balance sheet for equity. For example, if a director is offered the option to purchase 1,000 shares in three years' time, the fair value (IFRS 13) of options is estimated to be $900, which, if spread over three years, is $300 per year. For each of the next three years the income statement will be charged with $300 and balance sheet equity increased by $300.

Shareholders have a right to expect a company to inform them not only of what share option schemes are in operation but also of what options have been taken up by executives and at what prices. Where this information is available it can be incorporated in the analysis of directors' rewards suggested above (see Chapter 3).

The cost of the board

It is worth calculating the cost of the board of directors as a whole. The total remuneration package of each director, consisting of salary and fees plus any bonuses or other benefits, should appear in the annual report. If the total of these is added to the total number of directors' shares multiplied by the dividend paid, a reasonably accurate figure of the cost of the board of directors is produced. This figure can be expressed as a percentage of sales revenue or profit, as was suggested for the total employee cost, to produce ratios that can be used to compare the practice of different companies over a number of years. Where one company is seen to provide much higher directors' remuneration than similar companies, you may want to find out why this is the case. Has it proved worthwhile for the shareholders?

Average director's remuneration

If the total figure for directors' remuneration shown in the accounts is divided by the number of directors, a figure for the average director's remuneration is produced. The current year's figure can be compared with that of previous years to test for consistency and trends. It can also be compared with that of similar companies.

Who controls the board?

Ultimately, shareholders – although in practice this means the institutional investors who have substantial shareholdings – can overturn the directors' remuneration policy. In the UK shareholders should get the opportunity to vote on directors' remuneration policy. Indirect pressure from government, public opinion, professional bodies and stock exchanges may also influence board policy. However, there are many instances where boards have shown themselves to be thick-skinned when it comes to their remuneration.

Physical resource management

The decision on how to measure the efficiency of a company's use of its available physical resources – the assets employed – must be based on an understanding of the nature of its business. Different types of businesses demand different measures.

Starting point

A useful first step towards such understanding is to turn to the income statement to discover the broad cost structure of the company being analysed. The income statement provides outline details of a company's costs and expenses. The way the information is set out depends upon the nature of the business. For example, retail and manufacturing companies may set them out as follows:

Retail	**Manufacturing**
Cost of sales	Cost of sales
Staff costs	Distribution expenses
Occupancy costs	Administration expenses
Maintenance and renewals	Research and development

If each cost and expense heading is expressed as a percentage of sales revenue for the year and a number of years are considered or a number of companies are compared, trends and variations can quickly be highlighted for further investigation.

%			
Sales revenue	100		
Cost of sales	65		
		35	**% gross profit margin**
Distribution	12		
Administration	8		
R&D	1		
Other	4	25	
		10	**% operating profit margin**

Analysing the rate of return

A good single overall measure of a company's efficiency can be taken as the rate of return it produces on the assets employed. Rate of return ratios were discussed in Chapter 6. The target for almost any business is to make efficient use of assets to produce sales revenue from which profit is made. Dividing sales revenue by the assets employed in the business produces the asset turn ratio (see Chapter 6). This ratio is for most companies an eminently suitable measure of their efficiency in managing their assets.

Asset turn = sales revenue ÷ assets

A company displaying a low asset turn when compared with similar companies may be assumed to have some unproductive assets, some overvalued assets or inadequate management skills, or a combination of the three. The asset turn ratio is simple to produce, combining sales revenue from the income statement with the denominator – total assets, net assets, capital employed or whichever one is chosen. (Chapter 6 discussed the selection of an appropriate asset or capital employed figure from the balance sheet.) If calculated for a number of years, the ratio offers some insight into a company's continuing efficiency. When a number of companies operating in the same business sector are being studied, this ratio is an excellent basis on which to make judgments of comparative efficiency in the use of assets to generate sales and profit.

The overall rate of return of a company is produced from the combination of profit margin and asset or capital turn. The one multiplied by the other provides the ratio.

FIG 7.1 **The Du Pont model**

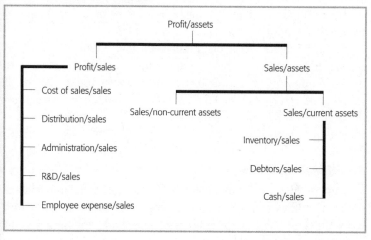

% rate of return = % profit margin × asset or capital turn

The use of the Du Pont or pyramid approach to presenting rates of return is discussed in Chapter 6 (see Figure 7.1). The two main component ratios of profit margin and asset turn can be further subdivided to offer insight into the way in which the rate of return is produced and the efficiency of a company at various stages of its production activities.

This pyramid of ratios can be helpful in analysing a company and in identifying which aspects of a business most affect its overall profitability. For example, it enables you to assess the impact on the rate of return of a decline in the inventory turn.

Ideally, it is the continuing business operations of a company that should be the focus of this analysis. In practice, however, where several companies operating from various country bases are being studied it is probably easier to take the total of both continued and discontinued operations for a year-by-year comparison.

For any company, the act of adding or removing businesses from its portfolio of operations can be significant, as can precisely when in the financial year this is done. The accounting treatment of acquisitions, in particular, can influence the profit displayed for the year. Whether a proportion of the full year's profit or the total profit of the acquired company is brought into the income statement can have a direct influence on apparent profitability.

Once the figures have been translated into a table, it is easy to see whether there is a consistent approach by which a company is, over a number of years, managing to achieve its profit margins. If similar data can be collected for similar companies, benchmarks can be selected for the measurement of comparative performance (see Chapter 9).

Additional measures

A company may, in its annual report, provide additional information on its operations and performance. Needless to say, a company that has nothing to boast about will not often provide anything beyond the minimum required.

Companies that provide more information than that stipulated by legislation or accounting rules and practice may adopt any form of presentation they wish, and the figures published are not necessarily subject to the normal independent checks and verification by an auditor. Furthermore, the provision of additional operating details in one year's annual report does not commit a company to provide the same details in other years or, if it does, to ensure that the figures are presented on a consistent and therefore comparable basis.

Many retail companies give details of the number and size of their outlets and total sales area. These provide a basis for calculating ratios of sales and profit per square foot or square metre of selling space. For any retailer, a practical measure of its efficiency is that of its ability to generate sales and profit per unit of sales space, and operating targets are often set to try to improve both of these ratios.

Such measures are an excellent means of assessing one company's performance over a number of years and of comparing several companies. But differences between companies may be explained partly because they are in different sectors of the business. For example, a food retailer can be expected to sell more per square metre than a department store but to be operating at a lower profit margin and therefore probably a lower profit ratio.

It may prove useful to calculate the asset turn ratio using only non-current assets as the denominator:

Sales revenue ÷ non-current assets

If all the companies being analysed are in the same business sector, the differences between them shown in this ratio may be worth further investigation. However, remember that if they are diversified companies there may be issues of non-comparability. If so, use the information provided in any segment analysis that is available.

Output or level of service ratios

Other businesses may provide statistics on their output or levels of service. A transport company may publish the number of passengers carried or the passenger miles travelled in a year. These figures can be used as the denominator in ratios to assist the study of a company's historical performance and to compare one company with another.

The cost and profit per passenger or per passenger mile can be calculated in a similar way to provide another measure of how efficiently companies deliver transport services. The staff cost of one company can be linked to the number of passengers, or ideally passenger miles, to allow comparison with previous years and with other transport companies. Transport companies in other countries may usefully be included in the analysis to produce the average amount paid by a passenger.

An electricity generating or supply company may provide details of the amount of electricity (megawatts) produced during the year. A motor manufacturer may disclose how many cars or tractors were produced during the year. Whenever a suitable common denominator for a business sector can be determined, this should be used as the basis for the preparation of a series of ratios to measure efficiency and performance.

Other sources of information

Additional information on a company or business sector can usefully be obtained from sources other than annual reports. Newspapers, journals, magazines and government and trade publications may offer data and information that can effectively be incorporated in performance and efficiency measures.

It is often possible to obtain national statistics relevant to a business sector – for total retail sales, total amount of electricity generated, number of cars and trucks manufactured and sold, for example. Even if the financial year end of a company does not match the calendar or fiscal year on which the statistics are based, it is still worth estimating the market share of a company to see how this has changed over the years.

Declining assets

Some indication of the age of assets employed in the business may help in the assessment of a company's current and likely future efficiency. Details may be provided in the notes accompanying the balance sheet; there should at least be a statement on when the assets were last valued. A general guide to the expected future effective working life of assets can be arrived at by dividing the balance sheet value of the tangible non-current assets by the depreciation charged for the year in the income statement. The resulting figure indicates how many years it will be before the assets are completely written off and may be taken as a measure of their estimated future useful working life.

Estimated life of assets = tangible non-current assets ÷ depreciation

If tangible assets are shown in the balance sheet at $100 and the income statement includes $10 for depreciation, this implies a ten-year useful working life for the assets. Of course, there are many factors and events that can render this ratio ineffective. A company may acquire a major asset at the end of the year and decide not to make any depreciation charge for it in the accounts. It may revalue all or part of its assets, or it may change its depreciation policy. But this quick and simple ratio provides a starting point for more detailed analysis of tangible non-current assets.

In the income statement notes a company should provide details of its depreciation policy, giving for each class of asset the rate and method of depreciation being charged. The most common depreciation methods are discussed in Chapter 3. Depreciation policy can have a significant impact on reported profit.

Asset replacement rate

The rate at which a company is replacing its assets can provide an indication of its ability to keep pace with technological change – an important factor for most companies and crucial for many. One means of determining the rate is to divide the tangible non-current assets shown in the balance sheet by the amount of capital expenditure for the year.

Asset replacement rate = gross tangible non-current assets ÷ capital expenditure

The figures for the gross, undepreciated value of tangible non-current assets and capital expenditure are given in the notes in the annual report. Alternatively, although it is not ideal, the capital expenditure figure in the statement of cash flows can be used. A company with gross tangible assets of $1,000 and capital expenditure for the year of $125 can be assumed to be replacing its assets approximately every eight years. Ideally, this ratio should be calculated for a number of years so the trend and consistency can be studied, and one company can be compared with others to see whether it is above or below the average or standard levels for the business sector. The ratio of accumulated depreciation to total non-current assets may be calculated to support the analysis; a high ratio suggests a low replacement rate.

It is possible to calculate the net capital expenditure each year as follows:

Year-end net non-current assets
Less beginning of year net non-current assets
Plus depreciation
= **net capital spending**

Capital expenditure turnover

The way a company's capital expenditure is maintained or moving in relation to sales revenue can be measured by dividing sales revenue by capital expenditure to produce a ratio of capital expenditure turnover.

Capital expenditure turnover = sales revenue ÷ capital expenditure

If the ratio is decreasing, this may indicate that a company is increasing its investment in tangible assets to support the continuing generation of sales revenue. An increasing ratio may indicate a reduction in investment due to a lack of available funds or a lack of confidence in the business's prospects.

The asset ownership ratio

In studying the tangible assets of a company, it is worth seeing what proportion of the non-current assets is owned and what proportion is leased. Is the foundation of growth to be on owned or leased assets? What may be the implications of this policy and what is the practice of other companies in the same business sector? The notes in the accounts give details of the division not only between owned and leased assets but also between long and short leases and operating and finance leases. This additional information may be of use when looking at the trend exhibited by a company over a number of years as it grows and develops.

Leasehold proportion = 100 × (leased assets ÷ total tangible non-current assets)

Research and development

A crucial function that often acts as a direct link between physical and human resources is research and development (R&D). The successful and profitable move from basic research to the development of commercially viable products and services is normally achieved through the application of the talents of highly skilled employees using sophisticated machines and instrumentation.

As described in Chapter 3, for most companies in most countries the total amount of R&D is written off in the year in which the expense is incurred; it is not usual to capitalise all or part of the R&D expense. If a company incurring an R&D expense of $100 follows the generally accepted accounting practice of writing the total amount off through the income statement, a loss may be disclosed as in company A below:

$	A	B
Income statement		
R&D	100	10
(Loss) profit	(Loss)	Profit
Balance sheet		
R&D	n/a	90

The income statement is charged with the total $100 of R&D expenditure and none is capitalised in the balance sheet. If the company is allowed to spread the R&D expense over a ten-year period, arguing that this is the time period over which the benefits of the investment will be gained, the position will be that of company B. Nothing has really changed, but a loss has been turned into a profit of $10 and the balance sheet value of the company is $90 larger because a new asset of R&D has appeared reflecting the capitalisation of the balance of the expense, which will be written off over the next nine years. This might be acceptable if there was no uncertainty about the survival of the company over the nine years, but were the company to run into problems immediately after the publication of its annual report, it is debatable whether the R&D asset in the balance sheet could be sold for $90. R&D is an intangible asset and accountants generally consider that its real value is too subjective for quantification in the accounts. Referring to Chapter 1, the rule of "when in doubt, write it off" applies.

A simple test of the effectiveness of a company's R&D investment is to see whether or not it produces results. There is no commercial benefit to a company in investing resources in interesting research projects if these do not result in products and services reaching the marketplace. There is equally no point in a company investing large sums in R&D when there is no call for this from its customers. For retail companies only a limited amount of R&D is worthwhile, but for their suppliers more substantial investment in this area may be essential. Sectors in which sizeable and continuing investment in R&D is crucial include pharmaceuticals, defence and information technology.

A company's annual report contains details of the amount spent on R&D and may also provide information on new products developed and launched, together with details of any breakthroughs that have taken place. All this is of at least some help in assessing the effectiveness of a company's R&D programme.

R&D to sales ratio

One way of determining the consistency of a company's policy on R&D is to divide the amount spent on it by sales revenue. The result multiplied by 100 gives the R&D to sales ratio.

$$\textbf{R\&D to sales} = 100 \times (\text{R\&D expense} \div \text{sales revenue})$$

For most companies, a reasonably constant level of investment in R&D is to be expected. A decline in the ratio may be because R&D expenditure is constant but sales revenue is rising, but a sudden reduction in the ratio may be an indication of corporate malaise. An easy way to improve profit when business is tough is to cut expenditure on things such as R&D. As discussed in Chapter 10, such action may bring short-term profit, but it may also damage long-term prospects.

Problems with percentages

Calculating a ratio as a percentage removes any necessity for currency conversion where international comparisons are being made, but it does not overcome the size differences of companies. If two companies invest 1% of their sales revenue in R&D, the ratio would not distinguish between them. However, if one company had sales of $10m and the other had sales of $1m, the amounts being invested in R&D by each are very different. For example, a big computer company may spend more on R&D than the total sales revenue of some of its smaller competitors.

Another problem is that many companies set their R&D budget as a regular percentage of sales revenue. This has the merit of consistency, but it may lead to difficulties. If revenue is declining, because of a lack of competitive edge in a company's products, reducing spending on R&D in line with the set R&D to sales ratio is likely to exacerbate the decline.

Additional sources of information

Well-informed media coverage and reports from analysts who are experts in the relevant sector will help in assessing a company's R&D performance. However, a simple but effective rule for anyone thinking of investing in a company is: "If you can't see it, don't buy it." Before investing money in a company, try to get some first-hand knowledge of its products or services. Are its products and the range offered as good as, if not better than, those of competitors? Do its staff give the impression of competence and enthusiasm? If you are not impressed, why should anyone else be? Have a look at some big internet companies, such as Amazon, to see what customer reaction is to their products or services.

When you have invested in a company, regular physical checks on its products and services are as important as the financial analysis suggested in this book. This may seem like hard work, but it can be interesting and it is definitely a safer approach.

Financial resource management

Chapters 8 and 9 deal with many aspects of financial management efficiency, but there are some that are properly covered here.

The treasury function

The role of a company's treasury department has become more important in recent years, mainly as a result of the increase in international business and the complexity of cash flows. Not long ago, a finance director might have spent a few minutes now and then considering the implications of currency movements for a company. Today, every major company has full-time staff overseeing the management of finance and cash flows.

For a company with its head office in the UK and a subsidiary operating in the US, a shift in the exchange rate between the pound and the dollar can have a dramatic impact on group profitability. If the subsidiary has a profit of $100 and this is "sent" to head office when the exchange rate is $1.55, £64.52 profit is brought into the group accounts. If the exchange rate is $1.65 or $1.45, the profit is £60.60 or £68.96. Thus the equivalent of a 10% change in the apparent profits of the subsidiary can be brought about simply by fluctuations in the exchange rate. The accounting treatment of international transactions is discussed in Chapters 2 and 3. Companies should do their best to avoid undue exposure to the risks of exchange-rate movements. In recent years, there have been some notable examples of companies that have lost large amounts of money because they were in effect betting on how currencies would move in relation to each other rather than hedging their risk from exchange-rate fluctuations. Managing currency transactions is a core responsibility of the treasury department.

Interest cover ratio

One financial efficiency measure for a company is its ability to pay the interest on its borrowings from operating profits. When profit before interest and tax (PBIT) or earnings before interest and tax (EBIT) is divided by the amount of interest paid, the resulting interest cover ratio shows how many times a company's profit covers the interest payments it has to make.

$$\textbf{Interest cover} = \text{pre-interest and tax profit} \div \text{interest}$$

The higher the figure the safer is the company. A company with an interest cover ratio of 2 could suffer a 50% drop in profit and still meet its interest payments. A company with a ratio of less than 1 would have to dip into its cash reserves or sell assets or raise additional finance to meet its interest payment commitments if there was any reduction in profit.

Summary

- Efficiency is normally associated with the control of costs and expenses and with the productive use of all the available resources of a company to deliver its products or services to the marketplace at a competitive price.
- The efficiency of a business can be measured in various ways. It can be argued that the acid test of efficiency is profit. The development of a suitable set of performance measures linked to profitability is described in Chapter 6. However, a company

may be highly efficient in managing its costs and expenses but face factors beyond its control that limit its ability to generate profitable revenues. There may be a recession or oversupply, or there may be a price war within the sector. In such circumstances, the lower profitability of the company may not indicate a lack of efficiency.

■ After you have gathered relevant data for as many years as possible, a useful first step is to reduce the income statement to a common factor basis by expressing costs and profits as a percentage of sales revenue (see Chapter 6).

	Year 1 $	Year 2 $	Year 1 %	Year 2 %
Sales revenue	7,200	8,500	100	100
Cost of sales	4,680	6,125	65	72
Gross profit	2,520	2,375	35	28

Using this approach makes it much easier to pick out changes and trends, either from year to year for one company or when comparing one company with another, particularly if they are operating in different countries. The profit margin ratio strips out problems of size and currency.

■ Profit per employee is probably the best measure of the efficiency of use of the human resource element of a company.

■ The rate of return ratio is the best single ratio to use as a measure of the overall efficiency of a company (see Chapter 6). An efficient company is more likely to produce a profit than an inefficient one, and is thus more likely to produce consistently higher rates of return.

■ In assessing the ability of a company to make use of its available resources, the asset turn ratio is ideal. It is quick and simple to calculate. Sales revenue is taken from the income statement and a figure for assets taken from the balance sheet; one divided by the other produces the asset turn for a company. If each time a company makes a sale it takes a profit, the more sales are generated the more profit is produced. The higher the asset turn the better is the productive use being made of the assets employed in the business and the better is the eventual overall rate of return.

- Financial management can be encapsulated in the interest cover ratio. This displays the cost of a company's external borrowings as a proportion of pre-interest and tax profit for the year. The more a company finances operations from external sources on which interest is paid or the higher the interest rates being charged the lower is the ratio.

8 Working capital and liquidity

THIS CHAPTER CONCENTRATES on the ways of assessing the short-term financial position and health of a company. Although the terms solvency and liquidity are often used to refer to the same thing, each focuses on a different aspect of financial viability. Solvency (discussed in Chapter 9) is a measure of the ability of a company to meet its various financial obligations as they fall due, whether they are loan repayments or creditors' invoices. Liquidity is directly related to cash flows and the nature of a company's short-term assets; that is, whether there is an appropriate amount of cash on hand or readily available. You may have $1m invested in stocks and shares but not enough cash in your pocket to buy a bus ticket. You may be solvent but far from being liquid.

A simple check on the short-term financial viability of a company might be first to make sure a profit was made for the year, and then turn to the statement of financial position to see if there was a large cash balance at the end of the year. If the company made a profit and shows positive cash balances, you might think all is surely well. Unfortunately, you might be wrong; positive cash balances at the year end, even when combined with profit, do not guarantee corporate survival in the short term, let alone the long term.

The statement of financial position is a snapshot of a company's assets and liabilities at the end of the financial year. It does not claim to be representative of the position during the rest of the year. The income statement matches income and expenditure for the year. Income, and therefore the profit for the year, includes credit sales income and credit expenditure as well as cash transactions. A company might show a profit for the year but have numerous creditors, perhaps its major supplier of raw materials, requiring payment in cash within the next few weeks. It is also possible for a company to manipulate the year-end cash position. If towards the end of the financial year the company puts more emphasis and effort into collecting cash from customers and slows payment to creditors, this will result in an increase in cash balances.

Creditors provide finance to support a company and debtors tie up its financial resources. A company extending more credit to its customers than it, in turn, can take in credit from its suppliers may be profitable, but it is also running down its cash resources. This is called overtrading and is a common problem among small and rapidly growing companies. It is crucial for any business to maintain an adequate cash balance between credit given to customers and credit taken from suppliers.

Working capital and cash flow

The relationship between short-term assets and liabilities was discussed in Chapter 2. Current liabilities are set against current assets to highlight net current assets or net current liabilities. The net current assets figure is often referred to as the working capital of a company to emphasise the fact that it is a continually changing amount.

Current assets and liabilities change not only from day to day but also from minute to minute as a company conducts its business. Cash is used to pay the invoices of suppliers for the production of goods that are then sold, usually on credit, to customers, who in return pay cash to the company. The cash cycles around the business on a continuing basis (see Figure 8.1). On each turn of the cycle the company makes a profit, the goods or services being sold for more than the cost of their production, resulting in more cash available to expand the business and for the purchase or production of goods for sale.

The key to a company's short-term financial viability is to be found in the study of working capital. Current assets consist of cash or near-cash items listed under four main headings: inventory (or stock), prepayments, receivables and cash. In the standard balance sheet presentation these are set out in order of liquidity, with cash being the ultimate form of liquidity:

FIG 8.1 **The working capital cycle**

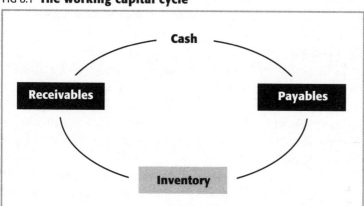

- Inventory – finished goods, work in progress, raw materials
- Accounts receivable (debtors) – trade and other
- Prepayments – advance payment of expenses
- Cash – cash and bank balances, short-term deposits and investments

Inventory

The least liquid current asset is inventory (stock). When inventory is sold to customers, it moves up the current asset liquidity ranking to become part of accounts receivable and lastly to become completely liquid as a part of cash and bank balances when customers pay their invoices.

For many companies the total figure for inventory in the balance sheet is further subdivided in the notes to give the amounts held as raw materials, work in progress and finished goods. For practical purposes it is safe to assume that finished goods represent a more liquid asset than work in progress, which, in turn, is likely to prove easier to turn quickly into cash than raw materials.

Most companies can be expected to sell their inventory and turn it into cash at least once each year. If this is not the case, there should be a good reason for the company to hold that item or amount of inventory. If inventory is not turning into cash, valuable financial resources are being tied up for no immediate profitable return.

Receivables

After inventory, the next item appearing within current assets is receivables. These are divided into receivables where the cash is expected to be received by the company within 12 months of the balance sheet date and those where the cash is expected later. Often it is necessary to refer to the notes to discover the precise make-up of the total figure.

If a group of companies is being analysed, the amount disclosed for receivables may include amounts owed by subsidiary companies. These are also divided into the amount due within one year of the balance sheet date and the amount due later.

It is reasonable to assume that receivables due within one year are mainly trade receivables; that is, customers owing money for goods or services provided during the year and expected to pay the cash due to the company under the normal terms of trade. If customers are offered 30 days' credit, they are expected to pay cash to the company within 30 days of accepting delivery of the goods or services provided.

To give the impression of income growth, a company may pursue a creative approach to sales revenue recognition – for example, counting future income in the current income statement. That something is amiss will be indicated by the much greater growth in trade receivables than in turnover. A company may opt to push inventory out to dealers on a sale or return basis and treat this as sales revenue for the year. In effect, the company is turning inventory into receivables. The income statement will show revenue and profit increasing, but there will be a mismatch evident when the growth trends of inventory and debtors are compared.

% increase in sales revenue **compared with** % increase in accounts receivable

Faced with an unacceptably large level of credit extended to customers, a company may factor or securitise trade receivables (see Chapter 2). This will result in a reduction in the level of receivables shown in the balance sheet – the true level is disguised. Always read the notes provided in the accounts for trade receivables. For a normal, healthy company, the growth in levels of turnover, inventory and trade receivables can be expected to be compatible. Any significant differences should be studied.

Receivables shown in the balance sheet may be assumed to be good debts. Customers owing the company money are expected to pay their bills when they fall due. Any known or estimated bad debts will have been written off through the income statement. Bad debts can be either deducted from sales revenue to reduce income for the year or charged as an expense in arriving at the profit for the year. Almost every type of business experiences bad debts. Customers may become bankrupt, flee the country or otherwise disappear; or there may be fraud.

Bad debts may be written off individually as they are incurred or there may be a regular percentage of sales revenue written off each year. Often a percentage charge is made, based on historical experience for the particular company and the sector in which it operates. If there is a substantial or material bad debt, the company may make reference to this in the annual report. If a major customer is declared bankrupt, this should be drawn to shareholders' attention in the annual report, even if the company hopes eventually to recoup all or most of the debt. Such an event is important when forming a view as to the future potential of the company. It may collect the debt but how is it going to replace the revenue involved?

Prepayments and accruals

Sometimes a company will show prepayments or payments in advance as an item within current assets. Prepayments are money the company has paid in the current year for goods or services to be received in a future year. For example, a company may pay the rent or insurance on property months in advance. For most forms of analysis, prepayments are treated as being as liquid as debtors.

Current liabilities often contain an amount for accruals. These may be considered the reverse of prepayments. Accruals are expenses relating to the current year that have yet to be settled in cash. Trade payables are the suppliers' outstanding invoices for goods and services delivered during the year. Accruals relate to other operating expenses, such as power and light, paid in arrears rather than in advance.

Cash

Cash is as liquid as it is possible to be. It consists of money in the company's hands or bank accounts. Cash is immediately available to provide funds to pay creditors or to make investments.

Why do companies need to hold cash? Cash as an asset is worthless unless it is invested in productive assets or interest-bearing accounts. Companies hold cash for the same reasons as individuals. John Maynard Keynes, a successful investment analyst as well as a notable economist, identified three reasons for keeping cash rather than investing it in other assets:

- Transaction
- Precaution
- Speculation

The transaction and precautionary motives should, ideally, dictate the appropriate size of a company's cash and bank balances. A company with no cash cannot continue in business. It would be unable to pay suppliers or employees. Cash is essential to fulfil the everyday routine transactions of the business. A company with insufficient cash in hand has no cushion to cover unbudgeted costs. Just as individuals try to keep some cash readily available, so companies need cash at short notice for the equivalent corporate experience.

Speculation, the third reason for holding cash, is generally less relevant to companies, since directors are on the whole not encouraged to gamble with shareholders' money. For individuals, surplus cash used for investment with a view to the longer term, perhaps planning for retirement, can be said to be precautionary, whereas that used to buy lottery tickets, back horses or play poker is definitely for short-term speculation – money that may be lost but life can still continue.

One important aspect of the internal financial management of a company is to achieve the delicate balancing act of having precisely the right amount of cash available at any time. To have too much is wasteful; to have too little is dangerous.

How much money a company needs depends on what it does. A company that can confidently look forward to regular cash inflows, such as a food retailer, has less need to maintain substantial cash balances than a company with more discrete or uneven cash inflows, such as a construction company or a heavy goods manufacturer.

The only way to assess whether a particular company's cash balances are adequate is to compare them with those of previous years and those of other companies in the same kind of business. The ratios described later provide useful measures by which you can make comparisons.

In assessing a company's liquidity, it must be remembered that the timing of the balance sheet may have significant implications for the level of cash balances. A retail company producing accounts in January, following the Christmas sales period, might be expected to show little stock but a high cash balance. The company would be more liquid at the end of January than in December.

Cash and cash equivalents

Companies often invest cash that is not immediately required for running the business in short-term marketable securities or even overnight on money markets. Such investments appear as part of current assets in the balance sheet and are assumed to be readily turned into cash. For financial analysis purposes they are treated as being as liquid as cash. US GAAP and IFRS define cash equivalents as including short-term non-risk investments that are readily convertible into cash and with no more than three months' maturity. IFRS allow bank overdrafts to be included in cash. The changes in cash equivalents can be tracked in the statement of cash flows (see Chapter 4).

Current liabilities

Current liabilities are the total amount of creditors due for payment within one year, indicating how much the company will have to pay in cash in the near future. Many of the ratios that measure and assess a company's liquidity and solvency use the total figure for current liabilities. For most purposes this is perfectly acceptable, but it will produce somewhat cautious results. Typically, five items appear in the balance sheet under this heading:

- Accounts payable (creditors) – trade and other
- Accruals – expenses not paid at the end of the year
- Bank loans – short-term loans and other borrowings
- Tax – amounts due for payment with the coming year
- Dividends – dividends declared but not yet paid to shareholders

Loans and other borrowings that fall due for repayment in the coming year are correctly shown as part of current liabilities in the balance sheet. Other short-term bank borrowing may also appear within current liabilities. Often, as with an overdraft in the UK, this is because they are repayable on demand. It may be argued that it is overcautious to include them among "creditors falling due within one year" when calculating liquidity or solvency ratios.

Measuring liquidity

Cash and receivables are defined as the liquid or quick assets of a company. A liquid asset is already cash or capable of being turned into cash within a fairly short time. To look only at the total of current assets in the balance sheet is not a sufficient guide to the liquidity of a company.

$	A	B	C
Inventory	50	25	25
Receivables	25	50	25
Cash	25	25	50
	100	100	100
Current liabilities	80	80	80
Operating profit	40	40	20
Depreciation	10	10	5

Although the three companies above have identical current assets of $100, their liquidity is quite different. Company C is the most liquid. At the year-end it has $50 in cash and can expect to receive $25 in the near future from customers. Although company B has the same amount of liquid assets as C ($75), it is not as liquid as it has less cash immediately available. Company A is the least liquid with 50% of current assets being held as inventory, which will probably take much longer to turn into cash than debtors.

Current ratio

A simple guide to the ability of a company to meet its short-term obligations is to link current assets and liabilities in what is commonly termed the current ratio. This appears to have been developed by bankers towards the end of the 19th century as one of their first and, as it proved, one of their last contributions to financial analysis. It links total current assets and total current liabilities.

Current ratio = current assets ÷ current liabilities

Current assets consist of cash balances, short-term deposits and investments, receivables, prepaid expenses and inventory. Current liabilities include payables, short-term bank borrowing and tax due within the coming year. The combination of the two in the current ratio provides a somewhat crude guide to the solvency rather than the liquidity of a company at the year end.

For the three companies in the example there would be no difference in the current ratio. As each company has $80 total current liabilities the ratio is:

$$\$100 \div \$80 = 1.25$$

For every $1 of current liabilities, each company is maintaining at the year end $1.25 of current assets. If the company paid all its short-term creditors, it would have $0.25 left for every $1 of current asset used. As a rough guide, for most companies, a current ratio of more than 1.5:1 can be taken as an indicating the ability to meet short-term creditors without recourse to special borrowing or the sale of any non-current assets.

Liquid ratio

However, its inability to distinguish the short-term financial positions of the three companies highlights the comparative uselessness of the current ratio. A stricter approach is to exclude the year-end inventory from current assets to arrive at what are called liquid assets. Liquid assets comprise cash and assets that are as near cash as makes no difference – cash and cash equivalents. This ratio is sometimes called the acid test, but it is more often termed the liquid or quick ratio.

Liquid ratio = liquid assets ÷ current liabilities

For the three companies the liquid ratio is as follows:

$	A	B & C
Liquid assets	50	75
Current liabilities	80	80
Liquid ratio	**0.62**	**0.94**

The liquid ratio is easy to calculate directly from the balance sheet and there are two reasons to support its use. First, it is difficult to know precisely what physically is included in the figure for inventory disclosed in the balance sheet. Second, even good inventory often proves difficult to turn quickly into cash. Where inventory consists mainly of finished goods ready for sale, valued at the lower of cost or net realisable value, a company trying to turn such inventory quickly into cash would be unlikely to achieve this value; potential buyers can usually sense when a seller is desperate to sell and will hold out for the lowest possible price. Thus a prudent approach to assessing the ability of a company to meet its short-term liabilities assumes inventory will not provide a ready source of cash.

Company A is now identified as being potentially less liquid than companies B and C. There is still no revealed difference between B and C. Both have an identical liquid ratio of 0.94:1. For most businesses, to have $0.94 readily available in cash or near cash for every $1 of current liability would be seen as very safe. Such a company could, without selling any inventory or borrowing money, immediately cover all but 6% of its short-term liabilities. A potential supplier, having first checked that the previous year's accounts disclosed a similar position, might justifiably feel confident in extending credit to such a company.

Whether the fact that company A has a liquid ratio of 0.62 would make suppliers unwilling to deal with it would depend on further knowledge and analysis. But clearly, through the use of the liquid ratio, company A is now isolated as being in a different short-term financial position from B and C.

Current liquidity ratio

Although the liquid ratio appears to be an improvement on the current ratio, it has still proved impossible to distinguish between companies B and C in the example. A further refinement is to consider current liabilities not only with current and liquid assets but also with a company's cash flow generating capability.

The simplest definition of cash flow is profit without any deduction for depreciation. Depreciation is merely a book-keeping entry and does not involve a physical movement of cash. If depreciation is added back to the trading or operating profit shown in the income statement, the resulting figure provides a rough indication of the cash flow being generated by the company during the year. On this basis, the cash flow for A and B is $50 and for C is $25.

A company wishing to pay creditors will first make use of its liquid assets. If it is assumed that inventory is not capable of being turned rapidly into cash, then, before borrowing money to pay creditors, the company will rely on cash being made available from its operations. The current liquidity ratio calculates how many days, at the normal level of cash flow generation, would be required to complete the payment of creditors.

Current liquidity ratio = 365 × ((current liabilities − liquid assets)
÷ cash flow from operations)

For the three companies in the example:

$	A	B	C
Current liabilities	80	80	80
Less			
Liquid assets	50	75	75
	30	5	5
Divided by			
Cash flow	50	50	25
	0.6	0.1	0.2
× *365*			
Days	219	36	73

If the only sources of finance other than liquid assets proved to be cash flow from operations, it would take company A 219 days, more than seven months, to complete payment of its current liabilities, whereas company B would require 36 days and company C 73 days. Assuming all three companies were operating in the same business sector, creditors assessing them would rightly feel least confident of company A.

Ratios in perspective

To explore further how the short-term financial position and viability of different companies can be analysed and compared, here is another example. Company D is a department store group, E is a food retailer, F is a heavy goods manufacturer and G is a restaurant chain.

$m	D	E	F	G
Inventory	75	38	193	10
Other	30	20	80	40
Trade receivables	80	5	162	30
Cash	120	15	215	190
Current assets	305	78	650	270
Trade payables	35	76	70	75
Other creditors	165	104	300	285
Current liabilities	200	180	370	360
Operating profit	130	60	160	300
Depreciation	20	25	35	20

From this the ratios covered so far in this chapter can be calculated.

	D	E	F	G
Current ratio	1.53	0.43	1.76	0.75
Liquid ratio	1.15	0.22	1.24	0.72
Current liquidity ratio	−73	601	−163	114

Companies D, F and G show a current ratio of close to, or better than, 1:1. For every $1 of current liability at the year end they have $1, or more, available in current assets. The food retailer (E) and the restaurant chain (G) can be expected to operate with a lower current ratio than the department store group (D) or the heavy goods manufacturer (F). Their business is based on the sale of food, with lower investment in inventory than for the other businesses represented in the example; and they do not normally offer long credit terms to their customers.

The differences between companies' financial positions are reinforced by the use of the liquid ratio. The manufacturer (F), with $1.24 in liquid assets for every $1 of current liability, shows the highest level of short-term solvency. As a potential creditor, possibly considering becoming a supplier, to company F, the 1.24:1 cover would provide reasonable confidence that invoices would be paid in full and on time.

However, before committing to a working relationship with F it would be necessary to compare this company with others in the same business to discover if 1.24:1 was typical. If a potential supplier to company E studied other food retailers, it would be seen that between 0.1:1 and 0.5:1 is typical. Thus on the basis of this ratio alone dealing with company E would appear reasonably safe.

As both the department store (D) and the manufacturer (F) have liquid ratios of more than 1:1, they will show a negative current liquidity ratio. They could pay all their short-term liabilities from liquid assets and still have some left over. In practice, having seen the negative values for the liquid ratio, potential creditors would not find it worth calculating the current liquidity ratio for these companies as this would not give them a better appreciation of their likely financial exposure in dealing with the companies.

The food retailer (E) discloses the highest figure for the current liquidity ratio. If the company used all its readily available liquid assets to pay current liabilities and there were no other immediately available sources of cash, it would require a further 601 days (20 months) of operating cash flow to complete payment. Before drawing any conclusions about the acceptability of this and any other ratio, it is necessary to obtain some benchmarks for comparison. If the food retailer's 601 days is compared with the department store's −73 days, it is clear that they have different short-term financial positions, and that, although they are both retailers, they are in completely different businesses.

The food retailer can confidently expect a more consistent and regular pattern of future daily sales than the department store. Customers make purchases more regularly in food supermarkets than in department stores. A creditor to company E can be reasonably confident that the next day some $2.7m, the average daily sales figure (see below), will pass through the cash tills in the supermarkets. The sales of the department store, although also averaging $2.7m per day, are more likely to be skewed in terms of their cash impact towards Christmas or other seasonal periods.

Creditors of the food retailer need not be concerned about the 601-day current liquidity ratio. In the UK and the US, current liquidity ratios of up to 1,200 days (four years) for food retailers are not unusual. In continental Europe, largely because of different working relationships with suppliers, ratios two or three times greater than this are to be found.

The key to interpreting this ratio, as with all others, is to obtain a sound basis for comparison. Different countries, as well as different business sectors, often have different solvency, liquidity and cash flow experiences and expectations.

Working capital to sales ratio

A good indicator of the adequacy and consistent management of working capital is to relate it to sales revenue. For this measure, working capital, ignoring cash and investments, is defined as follows:

Working capital = inventory + trade receivables − trade payables

For the four companies in the example the figures are as follows:

$m	D	E	F	G
Sales revenue	1,000	1,000	1,000	1,000
Inventory	75	38	193	10
Trade receivables	80	5	162	30
Trade payables	35	76	70	75
Working capital	120	−33	285	−35
Working capital to sales revenue (%)	**12.0**	**−3.3**	**28.5**	**−3.5**

A negative figure for working capital denotes the fact that a company had, at the year end, more trade payables than inventory and trade receivables. This is acceptable, providing creditors have confidence in the company's continuing ability to pay its bills when they fall due. Normally, such confidence is directly linked to its business sector and its proven record of cash flow generation. What is acceptable for the food retailer and the restaurant chain is not acceptable for the heavy goods manufacturer, because its cash inflow over the next few days is much less certain.

As a general rule, the lower the percentage disclosed for this ratio the better it is for the business. If the department store group were to increase turnover by $1m, this ratio suggests that an additional $120,000 of working capital would be required. For the heavy goods manufacturer, an additional $285,000 would be required to support the same $1m sales increase. However, for the food retailer and restaurant chain, for which the ratio is negative, an increase in sales revenue would appear to lead to a decrease in their working capital. This might well be the case for a company experiencing steady growth and maintaining creditors' confidence.

Alternatively the sales to working capital ratio could be used. This produces ratios of:

	D	E	F	G
Sales to working capital	8.3	−30.3	3.5	−28.6

What is the trend in this ratio over a number of years? Is it showing improvement or decline? How may the movement be explained? A company may be increasing sales revenue by dealing with lower-quality customers who take longer to pay – or never pay. A company increasing inventory in order to give customers a better service may see a decline in the ratio.

Receivables to payables ratio

More detailed analysis can be completed using specific ratios focusing on particular aspects of the working capital management and structure of companies. For example, the relationship between credit given to customers and credit taken from suppliers can be assessed and compared by linking trade debtors and creditors.

Trade receivables ÷ trade payables

For the four companies in the example the figures are as follows:

	D	E	F	G
Receivables ÷ payables	2.3	0.1	2.3	0.4

This ratio shows that for every 100 units of credit taken from suppliers, company D, the department store, and company F, the heavy goods manufacturer, were extending 230 units of credit to their customers. Company G, the restaurant chain, gives only 40 units of credit to its customers for every 100 units of credit it receives from suppliers. Further evidence of the aggressive use of suppliers' finance by company E, the food retailer, is provided as this ratio shows that for every 100 units of supplier credit the company extends only 10 units to its customers.

In normal circumstances, this ratio should remain reasonably constant from year to year. Large and erratic shifts either way may signal a change in credit policy or business conditions.

Average daily sales and costs

Another indicator linking a company's short-term cash flows and financial position is its average daily sales (ADS) and average daily costs (ADC). You can divide the total sales and cost of sales by 240 to more closely represent the number of working days in the year, but, given the broad nature of the analysis, it is as effective to use 365 days as the denominator.

The cost of sales is found in the income statement in most annual reports. The figure normally includes purchases but not always staff wages and associated expenses. If there is difficulty in obtaining a truly comparable cost of sales figure for all the companies being analysed, then, by deducting the operating or trading profit from sales revenue, you will get an approximation of cost of sales.

$m	D	E	F	G
Turnover	1,000	1,000	1,000	1,000
Average daily sales	*2.74*	*2.74*	*2.74*	*2.74*
Cost of sales	650	920	840	620
Average daily cost	*1.78*	*2.52*	*2.30*	*1.70*

Although comparing the ADS and ADC gives a broad idea of how much more a company receives than it spends each day, in reality companies whose trade is seasonal will spend much more than an average amount to build up stock before their peak periods for sales. They will also receive more than average from sales during peak periods.

The cash cycle

The management of working capital is critical to company survival. Continual and careful monitoring and control of inventory levels and cash payment and collection periods are essential. Working capital, particularly in connection with inventory, is also a popular focus for fraud and misrepresentation. Inventory can be overvalued or phantom inventory devised to produce an apparent improvement in profit.

The best way to monitor working capital and cash position is to use the liquid ratio, which is calculated directly from the balance sheet, and the cash cycle, which effectively combines operating activity with year-end position. The liquid ratio assumes that any inventory held has no immediate value. These two ratios should then be compared with those of previous years to test for consistency and identify any trends and, with appropriate benchmark companies, to assess conformity with the business sector.

The ability of a company to react to unexpected threats or opportunities by adjusting the timing and level of cash flows – its financial adaptability – is an important consideration. One way of assessing this from a more pessimistic viewpoint is to use the defensive interval, which indicates how long the company might survive and continue operations if all cash inflows ceased (see below).

When combined with other information from the balance sheet, ADS and ADC can help you understand the way in which the cash is flowing around the business in the cash cycle or working capital cycle ratio.

Inventory

To discover how long a company's cash is tied up in inventory, the balance sheet figure for inventory is divided by ADC to give the number of days that inventory appears to be held on average by the company. The ADC figure is used because inventory is valued at the lower of cost or net realisable value so there is no profit element involved. To use ADS would result in the number of days being understated.

$m	D	E	F	G
Inventory	75	38	193	10
ADC	1.78	2.52	2.30	1.70
Days' inventory	**42**	**15**	**84**	**6**

The longer inventory is held, the longer financial resources are tied up in a non-profit generating item; the lower the number of days' inventory shown, the faster is the turnover of the inventory. Each time inventory is turned the company makes a profit and generates cash.

In the example, the companies hold, on average, 37 days of inventory. As you would expect, the heavy goods manufacturer (F) has the highest level and the restaurant chain (G), with fresh food, the lowest. The crucial factor is how these levels compare with those of other similar businesses.

Another way of looking at the efficiency of inventory levels is to calculate the inventory turnover for the year; this can be done by dividing the annual cost of sales by year-end inventory. The higher the resulting figure, the more effective is a company's management of inventory. However, a company with a high inventory turnover may be maintaining inventory levels too low to meet demand satisfactorily, with the result that potential customers go elsewhere.

$m	D	E	F	G
Cost of sales	650	920	840	620
Inventory	75	38	193	10
Inventory turnover	**9**	**24**	**4**	**62**

These figures provide an alternative view of how effectively companies are managing their inventory.

Trade receivables

To discover the level of credit being offered to customers (trade receivables), average daily sales (ADS) is used as the denominator. The figure for trade receivables is usually found in the notes to the accounts and not on the face of the balance sheet.

$m	D	E	F	G
Trade receivables	80	5	162	30
ADS	2.74	2.74	2.74	2.74
Days' receivables	**29**	**2**	**59**	**11**

In the example, the average figure for what is sometimes called the credit period is 25 days. In effect, the companies are lending their customers money for that period until cash is received, and they must provide the necessary finance to support this.

In the case of the department store group (D), it can be assumed that cash is used to purchase inventory, which is displayed for 42 days before it is bought by a customer, who does not actually pay for it for another 29 days. The time from taking the cash out of the bank to receiving it back, plus a profit margin, is 71 days. The faster the cycle, the better it is for the company.

For example, if the ADC for the department store is $1.8m and it proved possible to reduce the level of inventory by one day, the cash cycle would speed up, the profit margin would be achieved one day earlier and more profit would be made in the year. Also the assets employed in the business would decrease by $1.8m, being one day's less inventory. If the time taken to collect cash from its customers could be reduced by one day, there would be a reduction of assets employed in the business of $2.7m and a corresponding increase in rate of return.

Cutting inventory or receivable levels reduces the assets employed in the business and increases profit, thus increasing the return on total assets (see Chapter 6). There is a direct link between the efficient management of cash flows and the overall profitability of a business.

Trade payables

Trade creditors represent the amount of money the company owes its suppliers for goods and services delivered during the year. These are normally found, as are trade receivables, not on the face of the balance sheet but in the notes to the accounts. As trade payables are shown at cost in the balance sheet, they are divided by average daily cost.

$m	D	E	F	G
Trade payables	35	76	70	75
ADC	1.78	2.52	2.30	1.70
Days' credit taken	**20**	**30**	**30**	**44**

In the example, the average length of credit the companies are taking from their suppliers (the reverse of credit given to customers) is 31 days.

Calculating the cycle

Cash flows out of the bank into inventory, from inventory into customers' hands then back into the bank. The suppliers of the inventory are paid cash and the cash cycle is complete. The three ratios can now be combined to give the cash cycle or working capital cycle.

Cash cycle = days' inventory – days' trade payables + days' trade receivables

$m	D	E	F	G
Days' inventory	42	15	84	6
Less				
Days' credit taken	20	30	30	44
	22	−15	54	−38
Plus				
Day's credit given	29	2	59	11
Days' cash cycle	**51**	**−13**	**113**	**−27**

The average cash cycle is 31 days. The two extremes are the heavy goods manufacturer (F) with a cash cycle of 113 days and the

FIG 8.2 **The average cash cycle for the example companies**

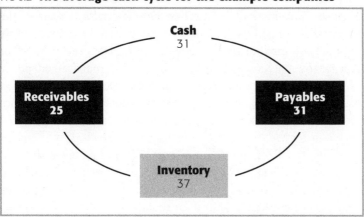

restaurant chain (G) with −27 days. It is possible now to return to the simple representation of the cash flow cycle shown earlier in this chapter and apply the average figures produced from the analysis (see Figure 8.2).

The average cash cycle experienced by the companies was for cash to be tied up in inventory for 37 days; after goods had been sold to customers it took a further 25 days for the cash to be received. The average company therefore required 62 days' finance to cover inventory holding and credit extended to customers. As the average company took 31 days' credit from its suppliers, it had to finance only 31 days of the cash cycle itself. Suppliers provided 31 out of the required 62 days' finance for the average company's investment in working capital.

The cash cycle can provide an indication of the short-term financial implications of sales growth. If the average cash cycle of 31 days is used, this suggests that for every $100 of sales $8.50 working capital is required.

$$31 \div 365 \times 100 = 8.50$$

If the company plans to increase sales by $1m, some $85,000 additional working capital must be found to support the growth.

Using creditors for finance

The use of creditors to finance this operating cycle is normal. The degree to which short-term creditors' money is used depends partly on what is normal or acceptable within a business sector, and thus accepted by suppliers, and partly on the financial management policy of the individual company. In retail companies, particularly food retailers, it is not uncommon for trade creditors to be used to finance the business to the extent that a negative number of days is disclosed for the cash cycle.

A negative figure for the cash cycle indicates an aggressive and positive use of suppliers' money to finance a company's operations. A cash cycle of –10 days could be interpreted as the company taking cash out of the bank, holding it for 10 days as inventory and selling it to customers who pay within 1 day: a total of 11 days. Then the company retains the cash, including the profit margin, in the business, or invests it for interest, for a further 10 days before paying suppliers the money owed.

However, most businesses do not have negative cash cycles. Food-processing companies supplying retailers, for example, will have comparably high cash cycles.

Manufacturers can be expected to hold much more inventory than retailers. In the case of company F, there is some 84 days' inventory including raw materials, work in progress and finished goods. Manufacturers are not cash businesses as are many retailers, and they are unable to collect cash from their customers as quickly. Company F, on average, is offering customers 59 days' credit, twice as long as the department store group (D). This is supported by the average days' credit being taken by the retailers. The credit taken by retailers is often the credit given by manufacturers. Lastly, manufacturers are unlikely to be able to take much more credit from their suppliers than can retailers. The heavy goods manufacturer (F) takes some 30 days' credit from its suppliers, as does the food retailer (E).

The heavy goods manufacturer therefore experiences a cash cycle of 113 days, representing the finance the company must provide for working capital. Different types of businesses produce different standards of ratios.

It could be argued that the cash cycle should be produced by taking the average of opening and closing inventory, receivables and payables. This is found by adding the current and previous year's figure for each item and dividing the result by two. Given the broad nature of the analysis being undertaken, it is probably just as effective to use the year-end figures set out in the most recent balance sheet.

Assessing the cash position

Current assets include the year-end cash balances of the company. At the same time, current liabilities may show some short-term bank borrowing. It may seem odd that a company can have positive cash balances on one side of the balance sheet and short-term bank borrowing on the other. Such a situation is normal, however, particularly when dealing with a group of companies. If subsidiary companies are, while under the control of the holding company, operating independent bank accounts, one may have a short-term bank loan and another may have positive cash balances. In the assessment of liquidity, short-term bank borrowing should be set against positive cash balances to provide a net cash figure.

It is not normally possible to gain detailed information concerning a company's banking arrangements from its annual report. Moreover, the level of short-term borrowing shown at the year end as part of current liabilities may not be representative of the rest of the year.

What constitutes a good cash position?

Too little cash might indicate potential problems in paying short-term creditors. Too much cash, as an idle resource, may indicate poor financial management. Cash itself is no use unless it is being used to generate additional income for the company. Cash balances may produce interest when deposited in a bank, but a company should be able to generate more net income by investing the money in its own business.

Too much cash may make a company an attractive proposition to a predator. A company that is profitable and well regarded in the marketplace, with an appropriately high share price, may not have substantial cash balances. All available cash may be reinvested in the business to generate more profit. Such a company may regard a less profitable but cash-rich company as an attractive target for acquisition.

Various ratios can be used to gain some indication of the adequacy of a company's cash position. It is useful to have some idea of what proportion of current assets is being held in the form of cash and short-term investments. Short-term investments may be treated as the equivalent of cash.

For the example companies, the percentage of cash to total current assets is as follows:

	D	E	F	G
Cash ($m)	120	15	215	190
Current assets ($m)	305	78	650	270
Cash holding (%)	**39**	**19**	**33**	**70**

The more liquid a company is, the higher is the proportion of current assets in cash or near-cash items. The restaurant chain (G) held almost twice as much cash, represented as a proportion of current assets, at the year end as the department store group (D). The heavy goods manufacturer (F) and food retailer (E) maintained lower levels of liquidity.

It might also be of interest to see what proportion of a company's total assets is held in liquid form either as cash or as short-term investments.

	D	E	F	G
Cash ($m)	120	15	215	190
Total assets ($m)	850	600	980	1,130
Cash holding (%)	**14**	**3**	**22**	**17**

Under this measure, there is little difference to be observed between D, F and G. For every $1 of total assets, company F had more than 22¢ retained in highly liquid assets. Company E is the least liquid, holding just over 2% of total assets as cash or short-term investments.

The speed with which cash circulates within a company can be assessed by linking sales revenue for the year with year-end, or average, cash balances.

	D	**E**	**F**	**G**
Sales revenue ($m)	1,000	1,000	1,000	1,000
Cash balance ($m)	120	15	215	190
Cash turn	**8.3**	**66.7**	**4.7**	**5.3**

The higher the figure for cash turn, the faster the cash circulation and the better it is for a company; each time it completes the circuit its profit margin is added. Once again, different levels of cash turn are expected and acceptable for different types of business. The food retailer has the most rapid cash turnover (66.7 times in the year) and the heavy goods manufacturer the slowest (4.6 times).

	D	**E**	**F**	**G**
Sales revenue ($m)	1,000	1,000	1,000	1,000
Operating cash flow ($m)	150	85	195	320
Total assets ($m)	850	600	980	1,130
Cash flow margin (%)	**15.0**	**8.5**	**19.5**	**32.0**
CFROA (%)	**17.6**	**14.2**	**19.9**	**28.3**

For any company, the main source of cash should be its normal business activity. The way in which a company finances its operations depends partly on the type of business and partly on its stage of growth and maturity. The restaurant chain (G) has the highest cash flow margin (32%) and cash flow rate of return on assets or CFROA (28.3%). A high level of internally generated cash is to be expected of a mature and successful company, whereas a younger and rapidly growing company is likely to have a different balance between sources of cash inflow.

To gain a better picture of the operating performance of a company, calculate the CFROA or the cash flow rate of return on investment (CFROI) and treat this in the manner described for ROTA analysis in Chapter 6. The higher the operating cash flow to total assets ratio the better. It shows the ability of the company to reinvest in the business or that more cash is likely to be available for future upgrades and replacements. Company E again falls behind in this respect.

The cash flow margin and CFROA provide a useful supplement to the statement of cash flows in showing the ability of a company to generate cash flow from operations. They also offer an insight into how successful a company is in converting sales revenue into cash. For every $1 of sales revenue, company D produces 15¢ of cash flow and G produces 32¢. The higher this ratio the better it is for a company.

Defensive interval

Another measure of the adequacy of liquid resources is the defensive interval. If an extreme position is taken and it is assumed that a company, for whatever reason, ceases to have any cash inflows or sources of credit, its survival would be limited to the length of time that existing cash balances and short-term investments could support operations before the company was forced to rely on another source of finance to meet its obligations. This ratio, the defensive interval, is calculated by dividing cash and investments by ADC.

Cash and cash equivalents ÷ average daily cost

The more liquid a company the longer is the defensive interval.

	D	**E**	**F**	**G**
Cash ($m)	120	15	215	190
ADC ($m)	1.8	2.5	2.3	1.7
Defensive interval	**67**	**6**	**93**	**112**

The previous ratios showed the restaurant group (G) to be the most liquid company, so it should come first when the defensive period is calculated. If all other sources of finance were closed to company G, it would theoretically be able to maintain its basic operations for almost four months (112 days) before running out of liquid resources. The food retailer (E) would, on the basis of a similar calculation, have cash flow problems within one week.

Another way of calculating the defensive interval is to use the average daily operating cash outflow of a company. If operating profit is deducted from sales revenue and depreciation is added back, a rough indication of total operating cash outflows is produced. Alternatively, the statement of cash flows can be checked to see if it provides details of cash payments to suppliers and employees' remuneration.

Lastly, when assessing liquidity, the figure for cash shown in a company's balance sheet will truly reflect the cash in hand or in the bank at the end of the year. It does not necessarily provide information on what currencies are involved or where the cash is actually held.

Profit and cash flow

There need be no short-term relationship between the profit a company displays in the income statement and the amount of cash it has available at the year end. There are a number of reasons for this. For example, a charge is made each year in the income statement for depreciation that does not affect cash balances. Differences between changes in cash position and reported earnings normally result from the following:

- **Operating activities.** There may be timing differences between the impact of cash flowing in or out of the business and that of transactions appearing in the income statement. Non-cash expenses such as depreciation are recognised in the income statement.
- **Investing activities.** Capital investment – purchasing fixed assets – or corporate acquisition or disinvestments may be contained within the balance sheet but not the income statement.
- **Financing activities.** Raising capital or repaying loans will change the cash position but not the profit in the income statement.

It is worth looking at the relationship between operating cash flow and profit (before any exceptional items appearing in the income statement).

Cash flow from operations ÷ profit from operations

This ratio should be higher than 1, and to make sure it is consistent it should be calculated for a number of years. Cash flow should be greater than profit – there is no deduction for depreciation – to give confidence in the quality of earnings. If net income is greater than operating cash flow, creative accounting may be being used to massage income. Or there may be potential liquidity problems with insufficient cash available to cover operating costs, dividends or for future investment. A high ratio may indicate a conservative depreciation policy masking true profitability.

The working capital cycle discussed earlier can be disrupted if it is necessary for a company to use financial resources outside the current assets and current liabilities area. When a company makes capital investments, or pays dividends to shareholders, interest on borrowings or tax, the amount of cash within the working capital area is reduced.

Financial management indicators

The interest cover ratio neatly combines profitability and gearing (leverage); a low-profit company with high debt will have a low interest cover. Gearing is an important factor in survival assessment. A highly geared low-profit company is more at risk than a low-geared high-profit company. A broad measure of the way in which a company is financed is provided by the debt/equity ratio. An alternative is the debt ratio, which expresses total debt (liabilities) – long-term loans and current liabilities – as a percentage of total assets, allowing appreciation of the contributions by debt and equity (see Chapter 9).

$	D	E	F	G
Equity	500	100	400	400
Long-term loan	150	320	210	370
Current liabilities	200	180	370	360
Total liabilities	850	600	980	1,130
Total debt (%)	**41**	**83**	**59**	**65**
Equity (%)	**59**	**17**	**41**	**35**

The total debt ratio measures the proportion of total assets financed by non-equity and gives an indication of short-term future viability. The higher the proportion of assets seen to be financed from outside sources rather than by shareholders, the higher is the gearing and the greater is the risk associated with the company. A general rule is that if the ratio is over 50% and has been steadily increasing over the past few years, this is an indication of imminent financial problems. For almost any type of business, a debt ratio of over 60% shows a potentially dangerous overreliance on external financing.

In the example, the highest geared company E with a total debt/equity ratio of 320% ($320 ÷ $100) has 83% of total assets financed by debt and 17% by equity. Another way of expressing this would be to use the asset gearing ratio. When equity is funding less than 50% of the total assets, the ratio moves to above 2. Company E has an asset gearing of 6 ($600 ÷ $100) and D's is 1.7 ($850 ÷ $500).

Cash flow indicators

Cash flows are difficult to manipulate, so the statement of cash flows offers a valuable source of information about the financial management of a company (see Chapter 4). It can be helpful to express the figures in the statement in percentage terms, especially when comparing several years or several companies. It also helps to highlight trends (see Chapter 5). Chapter 6 discussed how substituting operating cash flow for profit in some of the ratios of profitability and rates of return can assist the appreciation of a company's performance.

Companies producing regular positive cash flow are better than those that "eat" cash flow. Operating cash flow is a crucial figure, representing the degree of success management has had in generating cash from running the business. It can be used in several illuminating measures of performance and position:

> Operating cash flow ÷ interest
> Operating cash flow ÷ dividend
> Operating cash flow ÷ capital expenditure
> Operating cash flow ÷ total debt

The first three ratios will show what proportion of a company's cash flow is being allocated to pay for external finance, reward shareholders and reinvest in the fixed assets of the business.

For most companies, an operating cash flow ÷ interest of at least 2 or 200% is to be expected. Linking operating cash flow to dividend payments provides some assurance that sufficient cash was produced directly from the business in the year to cover the payment of dividends. All the ratios should be calculated for a number of years to assess their consistency.

Companies cannot easily manipulate or disguise their cash flows or disguise their financial structure. These can be combined in the cash flow/debt ratio. The higher the ratio the safer is the company. A minimum of 20% is often used as a guide level, indicating that it would take five years of operating cash flows to clear total debt. If the ratio were 10%, ten years' cash flows would be required. The cash flow from the business expressed as a percentage of the total of all non-shareholder liabilities indicates the strength of cash flow against external borrowings.

	D	E	F	G
Cash flow/total debt (%)	43	17	34	44

The poor cash flow of E, the least profitable of the companies, produces a cash flow/total debt ratio of 17%. Another way of interpreting this ratio would be to say that it would take E 5.9 years ($500 ÷ $85) of current cash flow to repay its total debt. The period would be 2.3 years for D and G, and 3.0 years for F.

The statement of cash flows can be used to assess what a company is doing with its available cash. Is it being used to pay tax and dividends or for reinvestment in the business in non-current assets? A comparison with previous years' figures will reveal whether the company has a consistent policy on the level of investment.

The statement can also be used to spot signs of potential problems. A company suffering from growth pangs or overtrading may show an increase in the level of receivables linked to sales revenues as more customers are offered extended credit terms. At the same time credit taken from suppliers increases to an even greater extent as the company finds it difficult to make the necessary payments on time. During this process cash balances and short-term investments decline rapidly as cash is used up. Any major changes observed in the levels of inventory, debtors, creditors and liquid balances shown in the statement of cash flows may reflect either the careful management of working capital or a lack of control by the company.

Lastly, the statement can be used to help decide whether the costs of capital and borrowings are consistent and of an appropriate level. Each year the proportion of cash flow being used to pay dividends to shareholders (cash dividend cover) and interest on borrowings (cash interest cover) should be checked.

Cash dividend cover = operating cash flow ÷ dividends

Cash interest cover = operating cash flow ÷ interest charge

Summary

■ Reading the annual report and discovering that a company made a profit for the year and has several million in cash in the bank at the year end is not sufficient evidence that it is safe.

■ The statement of financial position and the statement of cash flows are crucial in understanding the short-term financial position of a company. The year-end short-term assets and liabilities are set out in the statement of financial position; details of the major sources of cash inflows and the uses made of these during the year are provided in the statement of cash flows. This statement also shows, normally as its starting point, the amount of cash generated from a company's operations during the year through the income statement.

■ The liquid ratio (quick ratio) is the simplest and probably most effective measure of a company's short-term financial position. It is assumed that inventory will not prove an immediate source of cash so it is ignored. It is easy to calculate this ratio for the current and previous year directly from the balance sheet. The result gives a simple indication of the liquidity of a company and to what extent this is consistent between the two years. The higher the ratio the greater confidence you can have in the short-term survival of the company. A 1:1 ratio indicates that for every $1 of its short-term creditors and borrowings the company is maintaining $1 in cash or assets that can realistically be turned into cash in the near future.

■ As with all ratios, before interpreting the figures, it is essential to compare the subject company with others either in the same industry sector or of similar size or business mix. A low liquid ratio may be perfectly acceptable for a food retailer but not for a construction firm.

■ The liquid ratio is no guide to the profitability or cash flow generation of the company. A profitable company with a healthy cash flow is less likely to suffer short-term financial problems than one with a less positive performance. Yet both companies might have an identical liquid ratio. The current liquidity ratio provides a useful means of combining a company's liquidity with its cash flow generating capability. The lower the number of days in the current liquidity ratio the safer the company is likely to be from short-term liquidity and solvency problems. As a rough rule for most businesses, warning bells should sound if the ratio is seen to be moving to over 1,500 days (four years).

■ The liquid and current liquidity ratios provide a fairly straightforward indication of a company's short-term position. But to gain real insight into its liquidity and financial management, you should study the statement of cash flows, covering at least two years. If the cash inflow from operations (profit plus depreciation) is not consistently the major source of the company's funds, try to find out why and then decide whether it is reasonable to assume that this state of affairs can continue.

■ The ability of a company to react to unexpected threats or opportunities by adjusting the level and timing of its cash flows – its financial adaptability – is an important consideration. One way of assessing this from a more pessimistic viewpoint is to use the defensive interval. This indicates for how long the company might survive and continue operations if all cash inflows ceased.

■ The cash cycle helps you see how a company is managing cash flows through investment in inventory, credit provided to customers and credit taken from suppliers. The faster the cash circulates through the business the lower is the amount of capital tied up in operating assets and, as every time the cash completes the circuit a profit is taken, the higher is the rate of return achieved.

9 Capital and valuation

AN IMPORTANT ASPECT in the overall assessment of a company's financial position is its sources of finance and the performance measures applied by investors. The statement of financial position is a good starting point for seeing how a company is financed: the proportions of the total capital employed provided by shareholders and other sources of finance.

Equity and debt

A statement of financial position has three broad classifications of liabilities: equity (shareholders' or stockholders' funds), non-current liabilities (long-term creditors) and current liabilities (short-term creditors). These reflect the three potential sources of finance open to any company. Finance can be raised from shareholders, through long-term or short-term borrowing, or through the management of working capital. The raising of any form of finance – debt or equity – is completed by means of a "financial instrument".

The shareholders' contribution to the finances of a company may be given a variety of names:

- equity;
- net worth;
- net assets;
- capital and reserves;
- shareholders' (stockholders') funds.

Equity is the term most commonly used to identify the ordinary shareholders' investment in a company. The balance sheet figures for equity may include preference shares or other non-voting shares a company has in issue, but such shares should not be included in the definition of equity. Equity and any equity instruments have a "residual interest in the assets of an entity that remain after deducting its liabilities".

Any finance other than equity is referred to as debt, which can be divided into long-term and short-term borrowings and creditors. Borrowings with a life of less than one year appear within current liabilities and are short-term. Long-term borrowings appear as part of non-current liabilities. A note will detail their date of repayment and interest rate.

Equity shares provide a company with long-term finance. They are not normally redeemable and have no guarantee of income, through the payment of dividends, attached to them. Debt is normally borrowed for a fixed term with a fixed rate of interest. With debt, interest charges have to be paid and at some time the money borrowed will have to be repaid. With equity there is no expectation of capital repayment and any dividend paid is under the control of the company. The relationship between debt and equity is crucial to an appreciation of the financial structure of a company and its viability.

Leverage or gearing

Raising finance from external sources increases a company's risk because, in the case of loans, there is a cost (interest) and an obligation to repay the loan. If it is a convertible loan, it can reduce the degree of control that existing shareholders have over the company when new shares are issued. In the UK and the US companies are mainly financed by shareholders. In France, Germany and Italy it is mainly banks that provide corporate capital.

The relationship between debt and equity is referred to as leverage or gearing. Management should make sure that the balance between debt and equity finance is appropriate for the business being conducted. Too much debt and a company is said to be highly geared; a low-geared company is financed mainly by its shareholders. The higher the level of debt in relation to equity the greater is the potential risk to shareholders of not receiving a dividend or getting back the capital they have invested. Interest on debt must be paid before any dividends, and all borrowings must be repaid before anything becomes available for shareholders.

Debt/equity ratio

The relationship between internal (equity) and external (debt) sources of finance can be expressed as a percentage or a ratio: the debt to equity ratio.

$	A	B	C
Equity	250	500	1,000
Non-current liabilities	500	500	500
Current liabilities	250	250	250

Debt/equity ratio = (non-current liabilities + current liabilities) ÷ equity

For the three companies the debt/equity ratios are:

	A	B	C
%	300	150	75
×	3	1.5	0.75

The debt/equity ratio is the most commonly used measure of the relationship between internal and external finance. Company A with equity of $250 and debt of $750 has a debt/equity ratio of 3 or 300%. This can be interpreted as indicating that for every $1 of shareholder investment in the company, outside borrowings and creditors provide $3. Company C has only $0.75 of debt for every $1 of equity. Thus company A is the most highly geared company.

Another approach is to take the long-term borrowings – to be found in non-current liabilities – as the numerator and add it to the equity as the denominator to provide a long-term debt ratio.

Long-term debt ratio = long-term borrowings ÷ (long-term borrowings + equity)

	A	B	C
%	66.7	50.0	33.3

It is to be expected that equity outweighs long-term liabilities – the ratio is less than 1. If the ratio is greater than 1, lenders have more of a stake in the company than the shareholders.

Non-current liabilities ÷ equity

	A	**B**	**C**
%	2	1	0.5

Defining debt and equity

There is no standard definition of gearing, and there are often considerable practical difficulties in making the distinction between equity and debt. Although a debenture or bank loan is clearly part of debt, how do you classify a convertible loan, which carries a fixed rate of interest and is capable of being repaid on an agreed future date or of being converted into equity shares?

Using the balance sheet and its notes it is possible to identify all of a company's long-term and short-term borrowings. What remains are other non-current liabilities – including taxation and provisions – and other current liabilities – including trade payables, taxes payable and provisions. You may use these refined figures of debt and equity in any analysis. A sound rule in financial analysis is to be conservative; when in doubt, treat an item as debt.

The time for which debt is scheduled for repayment is an important factor influencing the interpretation of any gearing ratio. Any borrowings not scheduled for repayment within one year are included in debt. A company not required to repay loans for five years may be viewed differently from one where repayment will take place in two years. The gearing ratios of the two companies may be identical, but the underlying implications are different. The notes accompanying the financial statements will provide details of debt repayment terms and their interest rates.

Off-balance-sheet items

When a company raises finance or acquires assets and there is no identifiable change in the balance sheet, it is referred to as an off-balance-sheet transaction. There is nothing new in off-balance-sheet items: just because a transaction is not reflected in the balance sheet does not make it automatically suspect. Off-balance-sheet items caused considerable concern in the 1990s, as financial experts offered a range of such items to assist companies reduce the disclosure of costs and the risks of finance. They followed precisely the requirements of GAAP and accounting standards but failed to show the real picture.

Joint ventures are a good example of the potential for off-balance-sheet financing. Two companies (X and Y) set up a joint venture, and each invests $100 in the new company (Z) for 50% of the equity. They jointly act as guarantors for a bank loan of $1,000 to set Z up in business. The balance sheets of X and Y show only the $100 investment in the joint venture. The liability for the loan of $1,000 does not appear; it is an off-balance-sheet item. The figure of $100 will increase under the equity method of valuation as X and Y make further investments in Z or the joint venture begins to make a profit. Each company takes 50% of Z into its balance sheet.

The greater the assets and the lower the liabilities in a company's balance sheet, the happier everyone is. A bank lending money to a company will want to minimise the risks involved; it may stipulate a maximum level of debt to equity (gearing) for the company. If the company exceeds this level, the bank can require the loan to be repaid immediately. Similarly, analysts, as a simple measure of creditworthiness, may set "safe" levels of gearing that the company should not exceed. In such cases there is pressure on management to minimise the liabilities appearing on the face of the balance sheet. For companies X and Y, in effect their level of debt has increased by $500, but there is no evidence of this in their balance sheet gearing ratios.

Accounting standards have significantly limited the scope for off-balance-sheet manipulation. Legislation has also played a part. The US has the Sarbanes-Oxley Act, and from 2008 UK companies were required to disclose the potential impact of off-balance-sheet items (Companies Act 2006). Where such items are found to exist they should be included in the definition of a company's debt for the purpose of analysis. The IASB and the FASB have improved the reporting of off-balance-sheet items with IFRS 10, 11 and 12 and SFAC 166 and 167.

Debt ratio

A simple measure of a company's gearing is provided by the debt ratio.

Debt ratio = total debt ÷ total assets

	A	B	C
%	75	60	43
×	0.75	0.60	0.43

The debt ratio can be calculated either directly from the balance sheet or from a common size statement. The higher the ratio the higher is the gearing. A ratio of 50%, commonly viewed as the limit for accepting without question a company's level of gearing, indicates that for every $1 of assets 50¢ has been financed by long-term and short-term debt. Using this guideline, company A is highly geared with 75% of total assets financed by debt, whereas company C is low geared at 43%.

Interest cover ratio

Interest paid on debt is charged as an expense before arriving at the profit for the year attributable to shareholders. An increase in external borrowings brings higher gearing and a greater interest charge in the income statement. Once a loan is taken, the interest payments must be made in cash and the capital sum repaid on the agreed date. A company not generating enough profit to cover interest payments or having insufficient cash available to repay the loan faces serious difficulty.

An effective ratio for combining profitability with the impact of gearing is interest cover. This measures the ability of a company to generate sufficient profits to allow all interest on borrowings to be paid. It is calculated by dividing the profit before interest and tax (PBIT) by the interest charge for the year. The figure for PBIT should exclude any exceptional or extraordinary items, and so represent the profit being generated from regular trading operations.

Interest cover = profit before interest and tax ÷ interest paid

The figure for interest used in the ratio should be that due for payment during the financial year, and care should be taken to add back to the figure appearing in the income statement any interest that has been capitalised or interest received that has been deducted. This information will be found in the notes accompanying the income statement or the statement of cash flows.

$	A	B	C
PBIT	200	100	400
Interest	50	50	50
Interest cover	**4**	**2**	**8**

The higher the interest cover the lower is the risk that there will be insufficient profit available for payment of dividends to shareholders. Company C has the highest interest cover; profit could decline by eight times before it would be unable to cover the interest due on borrowings. The comparatively high interest cover of C is due partly to its profitability and partly to its gearing: C has the lowest gearing.

Interest cover can be used to assess the impact of changes in profitability on the risk of shareholders not receiving a dividend. For B a 50% decline in profit would result in there being nothing available for the payment of dividends; every $1 of PBIT is required to pay interest. In the same circumstances and ignoring tax, A would have $50 and C would have $150 available for the payment of dividends.

$	A	B	C
PBIT	100	50	200
Interest	50	50	50
Profit before tax	50	0	150

Attractions of high gearing

Simple arithmetic supports a decision by a company to take advantage of outside sources of finance. Shareholders will clearly benefit if a loan bearing a 5% interest charge is invested in the business where it is expected to generate a 10% rate of return. For no increase in their investment shareholders' return improves, through either increased dividends or capital growth, or a combination of the two.

The situation where there is a 50% decrease in profits has been considered, but what happens when profits double? Profit, subject to tax, becoming available to the shareholders of B increases by $100 and interest cover moves from 2 to 4 times ($200 ÷ $50).

$	A	B	C
PBIT	400	200	800
Interest	50	50	50
Profit before tax	350	150	750

When a company is confident that the costs of external borrowings can be covered through the increased profit flowing from the investment made in the business, it makes sense to increase gearing. An added incentive for debt is that interest is normally tax deductible but dividends are not. High gearing increases the risk associated with the investment, but it can provide shareholders with high returns.

Asset gearing and return on equity

In Chapters 6 and 7 the Du Pont Chart was used to analyse profitability and efficiency. The profit margin and asset turn were combined to generate a rate of return on assets employed. The same approach, using after-tax profit, can be used to calculate return on equity (ROE) – a key performance indicator for any company.

Return on equity = (after-tax profit ÷ assets) × (assets ÷ equity)

$	A	B	C
After-tax profit	75	25	175
Total assets	1,000	1,250	1,750
Equity	250	500	1,000
Return on equity (%)	**30.0**	**5.0**	**17.5**

With a little expansion this model can be highly effective in assessing the impact of gearing on a company's ROE.

The equity multiplier

How a company's assets are financed can be reviewed with the asset gearing ratio, sometimes referred to as the equity multiplier. This is directly linked to the debt ratio and identifies what proportion of the assets or capital employed is provided by shareholders. Assets may be defined as total assets or in any manner you intend to use consistently in your analysis – tangible operating assets (ROTOA) or net operating assets (RONOA).

The impact of gearing can clearly be seen; the higher the gearing the higher is this ratio.

Asset gearing = assets ÷ equity or
Equity gearing = (debt + equity) ÷ equity

$	A	B	C
Total assets	1,000	1,250	1,750
Equity	250	500	1,000
Asset gearing	**4.0**	**2.5**	**1.75**

Company A's shareholders are supporting only one-quarter of the total assets employed in the business. For each $1 of equity in company A there is $3 of debt and creditor finance ($750 ÷ $250). Company C shows only $0.75 ($750 ÷ $1,000). This can be viewed as the multiplier working for shareholders to increase the profitability of their investment. Any interest payable has been deducted in arriving at the after-tax profit. If two companies have the same total assets and after-tax profit, the one with the greater asset gearing will show the higher ROE.

Financing a business with debt can increase shareholder returns. For every $1 of equity in company A there is $4 of assets. This acts to increase the profits available to shareholders. For company A, if the after-tax profit margin (7.5%) is multiplied by the asset gearing ratio (4), the result is the ROE (30%). Company C has a higher profit margin (8.75%) but a lower asset gearing (1.75) producing a 17.5% ROE.

Return on equity can be seen to be the end result of three ratios.

ROE = (profit ÷ sales) × (revenue ÷ assets) × (assets ÷ equity)

Assuming that sales revenue for all three companies is $2,000, the ratios are:

$	A	B	C
Sales revenue	2,000	2,000	2,000
Total assets	1,000	1,250	1,750
After-tax profit	75	25	175
Profit ÷ sales	3.75	1.25	8.75
Revenue ÷ assets	2 .00	1.60	1.14
Assets ÷ equity	4	2.5	1.75
Return on equity (%)	**30.0**	**5.0**	**17.5**

If B and C increased their gearing level to that of company A (4), ROE would rise to 8% for B (1.25 × 1.6 × 4) and 40% for C (8.75 × 1.14 × 4). This illustrates the impact of gearing on shareholder returns.

This combination of ratios offers an effective tool to aid the analysis of a company's rates of return and financial structure. Capital structure measures are combined with the ability to produce profit (profit margin) and to use assets to generate revenue (asset turn). It can also be used to assess the implications of any likely changes in the business – what happens if profit margin declines and gearing increases?

Dangers of high gearing

The more a company relies on debt the less control it has over its finances and the more it is at risk. A highly geared company may find that lenders are less likely to accept changes in the terms of a loan agreement than shareholders are to accept a lower or even no dividend as the company runs short of cash or needs money to invest in assets.

High gearing can bring high volatility in the level of profit available to equity shareholders. For a highly geared company, a small movement in profit can have a dramatic influence on equity earnings. A small decline in profit may result in the company having to use all of its profit to service debt rather than pay dividends.

When business is booming, a company may regard an increase in gearing as not only attractive but also essential. It can be seen as a sign of poor financial management not to borrow more to achieve returns greater than the cost of the borrowing. During times of inflation, when the real cost of debt decreases, the pressure can be irresistible. However, if the boom slows and/or ends in recession, a highly geared company faces difficulties as profits decline, interest rates rise and loans fall due for repayment.

The problems that many banks encountered in the 2008 financial crisis provide a further illustration of the potential problems associated with high gearing. Suppose company A found that 10% of its total assets ($1,000) – subprime mortgages – had become valueless. The assets' carrying value becomes $900 and shareholders' funds are reduced to $150. The debt ratio moves from 75% to 83% ($750 ÷ $900) and the debt/equity ratio from 4 to 5 times ($750 ÷ $150), now showing the company in a somewhat different light.

A further danger inherent in high gearing is that as the providers of debt see gearing rise they may, to reduce their own exposure, insist that certain restrictions are built into the loan agreement, such as an upper limit for gearing or tougher levels of interest cover or liquidity. The company loses some degree of control and flexibility of approach in its financial management. If it breaks the loan restrictions, it may be held in default and forced to make immediate repayment.

Share price and value

Shares are normally issued at a par value. The par value of a share is the nominal value at which it is issued and appears in the balance sheet. A company may issue 25¢ or $1 shares and this, rather than the market price, is the value consistently used in the balance sheet. When shares are issued at a price higher than par value the difference is shown in equity as share premium or capital in excess of par value. The par value of a share has no relevance to financial analysis. In the US, it is common for companies to issue shares of no par value.

In general, share prices reflect views of the future rather than the mainly historical perspective presented in an annual report. A balance sheet should not be expected to reflect the market price of shares. It is the share price quoted on the stock exchange that determines the value of an investment. Share prices and price movements of the previous day are given in the media together with the high and low points for the year.

Many factors can influence a company's share price. Some are clear and quantifiable; others are more esoteric and ephemeral. A company issuing a profit warning can expect a drop in share price. Rumours of a takeover, a technological breakthrough, changes on the board, a big order or a lost one can all influence share price. Share price will partly reflect the general mood of the market, which is in turn linked to the national and global, economic, political and social environment. General optimism produces a bull market (one in which share prices are rising) and pessimism a bear market (one in which share prices are falling).

There can be only one indisputable answer to the question: why did the shares go up by 5% yesterday? It is, as any market trader knows: because there were more buyers than sellers.

The prime trigger for a movement in share price is a change in investors' confidence in the ability of a company to produce profits in the future. Shares may have been purchased on the basis of the past performance of a company, but they are held in expectation of future returns: income and capital gain. The sector in which a company operates can also influence share price. If it is one that is seen as being static, this will hold back the share price, whereas the reverse is true for a dynamic or glamorous sector.

Each stock exchange has its own share price indicator. In the UK, the FTSE 100, commonly referred to as the Footsie, includes the share prices of the largest 100 listed companies. This is a good real-time indicator of the market; a rise in the FTSE can be taken to indicate a general upward movement in share prices. The US has the Dow Jones and NASDAQ, France the CAC General, Germany the DAX and China the Shanghai Composite.

Betas

For any given period, movements in both a company's share price and a selected stock-exchange index can be plotted to give an indication of the sensitivity of the company's share price to general movements in the market. This relationship is termed the share's beta – the beta rating, beta factor, beta coefficient – and it provides a measure of the volatility of a share relative to the market. In the UK the FTSE 100 or the FT All-Shares index is used; in the US it is the NYSE Composite (all stocks on the exchange). The statistical analysis supporting the calculation of betas is complex. You are unlikely to be involved in calculating a beta; all you need to know is what it is meant to indicate.

Both income and capital gains from each share are compared with the return from the selected market index over a number of years. Betas are incorporated into the capital asset pricing model (CAPM), which can be used to quantify the cost of a company's equity. The market's beta is 1. If a share moves precisely in tune with the market it will have a value of 1.0. This, by definition, is that of the average company.

If it was found that for every 1% move in the market a company's share moved 1.5%, applying the 1.5 factor to the market index should provide an indicator of the likely price of that company's shares. A beta of 1.5 suggests that for every 1% move in the market the share will move 1.5%. If the buoyancy of the market is directly linked to expectations for the economy, companies with high betas are likely to be directly affected by boom or doom. With a sound economy high-beta companies can be expected to generate extremely good returns, but in recession they will probably be poor performers.

Cyclical stocks are likely to be high beta. For example, cars are more likely to be purchased during good times. There is a direct link between an investment's potential return and its risk. A company with a low beta is likely to be little affected by changes in the economic environment. Government stocks or gilts have a beta of 0; the interest received is not affected by stockmarket fluctuations. Companies producing consumer goods that are purchased irrespective of the economic climate can be expected to have low betas.

The higher the beta – the greater the volatility – the higher will be a company's risk premium. A risk premium may be seen as the compensation for uncertainty or the extra return an investor can be expected to require to invest in the share. Low-risk (low-beta) shares will attract little or no risk premium. If the average risk premium – market risk premium (MRP) – is 5% and the company has a beta of 1.5, its shares can be expected to have a 7.5% (5 × 1.5) risk premium.

Net asset per share and market to book ratios

If a company is wound up and the assets are sold for their balance sheet values, after all external liabilities are settled what remains – net worth or net assets – is all that is available to repay equity shareholders. It is therefore worth calculating the net asset per share ratio to get an idea of the value of the assets supporting the share price. The higher the assets per share the lower is the shareholders' risk.

Asset backing = net assets ÷ number of shares in issue

$	A	B	C
Sale of total assets	1,000	1,250	1,750
Less			
Debt	500	500	500
Current liabilities	250	250	250
Net assets	250	500	1,000
Number of shares	250	500	1,500
Share price ($)	3.00	1.00	1.50
Net assets per share	**1.00**	**1.00**	**0.67**

If the assets are shown at their fair value, the net asset value (NAV) per share can be taken as a reasonable starting point to estimate the amount to be received for each share held in the company if it were liquidated.

For most companies, net asset backing per share will be lower than the current share price for the simple reason that there should be more to a company than just the book value of its assets. The same will apply when the total stock-exchange value – the market capitalisation or book value – of a company is set against the balance sheet value of net assets. This will provide the "market to book" or "price to book" ratio, which will normally be greater than 1. If this is not the case, it means that little value is being placed on expectations of growth or improved performance.

For major US companies before 2008, the ratio was close to 5:1 with only $1 of assets in the balance sheet to support $5 of stock-exchange value. Intangibles can be an important factor in this ratio.

Typically, internet or dotcom companies have a low net asset per share but high market to book ratio.

Where the share price is lower than the net asset backing, this can be interpreted in a number of ways. It may be that the company has not been performing as well as others in the same sector and there is general agreement that this is likely to continue, with the result that there is little demand for the shares. Where the net assets per share are much higher than a company's share price it may be seen as being past redemption, and almost certainly a target for takeover by someone who has spotted the chance to acquire assets cheaply. The 2008 financial crisis provided many examples of this.

Risk and the payback period

A simple and popular means of comparing investment opportunities is to calculate the payback period. An investment of $1,000 offering an annual income of $100 has a payback period of ten years. Another option might be to invest the $1,000 in a project offering a $200 annual income stream. A payback period of five years is likely to be more attractive than the first option: the shorter the payback period the better. Payback is used in investment project assessment and provides an indication of how long it will be before a project generates sufficient income to recover the capital investment. It takes into account the risk involved in the project. The longer the payback period the greater is the exposure to risk.

Finance and capital investment

The strategic report should outline the current level of capital expenditure together with an indication of future intentions for non-current asset investment and, ideally, that allocated to:

- marketing and advertising;
- employee training and development;
- research and new product development;
- maintenance programmes;
- technical support to customers.

FIG 9.1 **Financing the business**

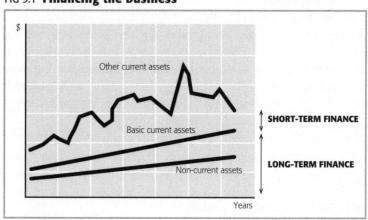

This kind of detail can be helpful in assessing how a company could, at least for a short time, reduce expenditure while maintaining the level of its current operations. Almost any expense might be cut for a short time without an immediate negative impact on profit.

To check on the consistency of asset investment, use the asset replacement rate and capital expenditure turnover ratios (see Chapter 7). The first provides an indication of the speed with which a company is replacing tangible assets, and the second links investment to turnover. Sudden shifts in these ratios can indicate a decision to reduce or halt investment in productive assets in an attempt to maintain liquidity or because finance has been refused.

The way in which capital investment projects are financed is worth investigation. The timescale of the planned investment should match that of the finance being applied. A company using short-term sources of finance to build a factory or make a long-term investment is more likely to run into difficulties than one using long-term finance.

You should expect finance for long-term assets to come from equity or long-term borrowings and for working capital to come from short-term loans or similar sources (see Figure 9.1). The annual report should make clear the link between borrowing requirements and capital expenditure plans.

What you generally want to see is some consistency in the debt/

equity balance and when finance is raised that it is being productively employed in the business. A simple source and application analysis of the balance sheet can give an insight into where funds are coming from and where they are employed in the business. A simple rule of financial management is that a company's long-term investment in assets should be financed from long-term sources. There should be a match between the length of time funds are tied up in investment and their repayment terms.

Peak borrowings

The annual report should include some discussion on cash flow linked to the statement of cash flows and liquidity. This can prove particularly useful where the cash flow generated from business segments is different from the profit disclosed for them in the segmental analysis report.

The annual report should make it possible to appreciate the level of a company's borrowings throughout the year not just that at the balance sheet date. That a company may have approached, or indeed exceeded, its borrowing limits during the year is an important factor in the assessment of its current financial position and future viability.

Price/earnings ratio

A company's earnings per share (EPS) can be incorporated in an equivalent to the payback measure: the price/earnings (P/E) ratio. Share price is dependent upon investors' opinions of a company's future earning potential as much as anything else. EPS (as last reported) can usefully be linked to current share price to provide some indication of expectations for future performance.

Price/earnings = share price ÷ earnings per share

	A	B	C
Share price (¢)	300	100	150
EPS (¢)	30	5	11.7
Price/earnings	**10**	**20**	**12.8**

For company A the P/E of 10 can be interpreted as showing that when a share is purchased for 300¢ this represents the equivalent of ten years' earnings of 30¢ a year – in other words, a payback period of ten years.

The higher the P/E ratio the greater the confidence investors have in the future prospects and performance of the company. A high P/E ratio indicates investors have confidence that the company will maintain and probably improve its current performance in the coming year.

High or low price/earnings?

The only way of deciding whether a company has a high or a low P/E ratio is to compare it with other companies. Companies are listed in the financial media by their sector of operation. The company with the highest P/E ratio is considered, on that day, to be the sector's best future performer for investors.

As EPS is dependent upon share price, the P/E ratio is influenced by forecast trends, rumours or myths of the moment. It is not unusual for the company with the highest ratio one year to be the first in the sector to succumb to recession or mismanagement. By definition, a high P/E ratio indicates that it is probably too late to invest in the company since the price to be paid will be too high. It may also indicate that a company is already overvalued. Experience suggests that the only way for a high P/E to move is downwards.

Prospective price/earnings

If a forecast is made of a company's likely future profits, this can provide a figure for likely future EPS. If company A is forecast to have a profit growth of 10% in the coming year, after-tax profit will rise to $82.50 ($75 + $7.50) and EPS to 33¢. If the current share price is divided by forecast earnings (300 ÷ 33), a prospective P/E ratio of 9.1 is produced. This prospective P/E is the product of arithmetic and is not influenced by real life.

If any item is left as unknown in the equation below, it is easy to discover its value.

Share price = earnings per share × price/earnings ratio

$$300 = 30 \times 10.0$$
$$330 = \mathbf{33} \times 10.0$$
$$\mathbf{300} = 33 \times 9.1$$

For company A, where only one variable in the equation is adjusted, EPS is forecast at 33¢ and the share price rises to 330¢. If the share price is held at 300¢, with 33¢ EPS the P/E ratio moves to 9.1. Prospective P/E ratios can only be estimated, but once some forecast is obtained for profit and P/E it can be used to indicate likely future share price movements. If for company A EPS is forecast at 33¢ and it is considered that the company should command a P/E ratio of 12, the likely future share price can be calculated as follows.

Future share price = forecast earnings per share × prospective price/earnings

$$\textbf{396} = 33 \times 12$$

Problems with price/earnings ratio

In most cases, the P/E ratio being used in analysis is that provided by the media, not one calculated by the user. This can cause problems. The profit used as the basis for a published P/E ratio is normally that shown in a company's income statement and it may therefore have been arrived at creatively. Furthermore, one side of the equation is historical profit, which is not guaranteed to be a guide to future performance, and the other side is current share price, which changes from minute to minute on the stock exchange. A rumour of takeover or a major technological breakthrough in product development will not alter historical earnings, but it will certainly have an effect on the share price.

Dividends

Companies normally make two dividend payments per year: an interim payment based on half-year profits and a final payment at the end of the year. These will appear in the statement of shareholders' equity and the statement of cash flows.

Investors see dividends as an indicator of current performance and future profits. An increased dividend signals that a company's directors consider performance and prospects to be good. Dividends also act as a signal to the market. Good news, indicated by an increase in dividend, usually triggers a rise in share price and bad news the reverse.

The strategic report should provide some information about

dividend policy and shareholder returns. It must be accepted, however, that it is difficult for companies to commit themselves to a predetermined dividend level. Next year the profit may drop, and for a variety of reasons the company may wish to move away from its previous dividend cover or payout level (see Chapter 6 and below). Many factors, other than profit, can influence the dividend decision, including the requirements of major institutional shareholders, how confident directors are that profit will improve quickly, general market expectations and what other companies are doing; if they are maintaining dividends, it may be difficult for one company to break the trend.

Dividend per share

The dividend per share (DPS) can be calculated using the same denominator as earnings per share. The total dividend for the year is divided by the weighted average of the number of shares in issue.

Dividend per share = dividend ÷ weighted average number of shares in issue

	A	**B**	**C**
Dividend ($)	25	20	87
Number of shares	250	500	1,500
Dividend per share (¢)	**10**	**4**	**5.8**

Remember, as with EPS, that it is not possible to directly compare different companies' DPS. Companies with an identical dividend but different share structures will not show the same DPS.

Retained profit per share

When the profit for the year attributable to equity shareholders is known, the next step is for the directors to decide what the dividend should be and how much of the profit should be retained for use by the company. If the dividend per share is deducted from the earnings per share (see Chapter 6), what remains is the retained profit per share for the year.

Retained profit per share = earnings per share − dividend per share

¢ per share	**A**	**B**	**C**
Earnings	30	5	11.7
Dividend	10	4	5.8
Retained earnings	**20**	**1**	**5.9**

Dividend cover

If after-tax profit attributable to ordinary shareholders is divided by the dividend, the result is the number of times the dividend was covered. As with interest cover, the higher the dividend cover ratio the better or safer is the position of a company. However, levels of what is considered acceptable cover vary across business sectors. If a company is operating in a sector that is reasonably unaffected by economic downturns, such as food manufacturing and retailing, a lower dividend cover ratio is more acceptable because the risk is lower.

Dividend cover = after-tax profit ÷ dividend

= earnings per share ÷ dividend per share

¢ per share	**A**	**B**	**C**
After-tax profit	75	25	175
Dividend	25	20	87
Dividend cover	**3.0**	**1.25**	**2.0**

Payout ratio

Another way of looking at the safety level of dividend payments is to show what proportion of profit is being distributed to shareholders.

Payout ratio = 100 ÷ dividend cover

	A	**B**	**C**
Payout (%)	33	80	50

The higher the payout ratio the lower is the dividend cover; the level of profit cover for dividend is just being expressed in a different way. A company with a high payout ratio is not retaining profit to reinvest in the business. You should always try to discover why. Is management not confident about the future prospects of the business, or are they taking a short-term view and keeping shareholders happy with a dividend payment rather than providing for future long-term growth? The reverse of the payout ratio is the retention ratio.

Gross dividend

Companies deduct tax and make a net dividend payment to shareholders. To allow comparison with other investment opportunities, tax should be added back to produce the gross dividend per share. Company A has a dividend of 10¢ per share. If the tax rate is 0.2 (20%), the gross dividend is 12.5¢; 2.5¢ covers the basic rate tax and 10¢ is paid to shareholders.

$$\textbf{Gross dividend} = \text{dividend} \div (1 - \text{tax rate})$$

Earnings yield

To obtain some indication of the return flowing from an investment, the current share price and earnings per share can be combined to give the earnings yield.

$$\textbf{Earnings yield} = 100 \times (\text{earnings per share} \div \text{share price})$$

	A	B	C
Earnings per share (¢)	30	5	11.7
Share price (¢)	300	100	150
Earnings yield (%)	**10**	**5**	**7.8**

Earnings yield is not an indicator of the actual return on investment. It is based on earnings per share not the dividend received by shareholders. If the P/E ratio is known, it is simple to calculate the earnings yield – it is the reciprocal of the P/E ratio. Company B with a P/E ratio of 20 has an earnings yield of 5 (100 ÷ 20) and company C 7.8 (100 ÷ 12.9).

Dividend yield

Dividend yield links the current share price to the dividend received.

$$\textbf{Dividend yield} = 100 \times (\text{dividend per share} \div \text{share price})$$

	A	**B**	**C**
Dividend per share (¢)	10	4	5.8
Share price (¢)	300	100	150
Dividend yield (%)	**3.3**	**4.0**	**3.9**

Movements in share price bring about a change in the dividend yield. As the share price changes there is an automatic adjustment in dividend yield, as illustrated below for company A, whose share price moves between 150¢ and 600¢.

Dividend (¢)	10	10	10
Share price (¢)	300	150	600
Dividend yield (%)	**3.3**	**6.7**	**1.7**

Shareholders' return

The return shareholders expect from their investment is a combination of the capital gain flowing from an improvement in share price and the income from dividends – total shareholders' return (TSR).

A change in share price is part of the total return on shareholders' investment. To calculate the current or the likely future TSR, the capital gain and the dividend yield can be combined. If company A's share price is forecast to rise to 396¢ and the dividend per share to 12¢, then the likely future return can be estimated as follows:

$$
\begin{aligned}
\text{Capital return} &= 100 \times (\text{share price change} \div \text{opening share price}) \\
&= 100 \times (96 \div 300) \\
&= 32\% \\
\text{Dividend yield} &= 100 \times (\text{dividend per share} \div \text{share price}) \\
&= 100 \times (12 \div 300) \\
&= 4\% \\
\text{Total return} &= 32\% + 4\% \\
&= \mathbf{36\%}
\end{aligned}
$$

Valuing companies

There is no simple way of arriving at the value of a non-quoted company. It is often necessary to do so not only to agree a price for a company's sale, but also to meet government requirements to place a value on a deceased person's estate for tax purposes. The annual report can be used as a basis for valuation; the statement of financial position offers comprehensive details of a company's assets and liabilities. The value of assets – fair value – shown in the statement can be used; but as the statement is not intended to offer a valuation, it can only be a rough guide.

Free cash flows, EBIT or EBITDA can form the basis of a rough and ready valuation. A company's cash flow or profit is multiplied by an appropriate factor to produce a value. It is possible to find on the internet suggested multiples for a variety of types and sizes of businesses. The multiple will always depend on a guesstimate as to what is appropriate for the company and its type of business.

The ideal would be to use discounted cash flow techniques to provide a valuation. Unfortunately, for most companies, the possibility of obtaining accurate forecasts of future cash flows is low. The only time there can be an accurate and indisputable value for a company is when it has just been bought or sold. At other times its value is an estimate based partly on science and partly on art.

Capitalisation

If a company's shares are quoted on a stock exchange, there is a ready source of data upon which to base a valuation. Multiplying the current market price of a share by the number of shares in issue provides an indication of the company's current stock-exchange value. This is its market value, or the capitalisation of the company.

	A	B	C
Share price (¢)	300	100	150
Number of shares	250	1,000	1,500
Capitalisation ($)	**750**	**1,000**	**2,250**

Company A has a capitalisation of $750. If you wanted to acquire the company, $750 is probably a better guide to the price to be paid than, say, total assets ($1,000) or equity ($250) in the balance sheet.

The financial media publish capitalisation figures for companies daily or once a week. This provides a basis for the comparison of the size of companies according to current stock-exchange values. In practice, if you decided to acquire A, as shares began to be purchased market forces would bring about a price rise. The capitalisation of $750 offers a guide to the minimum likely price for the company.

Earnings multiple

To calculate a company's capitalisation, after-tax profits can be multiplied by the P/E ratio. Company A has a P/E ratio of 10 and after-tax profit of $75, the product of which is the $750 capitalisation.

Capitalisation can be readily produced only for quoted companies. To calculate the value of a non-quoted company, you can use the P/E ratios of stock-exchange listed companies operating in an appropriate business sector. The internet offers numerous sources of real-time share prices. Otherwise newspapers normally contain a business section where the previous day's prices are published. The P/E ratio of three or four comparable companies or the sector average can be used as a basis for valuation.

Armed with an appropriate benchmark P/E ratio, it is possible to calculate a share price. For example, a company operating in a sector with an average P/E ratio of 16.66 has earnings per share of 5¢ but no quoted share price.

Price earnings ratio = share price ÷ earnings per share
Share price = price/earnings ratio × earnings per share
= 16.66 × 5¢
= **83.3¢**

Using the average P/E ratio for the appropriate sector produces a suggested share price for the company of 83.3¢. In most cases it should be possible to identify one or two quoted companies that reasonably match the activities or spread of business of the company being valued.

After-tax profit versus earnings per share

In the previous section the company's shares were valued at 83.3¢ using the sector average P/E ratio of 16.66. The basis of the valuation is the after-tax profit generated by the company and attributable to equity shareholders. This is not affected by the number of shares in issue or, ignoring tax implications, by dividend policy. It is therefore better and much simpler to use this as the basis for valuing non-quoted companies.

If the after-tax profit is $25 and this is multiplied by the 16.66 P/E ratio, the result is $416, which when divided by the number of shares in issue (500) gives the same share price of 83¢. It is easier and more practical to use $416 as a value for the company, but the individual share price may be important if shares are being transferred between family members in a private company.

Investing in a small private company is usually considered more risky than buying shares in a quoted company. To compensate for this, the P/E ratio used in valuing a private company may be adjusted by an appropriate amount, referred to as the risk premium. If the P/E ratio selected is 16.66 and a 35% risk premium is considered applicable, the multiple to be applied to value a company is 10.8 (16.66 – 35%). If the company has after-tax profits of $25, applying the 10.8 multiple gives a value of $270 and a share price of 54¢ ($270 ÷ 500).

Further problems are encountered if only a proportion of a company's equity is being valued. In this case the method detailed above can be used with discount factors applied to the multiple according to the quantity of shares involved. A 5% block of shares might be discounted by 60%, but if 51% of a company's shares are being acquired the discount might be only 10–20%.

The average P/E for the appropriate sector can be used, but in most cases it should be possible to find at least one suitable company to use as a basis for direct P/E comparison. A simpler alternative, for UK companies, is to use the FTSE Actuaries Share or Sector Indices. If there are no obvious sources of P/E ratios, a rule of thumb is that a multiplier of 10 should be applied to after-tax profits to provide an indication of company value. Where a company is making a loss, sales revenue multiples may be used.

Dividend valuation method

If it is assumed that the value of a share is the present value of its future dividends, then dividend can form the basis for valuing a company. The basic formula is:

$$\textbf{Value} = (\text{dividend} \times (1 + \text{dividend growth}) \div$$
$$(\text{required return} - \text{dividend growth}))$$

An appropriate discount factor can be applied to give the present value of the anticipated dividend stream. If the current dividend of a company is 6¢ per share, dividend growth is expected to be 5% per year and shareholders require a 15% rate of return, a share in the company can be valued at 63¢.

$$\text{Value} = (6.0 \times 1.05) \div (0.15 - 0.05) = 6.3 \div 0.1 = 63¢$$

Government bonds and rates of return

Investors can be assumed to look for different rates of return linked to the risk of a given investment opportunity. The lower the risk the lower is the required rate of return. The rate of return investors require has a direct influence on the cost of a company's capital. The higher the risk the higher is the rate of return required, and the more it costs a company to service through dividend and interest payments the finance provided. A good starting point is to look at returns from risk-free investments.

It is generally accepted that lending money to the government is risk free, as the interest rate and maturity date are fixed and certain. Thus the return from government securities can be regarded as that required from a risk-free investment. Investors in other securities, such as equities, require an additional return to compensate for the additional risk. This is called the risk premium. Using non-redeemable bonds, the interest yield can be calculated in a similar way to that of dividend and earnings yields.

Bond value ($)	100	100	100
Price paid ($)	100	50	200
Interest rate (%)	5	5	5
Interest yield (%)	**5**	**10**	**2.5**

If investors see that the returns from alternative sources are greater than 5%, they may sell their bonds to take advantage of the opportunity. The sale of bonds brings about a reduction in their price ($50) and their yield increases to 10%. When bonds are seen as a better investment, the price rises to $200 and the yield falls to 2.5%.

The base bank rate of interest, quoted daily in the media, can be used as an alternative to government securities to provide an indicator of the risk-free rate of return.

Equities risk premium

As well as the risk-free rate of return, investors can reasonably expect a premium for the risk involved in investing in equities. The equity risk premium has normally been between 5–10% on both the UK and US stock exchanges.

An additional premium is required when considering investment in private, non-quoted companies, which are generally assumed to be a more risky investment than quoted companies. As a general rule, a minimum of an additional 25% premium should be added to compensate for the risk of unlisted company investment. Many valuation experts, however, suggest that the premium should be 30–40%.

Cost of capital

The view investors take of the risk associated with buying shares in a company determines its cost of capital. The higher the risk the higher are the expected returns and the higher is the cost of raising finance for the company. Before a company returns a profit it must cover its cost of capital. Interest on borrowed funds will have been charged before arriving at the profit for the year, but the company will not necessarily have made an appropriate allowance for the cost of equity capital provided by shareholders.

The cost of debt can be estimated from the financial statements. There will be notes providing details of the interest rates applying to loans. The after-tax cost of borrowing $500 at 10% interest with a tax rate of 50% is 5%, and at a tax rate of 40% it would be 6%. Inflation reduces the real cost of debt financing. With a currency decreasing in value over time, the true rate of interest adjusts and so does that repaid at the end of the loan period. Calculating the actual cost of borrowings for loan or convertible stock not issued at par is complex. For most purposes, it is adequate to take the interest rate quoted as being an acceptable approximation of the actual real cost.

There are many ways of estimating the cost of equity. One is to use dividend yield adjusted for the impact of tax. This is only an estimate as it does not take account of the fact that dividend rates may change and, of course, that share prices change from day to day. A simple adjustment to allow for some rate of growth could be applied to the dividend yield, or the earnings yield could be used. The higher the P/E ratio the lower is the earnings yield. A high P/E ratio infers that investors have confidence in the future performance of the company so the cost of raising finance will be lower; of course the reverse also applies.

Investing in new and untested technology can offer huge returns if it is successful, but there is also the possibility of the investment having to be written off, so a high risk is involved. If investors are to be attracted to the investment, they must have some incentive. The cost of equity is the return required by investors to provide capital to a company; the higher the perceived risk of the company the higher is the cost of capital.

The CAPM offers an approach to calculating the cost of equity for a company.

Cost of equity = risk-free rate + beta (market rate − risk-free rate)

= 5% + 1.3 (15% − 5%)

= 18%

With a risk-free rate of return of 5% and a market rate of return of 15%, the equity risk premium is 10%. A company with a 1.3 beta has an estimated cost of equity of 18%. If the company had a beta of 2, the cost of equity would rise to 25%.

Another way of arriving at an approximation of the cost of capital is to take a simple weighted average for equity and debt. The cost of debt is taken as the interest rate applying to each item and the cost of equity as the dividend yield.

Where a company is financed 50% by debt, requiring 10% interest, and 50% by equity, requiring a 20% return, the weighted average cost of capital (WACC) is 15%.

Summary

- The debt/equity ratio is a well-tested and simple measure of the balance between the finance provided by equity shareholders and that derived from external borrowings (debt). Although the ratio may be subject to manipulation, it still provides the best starting point for an assessment of capital structure. The content of the denominator and numerator can be refined as appropriate. The lower the ratio the greater is the proportion of finance being provided by shareholders. A company with a low debt/equity ratio is said to be low geared.

- The debt ratio is helpful in interpreting the structure of a balance sheet. It shows what proportion of total assets has been funded by external sources of finance. For most businesses, when more than 50% of assets are debt financed it is advisable to complete a detailed analysis of the company and its likely future prospects before considering an investment. If only one measure of gearing were allowed, this would be the most attractive.

- Notes in the annual report will provide details of a company's debt, showing for the next five years the amount, rate of interest and date when the borrowings mature or are to be repaid. At first glance these notes may appear overwhelming, but they are worth studying. A simple indicator of the likely demands to be made on a company's future cash flow is created by taking the total annual interest charge and adding to it any capital repayments to be made for each of the next two or three years. Based on previous experience, does it look as if the company can meet these expected cash outflows without having either to sell assets or to initiate new borrowing?

- For shareholders, the efficiency of a company in making debt work for them is an important consideration. Shareholders' return is a combination of profitability and gearing. Two ratios can be combined to highlight how return on equity is being achieved.

- The interest cover ratio is an effective way of linking the level of gearing with profitability. A company borrowing money to finance its operations must pay the agreed interest in cash each year. The greater the interest cover provided by pre-interest and pre-tax profit the safer is the company's position. A high-geared company must guarantee to maintain a safe level of interest cover. A combination of high gearing and low interest cover is not a healthy sign.

- Similarly, the extent to which dividend is covered by profit is a useful indicator of the comfort or safety level for shareholders. The higher the dividend cover the greater is the proportion of retained profit being ploughed back into the company.

- A useful measure is to use cash flow as the basis for cash flow dividend cover. All interest, tax and non-equity dividends are deducted from operating cash flow and the result divided by the equity dividends. This ratio identifies the proportion of cash flow, after all external financing charges, available for equity dividends.

- Dividend per share should be combined with earnings per share in studying the historical record of a company. If earnings per share and dividend per share are plotted, the difference is the amount per share being retained in the business each year. Some consistency in the three figures should be evident.

- The financial media provide daily calculations of dividend yield and P/E ratios. When studying a listed company it is possible to make a direct comparison with the P/E ratios of similar companies, and to obtain some indication of the ranking given by investors. The higher the P/E ratio the higher are investors' expectations of a company's future performance.

- A company with a high P/E ratio is not necessarily a good investment. A high ratio indicates that the market has already taken into account the future prospects of the company and that it is probably already too late to buy.

- Published P/E ratios can be used to provide a valuation for non-listed companies. If the average ratio for the appropriate sector is found and applied as a multiplier to the after-tax profit of a company, the result is an indicator of total value.

10 Strategy, success and failure

WHEN ANALYSING A COMPANY three key areas should be examined: management, operating performance and financial position. Using annual reports and other published information to analyse the past and forecast the future in two of these three areas has been covered in earlier chapters. This chapter goes over some of that ground again, considers approaches to assessing the strength of management and discusses the unavoidable mix of the quantifiable and the qualitative necessary to make an overall assessment of a company's performance and its future prospects.

Sources of information

XBRL

Moves towards the standardisation of financial report information are leading to significant improvements in the quality, value and accessibility of corporate financial information. This is largely due to the adoption of Extensible Business Reporting Language (XBRL) and Extensible Meta Language (XML). An inline variant is iXBRL, which can be read directly by computers or opened with a browser and read as ordinary text.

Do not be put off by the names. This is where the future of both corporate reporting and analysis lies. There will be an international standardised form of presentation; language or terminology will no longer be a barrier to analysis. You can now import company data easily into your own spreadsheet and with little trouble make comparisons with other companies. There is increased certainty, reliability and consistency in the financial definition of each XBRL item used.

In the US, the SEC has accepted XBRL filings since 2005, and in 2006 it provided $5m to assist in the development of common electronic definitions for every accounting transaction. This involves "tags" – tagging all the individual items of information appearing in financial reports. In North America the Edgar database now provides direct access, through the internet, to company financial data, which can be taken into a spreadsheet for analysis and comparison. A number of companies may be compared with complete confidence in the comparability of the raw data being used. Visit the SEC website to discover more – "interactive data (XBRL)".

Using the website (www.sec.gov/searchedgar/company) you may select a company. Then use "interactive data" and "financial statements" – for the annual, 10-Q or 10-K reports – to select the item(s) of interest. Each line (tag) has an explanatory "details" description that is linked to US GAAP and XBRL taxonomy. This is a useful resource in its own right. If you want a definition of any item in an annual report, go to this section of Edgar, click on "details", and you should quickly find an explanation. It is to be hoped that Companies House in the UK will soon be able to offer a similar service.

Having decided what data you require, highlight this in the company file and then take it to your spreadsheet for analysis. Once you have done this a few times you will find it is a simple task providing quick access to comparable – and free – financial data. In the UK, HM Revenue & Customs (HMRC) has required companies to file their corporation tax returns using XBRL since 2011.

The internet

The internet is recognised as being the primary vehicle for corporate communications. All companies operate a website. You can access general business information, financial statements and annual reports with little trouble – just enter the company's name in a search engine. All listed companies have an "investor relations" section on their website. This is where annual reports are normally found as well as up-to-date financial information. Most major companies offer a translation service.

Using a webcast for the annual general meeting (AGM) or a

statement from the chief executive officer (CEO) is becoming standard practice, particularly with regard to institutional investors and analysts. Expect corporate communications to continue to become more interactive.

The media

Newspapers, journals, magazines, TV and radio, and professional or trade publications provide further information that may help interpret the facts given in the annual report or on developments since the report was published. Media reports may provide technical analysis of the company, its current and likely future markets and operating environment, or they may give more qualitative impressions with reports of lawsuits or gossip-column pieces about directors. However, bear in mind that Enron was "America's most innovative company" between 1996 and 2001 according to *Fortune*, and in 2000 was voted "energy company of the year" by the *Financial Times*.

The importance companies attach to their websites as a means of communication continues to grow. Xerox was one of the first companies to publish its interim statements online rather than mailing them to shareholders, saving some $100,000 per year. A company's website should be the first place you look to see what information is available.

The annual report: appearance may matter

Even though a hard copy of the annual report is becoming less important, it should not be underestimated as a visual presentation of a company and its directors. A dull report may indicate a dull company; a glitzy report may indicate a company too concerned with impressive presentation, perhaps in order to disguise poor performance – "never mind the quality, feel the width". How a company uses its website is also a good indicator of management's clarity and transparency of communication and presentation.

Photo opportunity for the board

The way in which the board is presented reflects the changing trends in corporate reporting. Before the internet took over, the printed annual report was the keystone of corporate communication. From the 1960s to the mid-1970s, reports often contained the classic "oil painting" profile of the chairman gazing into the far distance thinking deep strategic thoughts, showing that the company was led by a tough but fair father figure. There was little detail, beyond the statutory minimum, of the other directors.

In the late 1970s, it became important for the board to be seen to be managing the company as a team. It was recognised that a team was needed to support a dynamic leader to ensure success. The result was often a photograph of the CEO sitting in the boardroom surrounded by all the other directors (standing). Positive statements were made concerning the diversification policy the board was adopting.

The mid-1980s showed directors actively running the business. They were depicted walking around a shop or factory and talking to employees. Typically, the director was named and looking at the camera, while the employee was anonymous and stacking a shelf or working a machine. The annual report explained the importance of unbundling or restructuring the group.

By the end of the 1980s, with the growth in empowerment of employees, annual reports increasingly included photographs of employees working alone or in happy groups, with no directors in sight. The board was once more relegated to a single page in the annual report. Directors were faceless but beginning to expand their personal horizons. Their prime duty remained that of running a successful company, but they also made sure that their personal rewards and compensation were attractive. The fat cats were there but not yet visible.

In the early 1990s, as corporate websites were developed, directors were back as a group at the boardroom table or a selected site, not necessarily doing anything but looking quietly confident and in control. It was often difficult to identify the leader.

In the early 2000s more emphasis was placed on corporate responsibility, ethical practices and environmental reporting, with the company website quickly gaining a prime position. The terms "global", "value", "environmental issues" and "sustainable development" became common. Today there is more emphasis on the non-financial aspects of a company and narrative or integrated reporting. Shareholders need not only the figures but also some help in understanding how they were arrived at – what is behind them. For UK companies, the strategic report has replaced the operating and financial review (OFR) and business review as a forward-looking analysis of strategy and the key issues seen by a company as significant for its success. This is the equivalent of the management discussion and analysis (MD&A) statement for US listed companies.

Narrative and integrated reporting

One significant trend of the 2010s is towards increased narrative and integrated reporting. Companies are trying to find ways to successfully blend qualitative and quantitative information. In 2013 the International Integrated Reporting Council (IRRC) defined an integrated report (IR) as "a concise communication about how an organisation's strategy, governance, performance and prospects, in the context of its external environment, lead to the creation of value in the short, medium and long term".

Companies are being encouraged to improve their narrative reporting ("telling the story"), providing reasons and explaining decisions taken to support the financial statements. The primary purpose is to explain to providers of capital how a company creates value over time. Examples of IRs can be found at www.theiirc.org.

Narrative reporting aims to provide information on and insight into a company's objectives and strategies to allow its performance and position as set out in the financial statements to be better understood. It describes the non-financial information included in the annual report.

In 2012 the UK Department for Business, Innovation & Skills published *The Future of Narrative Reporting*, which for UK listed companies replaced the business review in the annual report with the strategic report. The 2013 (Strategic Report and Directors' Report) Regulations amended the 2006 Companies Act. This forms the core for company narrative reporting in their annual reports. In 2013 the FRC published *Guidance on the Strategic Report*, where it stated:

> *The overriding objective of narrative reporting is to provide information on the entity, insight into its main objectives and*

*strategies, the principal risks it faces and to complement, supplement
and provide context for the related financial statements.*

Corporate governance

Corporate governance embraces not only the way in which a company
is managed and its dealings with shareholders but also every aspect of
its relationship with society. Emphasis on corporate governance was
stimulated partly by apparent fraud and mismanagement in some
major UK and US companies and partly by the increase in corporate
failure rates during the recession years of the 1980s and early 1990s.
Shareholders and others dealing with a company wanted assurance
that it was being well and correctly managed. In 1992 the Cadbury
Committee established a code of best practice for UK companies. It
contained 19 points and required that the reasons for non-compliance
with any of these should be given in the annual report. Several other
committees followed, leading to the publication of the Combined
Code in 1998 and its revision by the FRC in 2003 – "The principles
on which the Code is based are those of openness, integrity
and accountability". In 2006 the Combined Code on Corporate
Governance (the Code) was issued and is now mandatory for all
listed companies (see Chapter 1), which must "comply or explain".

The OECD published *Principles of Corporate Governance* and in
2003 the European Commission issued *Modernising Company Law
and Enhancing Corporate Governance in the EU – A Plan to Move
Forward*. In the US, following the collapse of Enron and WorldCom,
the Public Accounting Reform and Investor Protection Act – normally
referred to as the Sarbanes-Oxley Act – was passed to improve investor
confidence and encourage full and transparent corporate reporting.
Section 302 requires senior management to certify the accuracy of the
financial statements and (Section 404) report on the adequacy of their
internal control systems.

The corporate governance report should provide the necessary
information to show how the mix and organisation of a company's
governance structures support the achievement of its objectives:

*To provide information that enables the assessment of whether the
entity has the right governance to execute its strategies and evaluate*

whether executive remuneration plans efficiently incentivise delivery of those strategies.

The board and its roles

The prime role of the board is to satisfy the company's shareholders through the successful implementation of the chosen corporate strategy. Ideally, the annual report should contain an organisation chart to show the reporting lines and areas of individual authority and responsibility. At least the direct business responsibilities of each member of the board should be identified. The board has three important committees that provide reports for inclusion in the annual report: audit, remuneration and nomination.

Audit committee

To comply with best practice, a listed company must have an audit committee made up of independent and reasonably financially acute non-executive directors. Details of its membership and duties will be found in the annual report.

The Sarbanes-Oxley Act in the US emphasised the importance of the audit committee, expanding its role to include responsibility for not only the proper treatment of employees' whistle-blowing but also all other internal and external complaints concerning financial matters. At least one member should be competent in finance. The Public Company Accounting Oversight Board (PCAOB) was set up in 2003 to work with the SEC to oversee the auditing of all US listed companies and to support the development of auditing standards.

The audit committee is responsible for overseeing a company's internal control systems, monitoring the integrity of the financial statements and dealing with every aspect of the auditor's work with the company. The audit committee's report should contain details of what are considered to be the main risks the company has faced during the year in relation to strategy and operations, and what might undermine its long-term viability. This, the FRC says, is to "improve the overall transparency of the reporting process and the accountability of all those involved in the financial reporting chain". A report from the audit committee should be on the agenda of the AGM and appear in the annual report.

Most companies have their own internal audit function, linked to but separate from the work of the external auditors, which should report directly to the audit committee. Internal audit is to ensure that all employees maintain and follow company procedures and systems. Best practice in corporate governance places an obligation on directors to ensure that all appropriate internal controls are applied, all assets are safeguarded, accurate accounting records are maintained, and that company risk is at an acceptable level.

Remuneration committee

Every public company should have a committee to oversee remuneration and terms and conditions for all executive directors, including the CEO and chairman. Best practice requires that its members are non-executive directors. The fact that directors' remuneration has been set by the committee should be recorded in the annual report. It is usual for the committee also to oversee the employment terms and remuneration of all senior staff, thus making sure that these are not solely dependent on the whim of the CEO. The intention is to have a transparent and consistent remuneration policy.

Nomination committee

The nomination committee leads the search for new board members, both executive and non-executive. If the committee has relied on an external recruitment or head-hunting firm, details should be provided. The process adopted to recruit directors and how this fits with the company's policy on diversity and gender should be explained.

Chairman's statement

The main task of a company chairman is to run the board and its committees, allowing the CEO to concentrate on running the business. For this to work there must be a good working relationship with the CEO and executive and non-executive directors. The development of good two-way communication with all company stakeholders is also expected. The chairman oversees the composition of the board and succession planning is an important role, particularly as the tenure of CEOs continues to reduce. The chairman is expected to provide good leadership in the process of achieving the company's objectives.

In their statements to shareholders, chairmen are free to make any comments and take any view they wish. They are not constrained by legislation, or accounting standards or even a code of best practice. The statement was originally intended to be a personal comment on the year by the chairman to shareholders. The auditors can probably be relied on to make sure that nothing too bizarre is included.

Investors read this section of the annual report carefully. Indeed, it is often the only section they read, perhaps in the naive expectation of an objective overview of a company's performance and position. Chairmen are well aware of this, so it is not unusual for their statements to concentrate on good news rather than the less positive aspects of the business. Some are little more than public relations statements: high on presentation and low on content.

The quality of a chairman's statement is a useful guide to the quality of the individual charged with leading the company's strategic thinking and managing the workings of the board. With the acceptance of corporate governance, there are signs of improvement and standardisation in chairmen's statements. However, there is a danger that in the process we will lose the chance to gain insight into the personal views of these key individuals.

Relationship with the City

Successful companies may run into difficulties because they fail to establish a good relationship with the financial institutions providing them with capital. This is most often seen with small, rapid-growth companies in the years immediately following their listing. A successful entrepreneur is not always best suited to dealing with institutional investors, who expect to be kept fully aware of what is going on. In the UK, guidance for institutional investors in their relationship with companies is provided in the FRC's 2012 UK Stewardship Code. The chairman normally takes the lead in shareholder communication and in maintaining a productive working relationship with any institutional shareholders.

The annual report lists a company's bankers and financial and legal advisers. Changes in the year of auditors, bankers, solicitors and advisers must be taken as negative indicators unless a clear and unambiguous explanation is given in the annual report.

Who are the directors and how good are they?

The annual report should contain sufficient information on directors to enable an assessment to be made of their competence and experience. At least each director's age and length of service should be recorded. A simple aid to assessing the board is to calculate the average age of the directors. If it is the late 50s for executive directors and over 60 for non-executive directors, the board may be getting past its sell-by date, with directors more concerned with serving their time than the shareholders' interests.

Financial analysts assess companies in three main ways: by studying the financial statements to discover underlying strengths and expose weaknesses; through general background research into the business sector and its future; and by visiting the company and talking to the executive team. Face-to-face meetings are extremely important; if senior management fails to inspire confidence support for the company will drop, even if there was a record profit in the previous year.

Non-executive directors

The role of non-executive directors (NEDs) is seen as increasingly important. They can provide a wealth of experience brought from other business sectors and companies, but their principal benefit should be independence of thought, view and personal income. They are not full-time employees of the company and so do not rely on it to maintain their standard of living. This places them in a powerful position to reinforce the stewardship role of the board and to act on its various committees. A non-executive director who is a customer, a supplier or a friend of the family, or whose only source of income is the directorship, is unlikely to fulfil the independence requirement.

In much of Europe, however, there is a two-tier board structure. Large companies in the Netherlands and Germany usually have a supervisory board made up of representatives of shareholders and employees. In France some companies have two-tier boards, but the majority have a single board with two-thirds of its members being non-executive. Best practice in the UK requires at least half of the board to be made up of NEDs to enable them to exert an independent influence on the direction of the company. NEDs are not expected to be on the board for more than six years; three years is a more common tenure. They are at the core of effective corporate governance. They are not involved in the day-to-day running of the business and should be ideal independent members of a company's main committees, such as the audit and remuneration committees. In 2011 Deloitte found that the average number of NEDs in major UK companies was three.

Directors' remuneration

Although money is not everything, it is clear that remuneration plays a crucial role in the motivation and retention of high-performing directors. Directors responsible for several billion dollars-worth of assets and thousands of jobs rightly expect substantial rewards. It is generally accepted that reward should be directly linked to performance, and that a significant proportion of a director's remuneration package should be performance related. The aim is to provide a match between directors' and shareholders' interests.

Managing an executive remuneration policy is a considerable undertaking. It is the acid test of the quality of the non-executive directors. The remuneration committee should make sure that there is a defensible policy, and where directors' remuneration is increasing out of step with company performance there should be an explanation.

When a company makes a loan to a director or executive (or any member of their close family) this should be disclosed in the annual report as a "related-party transaction" (IAS 24). The details should include not just the year-end balance but also the highest level of the loan during the year. This avoids the situation, sometimes referred to as "window dressing", where a director borrows money from a company and, each year, repays it just for the balance sheet day – no loan appears in the financial statements. It is always worth reading the related-party transactions details provided in an annual report.

Are they worth it?

The annual report provides details of company policy on executive directors' remuneration and the total remuneration and taxable benefits paid to each named directors is disclosed, together with details of their service contracts with and shareholdings in the company. These details can be compared with those of similar-sized companies to assess their generosity. Year-on-year changes can be set against the rate of inflation, the change in average wage rates, or growth in the company's turnover or profit to provide a benchmark to decide whether the cost of the board appears reasonable. Don't forget to include any dividends being paid to directors on their shareholding in arriving at their total package.

In the UK, it is unacceptable for directors to have, without shareholders' agreement, service contracts of more than three years. Most listed-company directors are put forward for re-election at the AGM.

Changes on the board

To be effective, directors must develop a set of individual and group working relationships to support their function as the top management team. Changes in the team are inevitable through retirement, accident, illness or career opportunity. However, it is reasonable to expect that any company has a core of experienced directors continuing to run the business from year to year.

Changes on the board can be a sign of existing and potential problems. The annual report provides a list of directors which can be compared with the previous year to see changes. Unfortunately, there is no requirement to provide the equivalent of comparative figures for directors, so it is often necessary to refer to the previous report. However, it is possible for someone to join and leave the board during the year and for this not to be noted in the annual report. Keep an eye on the company's website where any moves on the board will be reported.

There should be a statement giving the reasons for board changes (most often these will be for retirement or career moves). A popular euphemism to disguise board conflict and disagreement is a director leaving "to pursue other interests". A continually changing board should be taken as an indicator that all is not well with the company. It can be assumed there are potentially destructive tensions at the top of the organisation that will not improve confidence in its future prospects.

A good warning sign is a continuing turnover in directors. As a general rule, where more than 20% of a board is seen to change in consecutive years, the company should be treated with caution. Particular significance should be attached to a group of directors leaving at the same time, such as all the non-executive directors resigning. Although the reasons may not be made public, history suggests it is prudent to assume the worst.

As a rough guide, the expected lifespan for the CEO of a major UK company appears to be about four years. The departure of the CEO is an important event for a company, and it should provide a quick and clear statement of the reasons for the CEO's departure. A warning signal flashed when the CEO of Enron resigned for "personal reasons"; but it was probably too late when Bernard Ebbers left WorldCom. If there is no statement, but there is adverse press comment on the CEO's departure, the apparent conflicting personal relationships of directors or the operation of the board, this should be taken as a convincing black mark against the company. If the directors cannot demonstrate that they are working as a team and are in control, you should sell.

One person, two jobs

It can be argued that every company needs someone, particularly in its early growth period, in firm control offering effective leadership and direction. As a company grows and becomes a more complex organisation, it becomes more difficult if not impossible for one person to manage single-handed. There is eminent sense behind the separation of the roles of chairman and CEO, and this is required by the UK Code.

Sainsbury's, until the mid-1990s the UK's foremost food retailer, provides an example of the potential problems that can arise. In 1996, after profits fell for the first time in the company's history, there was immediate media comment. The *Times* (May 6th 1996) ran a headline

"Sainsbury's decline is blamed on arrogance and complacency" and drew attention to the fact that David Sainsbury was both chairman and CEO. In 1998 the final act took place, with the Sainsbury family being separated from the management of the company. Marks & Spencer, another major UK retailer, suffered similar problems in the late 1990s, with board conflict becoming public followed by a dramatic decline in profits and share price.

The combination of an entrepreneur and a non-participating board is usually fatal in the longer term. Companies may have their powerful personalities or leaders, but to ensure continued success they must be supported by an experienced and competent team of managers. The UK Code firmly states: "The roles of chairman and chief executive should not be exercised by the same individual."

Follow the finance director

The finance director, as head of the finance function, not only keeps the books but also plays a crucial role in ensuring good communications with all investor groups. The finance director must keep them abreast of the business and maintain their confidence in it. Nearly 20% of UK and US listed companies' directors are female; in 2013 there were nine female finance directors of FTSE 100 companies. A 2014 survey by *Finance Director* (www.financedirector.co.uk) found that the average earnings of a FTSE 100 finance director was £1.1m.

A sound working partnership between the CEO and the finance director or chief financial officer (CFO) is fundamental to the successful management of any company. The CEO of Enron pledged his "unequivocal trust" in his CFO the day before the collapse.

The departure of a finance director, other than for normal retirement or a non-contentious career move, is an important event. The finance director of Northern Rock, a UK bank that had to be bailed out by the government following the 2008 financial crisis, retired in January 2007. Try to discover the reasons for the departure and details of who is going to take over the job. The sudden departure of a finance director with 3–5 years' service, to be replaced by either the chief accountant with 20 years' service or the auditor, has in the past proved a firm warning signal.

Corporate strategy

Corporate strategy encompasses a planned approach to the achievement of defined objectives: knowing where you want to go and how to get there. The objectives or goals are the "ends" or the "where" and the strategy is the "means" or the "how" of successful implementation.

Every major company must have a strategy that is recognised and embraced by the board and ideally communicated to shareholders and accepted by all employees who are actively involved and participate in its development. The annual report should provide sufficient information in the strategic report to identify what the company's strategy is and how successfully it has been implemented. If you cannot gain a reasonable understanding of a company's objectives, you must assume that it is rudderless and adrift; it will either hit the rocks or someone competent will take the helm.

Going for growth

Growth is often seen as the best measure of corporate success. A company growing at a rate of 15% per year is doubling in size every five years. Rapid-growth companies can be defined as those with annual growth rates of 20% or more, and super-growth companies show a compound growth rate of around 40% per year.

Market share information can provide valuable support to the analysis and interpretation of changes in a company's turnover. The majority of companies provide turnover growth details in their annual report, but few offer any details of market share. Where turnover is known for several firms competing in the same market, it is possible to devise a simple alternative to market share information. Data on four competing companies are as follows:

	A		**B**		**C**		**D**		**Total**	
Year	1	2	1	2	1	2	1	2	1	2
Sales ($bn)	2.5	2.9	16.0	16.3	5.9	5.5	17.2	18.8	41.6	43.5
Share (%)	6	7	39	37	14	13	41	43	100	100

How their share of the joint total market changes can readily be seen. If this is done for a number of years, the analysis can form the basis for a performance comparison.

A common view is that a rapid-growth company is a safe and sound investment. However, evidence suggests that rapid growth cannot always be sustained. There are of course exceptions, but it is probably safer to assume that rapid growth, particularly if associated with diversification, will not continue. If high compound growth rates are matched by increasing debt financing, extreme caution is called for.

For some companies, turnover growth is seen as the prime objective and measure of success, even when it is being achieved at the cost of profitability. In the late 1990s, e-business provided many extreme examples of this. Analysts decided to use a multiple of turnover as the basis for valuing internet companies. As soon as this became known, companies focused all their efforts on achieving the required numbers, and turnover growth became the only target. Inevitably, pressure to deliver turnover growth stimulated creativity. If a big discount was offered to customers to get them to buy the product or service, the full price was taken into the income statement and the discount lost in marketing expenses. The provision for bad debts could be reduced. A company acting as an agent to sell holidays might take the full price of the holiday into the income statement rather than just the commission due on the sale. A single payment made by customers for the use of an internet site for a number of years might be taken into the current year's sales figure. These practices are clearly contrary to GAAP, but they were adopted to boost apparent income growth.

Being pushed towards diversification to fuel continued growth is often the final challenge for the one-person company. Having proved itself in one business sector it moves into new areas, commonly through acquisition. More often than not its old skills prove not to be appropriate in the new business, attention is distracted from the core business, and it is viewed as having lost the golden touch. Its survival may depend on new management and financial restructuring.

When a one-person company's growth slows and criticism mounts, two scenarios may occur. In one, the individual running the company begins to take increasingly risky decisions in the hope of returning to previous levels of profit growth. In the other, recognising that there is little that can be done immediately to improve operating performance, the individual steps outside the law and accepted business practice to sustain his or her personal image and lifestyle. Often in these companies other executives are reluctant to rock the boat and go along with the deception; Cal Micro, an electronic devices company, in 1997 was a good example of these problems.

Single solution is no solution

If a company appears to have decided that it has found a single, simple solution to its strategic problems, the likelihood is that it has not. Single solutions are often attractive, but they represent companies putting all their eggs in one basket. If the single solution does not provide the answer, there is nowhere else to go.

Potentially ambitious schemes that may take up valuable management time and attention and have adverse effects on other areas of the business include product development, new technology, acquisitions, diversification and high-value contracts.

Acquisition is often seen as a good solution to company problems. The operating profits flowing from acquisitions made during the year will improve apparent profitability with no compensating increase in costs. However, when acquisitions are clearly outside a company's proven area of competence, bringing about rapid and major diversification, the problems are compounded. Managing businesses in new markets or overseas can speed decline, even though the acquisition may improve reported profitability in the year in which it takes place.

When a substantial acquisition represents a major diversification, experience in both the UK and the US supports the view that the risk of the company failing has increased substantially. Diversification involves new areas of activity that have to be experienced and mastered before positive returns are generated.

Where to look for a strategy

The first place to look for some explanation of a company's strategy and objectives is the strategic report (see below) or the MD&A statement.

For many years *Forbes* magazine has published a list of the companies it believes are the best corporate citizens in the US.

They are assessed under seven headings: environment, climate change, employee relations, human rights, governance, finance and philanthropy. This list provides a good skeleton for any company's annual report. The seven headings can also act as a checklist for analysing a company's performance and comparing it with others in the same business sector.

Until 2013 UK companies followed the 2006 Companies Act provisions, and the directors' report, business review or the OFR were presented to assist in interpreting the financial statements and give additional non-financial information to users of the annual report. From October 2013 the strategic report, "which will be presented as a separate section of the annual report, outside the directors' report", became the prime vehicle for the delivery of such information.

The strategic report

The strategic report is intended to "provide shareholders of the company with the ability to assess how the directors have performed their duty to promote the success of the company for their collective benefit". All material information should be disclosed in the report, which should include:

- fair review of the company and its businesses;
- description of the company's strategy and strategic context;
- business model;
- description of the principal risks and uncertainties faced;
- chairman's and CEO's statement;
- balanced and comprehensive financial review of the year, development and performance during the year, and the company's position at the year end;
- three- or five-year historical financial record;
- key performance indicators used by the company;
- the main trends and factors likely to affect the company's future development, performance and position;
- information on environmental matters;

■ details of employee numbers, and the number of male and female directors and other senior managers.

All the above are self-explanatory except, perhaps, the business model requirement. A company's business model should define and explain how it "generates or preserves value, and how it captures that value". The Chartered Institute of Management Accountants (CIMA) provides a clear definition of a business model: "the chosen system of inputs, business activities, outputs and outcomes that aims to create value over the short, medium and long term".

There should be information to allow an understanding of how the company is structured and organised. The markets in which the company competes should be described – reference may be made to its position in the value chain – together with its main products, services, customers and distribution methods. The intention is to show how the company takes the inputs for its operations and generates outputs that create value and contribute to its strategic objectives.

Key performance indicators

Where appropriate reference should be made to any key performance indicators (KPIs) that the directors use in measuring their success in achieving their objectives. KPIs are defined as "factors by reference to which the development, performance or position of the company's business can be measured effectively". Ideally, these will be measures common to a company's business sector. Make sure you look at this section of the strategic report before starting any in-depth analysis of the company. You may find some useful ratios to include in your assessment. There may also be an independent assurance report from the auditors that gives confidence in using the information being supplied, such as "nothing has come to our attention that causes us to believe that the selected subject matter for the year ended 31st December 2013 has not been prepared, in all material respects, in accordance with the reporting criteria".

The strategic report should give details of developments that are likely to affect future profitability, such as the launch of a new product, a major capital investment programme or planned acquisitions and disposals.

Corporate social responsibility

Companies have corporate social responsibility (CSR) and can be expected to report on this. The 2006 UK Companies Act requires information to be disclosed on the impact of a company's business on the environment and social and community issues. The term "intrapreneurship" is often used to describe a positive approach to the working relationship with employees.

Sustainability

This is a key word for CEOs and chairmen when composing their annual statements, as it shows that they are not endangering the future environment for short-term profit. A good example of a company giving emphasis to sustainability is Walmart (www.walmart.com). In 2009 it issued a sustainability index for every product sold and required all its suppliers to give attention to sustainability. A saving of some $3 billion per year resulted from reduced packaging. In 2013 it published a *Global Responsibility Report*, which is similar to the integrated reports covered below.

There are, as yet, no standards on social or environmental reporting. The SEC requires companies to detail their environmental expenditure and the EU calls for a discussion of the environmental issues relevant to a company's operations.

Environmental reporting

Companies can now be expected to provide details of their environmental policies and activity. Typically this will include information on environmental policies, initiatives and improvements on previous years, key risks and how the company is responding, compliance with legislation, environmental expenditure and KPIs, ideally with industry benchmarks for comparison.

The integrated report

Flowing from Accounting for Sustainability (A4S), the IIRC was set up in 2010 and in 2013 published the *Integrated Reporting Framework*. The intention is to redirect attention from short-term earnings to the key drivers of corporate business value. The IIRC makes an annual award for sustainability corporate reporting. Marks & Spencer in its annual report presents its aim to be the most sustainable retailer in the world. It is already carbon neutral, contributing zero waste to landfill, and claimed a directly related bottom-line improvement of over £100m in 2013 when it was a highly commended finalist in the competition.

Integrated reporting may well be the future direction for the annual report. An integrated report tries to explain a company's ability to create value today, tomorrow and in the long-term. This is a useful basis for shareholders and other capital providers to understand not only what a company does but also how it does it and what it thinks the future holds. It is worth keeping an eye on the IIRC website (www.iirc.org) to monitor progress and see examples of companies developing an integrated framework.

Risk disclosure

There should also be discussion of the major risks and uncertainties facing the company and how these are being dealt with. Risk relates to future events that are quantifiable. Uncertainties are future events that are indeterminate and non-quantifiable. In the 1990s companies began to move from simple risk analysis to more proactive risk management.

The 1999 UK Turnbull Report recommended that companies should disclose their risk management practices. IFRS 7 deals with the risks associated with financial instruments (see Chapter 2). The main classes of risk are identified as:

- market risk – exchange rate, interest rate, or other price movements;
- liquidity risk – possible problems in making cash available;
- credit risk – customers fail to pay.

The intention is that where a company has "obligations ... to transfer economic benefits as a result of past transactions or events" this is fully disclosed in the annual report. It does not matter how the obligation was incurred or whether it is wrapped up in a complex financial instrument or accounting jargon. If there is an existing or potential liability, you need to know about this in order to properly assess the company.

The 10-K report is similar to the strategic report in offering a useful source of information on a company's risk profile. Item 1A, "Risk Factors", provides some insight into management's view of the risks seen to be facing the business. The risk factors are normally listed in order of significance. These may be related to a country's economy, or a company's industry or geographic location. Market risk – including interest rates, foreign exchange and commodity price risk – is dealt with in Item 7A, "Quantitative and Qualitative Disclosures about Market Risk".

"New" measure of risk

An alternative approach to company risk assessment has been offered. It is suggested that the number of times the word "new" appears in the annual report may provide a measure of risk.

Success or failure?

Future profit overrides current liquidity

The various ways of measuring profitability and liquidity were discussed in Chapters 6 and 8. Ideally, a company can be expected to focus on two principal objectives. The first is to provide an acceptable and continuing rate of return to investors, and the second is to maintain an adequate level of financial resources to support current and planned future operations and growth. A company can survive without profit as long as it has access to cash. A profitable company with no cash faces difficulties. No company can survive for more than a few days with neither profit nor cash.

A truism is that a profitable company is less likely to fail than an unprofitable one. The overriding factor in deciding whether to allow a company to continue in business is its profit potential, which is more important than its current liquidity. A company with low liquidity and a high profit potential will almost certainly be helped to overcome what may be regarded as a temporary problem. A highly liquid company with declining or no profit potential is unlikely to survive for long. Why should investors leave their funds to dwindle? The only decision facing such a company is whether to end operations immediately or to continue and see liquidity and profitability decline until matters are taken out of management's hands.

Creative accounting and failure

All companies can be expected to apply creative accounting techniques to some degree. For most companies, all the necessary detail and support information is set out in the annual report, but it is unrealistic to expect attention to be drawn as clearly to problems as to good news items. To some extent annual reporting is an art form, but there are clear rules that must be followed. Breaking the rules is not an act of creativity but of misrepresentation and possibly fraud. In 1987 the National Commission on Fraudulent Financial Reporting, the Treadway Commission, defined fraud as "intentional or reckless conduct, whether by act or omission, that results in materially misleading financial statements".

Creative accounting is not a cause of corporate failure, but it makes it more difficult for users of a company's financial statements to appreciate the underlying performance or financial position of the business. The question then is why the company thinks it necessary to adopt this approach. If the operations and finances of a company are so complex that you cannot fully understand them, walk away. If the terminology is incomprehensible, take this as a firm negative point.

Enron imploded with some $3 billion liabilities described as "special purpose entities", which enabled it to remove debt from its balance sheet and shuffle assets to create fictitious profits. Profits were overstated by $1 billion in 2001. A major frustration in the US, resulting in the Sarbanes-Oxley Act, was that although much of Enron's accounting was aggressive or creative, it was not necessarily illegal. A creative finance director may be justly rewarded; a fraudulent finance director should be imprisoned.

Any changes in accounting policy should always be examined carefully; this is particularly important when warning signals relating to the company have been picked up elsewhere. Is the change appropriate and rational, or is it made in order to give the year's profit a boost? Changes in depreciation policy, inventory valuation, use of provisions, capitalising expenses, and treatment of extraordinary and exceptional events can all indicate a desperation to improve profits rather than provide a true and fair view (see Chapter 3).

Credit rating

It is better to have several compatible measures than to rely on a single one in the assessment of a company. An early approach was to select a set of ratios considered to be good indicators of financial position and weight each of them to produce an index that would act as an overall credit assessment rating.

Ratio	Weight
Liquid ratio	15
ROTA	15
Interest cover	30
Cash flow/debt	20
Sales/inventory	10
Equity/debt	10
	100

Each ratio was calculated and then multiplied by the assigned weight, the results totalled and the index for the company produced. This was then compared with an average or standard for the business sector or type of company to provide a comparative credit rating. The higher the score of the company the better was its credit rating.

This approach is still valid. It does not require substantial computer resources or high statistical competence; it can be completed on the basis of experience or personal view of a sector or type of company. It is a straightforward task to select a set of ratios that are considered to be good indicators of performance or position for companies operating in the business sector, to weight them according to their importance, to combine them and to produce an overall index for each company. You should consider doing this as part of your analysis. Deciding which ratios to use for the companies that are appropriate for the type of business is a useful exercise in itself.

It is recommended that the ratios are kept to a maximum of five or six, and that each one can be directly and independently interpreted. The simplest form of weighting is to allow a total of 100 points and allocate these to each ratio according to its perceived importance. Each ratio can be calculated as a percentage, multiplied by its assigned weight and the results totalled to give an index.

It is simplest to select ratios where a high percentage rather than a low one indicates good performance or position; for this reason the equity/debt ratio is to be preferred to the debt/equity ratio.

	Equity/debt	Weight	Index
A	0.33	10	3.3
B	0.67	10	6.7
C	1.33	10	13.3

The result is a simple composite or multivariate index that can be used to compare companies. The benchmark index level can be that of the sector leader or the average or median of the sample companies.

Predicting failure

Directors must formally state in the annual report that they believe their company is a going concern. This statement most commonly appears in the strategic report. It is, however, sometimes hedged with reminders of the uncertainties of future events and the impossibility of guaranteeing continued operations. But at least it indicates that the directors think their company should survive the next year.

It is a truism that it is inadvisable to lend money to a company that is about to fail. The ability to predict corporate failure before the event has been the holy grail of financial analysis for more than 50 years. There is normally a few years' warning before a company fails; a sudden and unexpected collapse is unusual. Two companies that were apparently healthy one day and failed the next – Rolls-Royce in the UK and the Penn Central railway company in the US – stimulated research into whether it was possible to predict corporate failure. The first moves away from hindsight analysis were made in the late 1960s, when work in the US broke new ground in the development of the multivariate approach to failure prediction. It was similar to that described above for producing a credit rating index, but it made use of computer power and complex statistical analysis.

In 1966 William Beaver, an accounting researcher, claimed a link between failure and the ratio of operating cash flow to total debt. Total debt was defined as long-term and short-term borrowings appearing in the balance sheet. If the ratio was below 0.3, the company's future survival chances were low.

Z-score

In 1968 Edward Altman published his Z-score formula for predicting whether or a not a company would fail within the next two years. Five ratios were selected and weights assigned to produce a Z-score.

A = Net current assets ÷ total asset
B = Retained earnings ÷ total assets
C = Profit before interest and tax ÷ total assets
D = Capitalisation ÷ total debt
E = Sales ÷ total assets

Z = 0.012A + 0.014B + 0.033C + 0.006D + 0.999E

A Z-score below 1.8 was an indicator of probable failure, and a score of over 3 was seen as a clean bill of health. The model proved capable, for the sample companies, of predicting with an accuracy of 95% failure within one year and with an accuracy of over 70% failure within two years.

An advantage of this approach is that using a combination of several financial ratios makes it less likely that the result will be affected by manipulation of the financial statements. Each ratio attempts to provide a relevant measure of company performance or position and can be used independently as an indicator of financial viability. The greater the proportion of net current assets (working capital) compared with total assets the healthier is the short-term position. In the second ratio, retained earnings is the figure in the balance sheet representing the amount ploughed back from earnings to provide finance for the assets employed. The higher the figure the greater is the extent of the company's self-financing. In the third ratio, profit before interest and tax indicates the contribution of a company's profitability towards the end index score, profitable companies being less likely to fail than non-profitable ones. The fourth ratio brings market value (capitalisation) into the equation. The investors' view of the future potential of the company is set against total debt. This ratio represents the only figure – capitalisation – that is not guaranteed to appear in the annual report. The higher the ratio the more confidence the market has in the company's future and the lower its reliance on debt financing. The last ratio shows the ability of the company to use its assets to generate sales revenue. The higher the asset turnover the greater is the number of times cash from sales can be assumed to pass through the business each year. The higher the ratio the more productive are the assets and the greater is the amount of cash passing through the business.

In 1976 John Argenti published *Corporate Collapse: The Causes and Symptoms*. This identified non-quantitative indicators of "management weaknesses" and "accounting deficiencies" as signals of potential problems. Argenti's list still offers a useful basis for analysing a company from a qualitative viewpoint.

Since the 1970s, increasingly sophisticated and arcane models have been developed to aid the prediction of failure, and those undertaking the research have not always been prepared to share their findings or index weightings. Thus the rule "keep it simple" has been neglected, and many failure prediction techniques are beyond the comprehension of the average user. If you cannot understand why the ratios employed in the formula might be useful predictors do not attempt to use it.

F-score

Developed in 2000 by Joseph Piotroski, the F-score uses nine variables in three sections of analysis. One point is scored for each element passed.

- **Profitability** – net profit is positive; operating cash flow is positive; return on total assets is higher than the previous year; operating cash flow is greater than net profit (before extraordinary items).
- **Finance** – long-term debt/average assets is not increasing; current ratio has increased; no issue of ordinary equity.
- **Efficiency** – gross margin has improved over previous year; asset turnover has increased over previous year.

The aim is to highlight a company's potential for investors. A score of less than 2 indicates potential problems ahead – do not invest – while 8 or 9 predicts future success – buy. There is quite a body of support for the F-score.

M-score

In 1999 Messod Beneish published his original eight-ratio M-score as a means of detecting earnings manipulation. The eight ratios are compared with those of the previous year. Beneish later provided a five-ratio M-score by removing three of the less valuable indicators.

- DSRI – days' sales receivables index. Measures the number of days' sales held in receivables. A large increase could indicate manipulation.
- GMI – gross margin index. If this is above 1, the gross margin is declining. A company with poor prospects is more likely to be attracted to massaging profits.
- AQI – asset quality index. Measures non-current assets to total assets.
- SGI – sales growth index. May indicate possible pressure on the company to show growth.
- DEPI – depreciation index. Compares the current rate of depreciation with the previous year. An index of more than 1 suggests that the rate of depreciation is slowing. Is the company revising asset lives to improve apparent profitability?

$$M = 6.065 + 0.823DSRI + 0.906GMI + 0.593AQI + 0.717SGI + 0.107DEPI$$

A score greater than −1.78 provides a strong indication of income manipulation. It was claimed that the original M-score formula provided a success rate of 76% in identifying earnings manipulators.

Famous last words

Perhaps a more enjoyable, but possibly masochistic, pastime for the immediate future may be collecting the "last words" of chairmen and CEOs appearing in the media as they try to explain their disastrous performance and their company's collapse. As an example, an analyst neatly summed up his and the market's experience with the collapse of a UK bank as "at least we've learnt not to put a grocer in charge of a bank" (the bank's CEO had previously worked for a major food retailer). Charles Dickens created Mr Merdle, the swindling banker in *Little Dorrit*, an "illustrious man and great national ornament", who defrauded investors with a pyramid or Ponzi scheme. His last words were: "Could you lend me a penknife?" Some 150 years later Bernard Madoff, using exactly the same scam as Merdle but on a much greater scale, delivered the less memorable: "It's all just one big lie." The Methodist minister who was mistakenly put in charge of the Co-operative Bank in the UK scored well in 2013 with: "I did things that were stupid and wrong. I am sorry for this and I am seeking professional help." In July 2014 the CEO of Gowex, a Spanish Wi-Fi firm, resigned after admitting that he had manipulated the accounts for the past four years. Market value fell by $1 billion and the receivers were called in. His parting words were: "I apologise to all. I am heartily sorry." There will surely be more to collect.

Bill Mackey's list

A serious base to a light-hearted listing of possible indicators of corporate demise was provided by Bill Mackey, an insolvency expert working in the UK in the 1980s. These are my favourites – it is fun to bring the list up to date:

- Rolls-Royces with personalised number plates
- Fish tank or fountain in the reception area
- Flag pole
- Queen's Award to Industry (UK only)
- Chairman honoured for services to industry
- Salesman or engineer as CEO
- Recently moved into new offices
- Unqualified or elderly accountant
- Products are market leaders
- Audit partner grew up with the company
- Chairman is a politician or well known for charitable works
- Recently announced a huge order in Afghanistan (or equivalent)
- Satisfied personnel with no strike records
- Recently announced a technical breakthrough

Yes to three or more? Call the creditors together, you're broke!

Appendices

1   Useful benchmarks

Practical examples of ratio analysis

This section provides some useful examples of the application of ratio analysis. A number of reasonably representative benchmarks for five sectors and six countries are provided against which you can compare companies you are interested in. The ratios are, as far as possible, calculated from the 2011–13 financial statements of mature quoted companies with a track record of consistent performance in their sector.

	Construction	Food	Hotels	Pharmaceuticals	Retail
Operating profit %					
France	5.7	4.6	15.3	17.0	2.7
Germany	5.4	9.1	2.6	12.3	4.5
Italy	4.1	8.0	11.1	20.5	15.8
Netherlands	0.8	16.4	11.4	21.4	4.5
UK	8.1	5.1	15.6	24.5	5.5
US	4.7	19.5	23.9	31.3	6.2
Pre-tax profit %					
France	3.9	3.2	8.2	15.2	2.0
Germany	2.8	4.0	1.6	10.6	2.0
Italy	3.2	4.4	9.4	19.3	13.9
Netherlands	−1.6	14.4	7.7	18.7	3.5
UK	7.7	4.1	22.5	22.8	4.3
US	5.4	12.2	5.6	20.3	5.7

Sales/total assets

France	0.9	1.2	0.8	0.3	2.0
Germany	1.3	1.1	1.4	0.7	2.3
Italy	0.6	1.6	0.7	0.7	0.4
Netherlands	1.3	1.4	0.4	0.8	2.0
UK	1.3	1.4	0.3	0.6	1.4
US	1.8	1.0	0.9	0.4	2.5

Operating profit ROTA %

France	4.1	5.4	11.7	5.9	5.0
Germany	8.1	15.8	3.6	8.6	8.8
Italy	2.9	9.7	4.2	15.3	6.4
Netherlands	0.2	9.2	4.8	23.0	9.0
UK	7.0	7.4	5.1	15.2	7.5
US	9.9	17.7	12.8	9.5	12.6

Pre-tax profit ROTA %

France	3.1	3.8	6.3	5.3	3.7
Germany	3.0	4.1	2.2	7.5	3.9
Italy	2.3	5.2	7.1	14.4	5.6
Netherlands	−1.6	9.5	3.2	18.2	7.1
UK	6.8	6.0	6.5	14.3	6.0
US	8.0	10.7	5.5	6.4	12.1

Operating profit RONA %

France	24.4	16.6	29.9	10.1	12.1
Germany	20.1	62.3	23.7	21.4	20.9
Italy	9.1	22.3	0.6	26.5	13.1
Netherlands	5.0	22.9	6.1	5.3	22.8
UK	16.8	14.7	9.2	46.0	21.4
US	22.2	56.5	33.8	18.4	39.1

Pre-tax profit RONA %

France	22.9	7.6	15.9	9.1	9.5
Germany	10.4	7.9	14.1	18.7	9.5
Italy	7.2	5.3	8.9	25.0	11.6
Netherlands	−8.4	17.2	8.2	23.9	17.9
UK	19.8	12.0	11.5	37.8	17.0
US	18.0	27.3	11.9	12.2	38.8

After-tax profit ROE %

France	22.8	7.6	4.1	7.8	18.0
Germany	7.0	7.9	8.0	13.9	6.6
Italy	14.3	5.3	13.0	18.5	10.7
Netherlands	−7.2	17.2	6.7	9.5	16.1
UK	14.0	12.0	9.8	28.2	14.5
US	16.4	27.3	7.8	9.8	25.2

Liquid ratio

France	0.9	0.7	1.1	1.2	0.6
Germany	1.0	0.3	0.3	0.9	0.3
Italy	1.1	1.4	1.2	0.8	0.8
Netherlands	0.9	1.0	0.6	1.5	0.9
UK	0.9	0.8	1.1	1.3	0.5
US	1.2	0.8	0.8	1.6	0.4

Cash/current assets %

France	40	13	65	31	27
Germany	27	4	30	16	10
Italy	23	25	35	12	33
Netherlands	15	16	11	11	49
UK	26	18	38	26	17
US	36	17	19	27	17

Defensive interval days

France	116	22	182	242	28
Germany	49	11	56	88	9
Italy	231	53	115	53	171
Netherlands	37	27	16	16	42
UK	44	27	194	314	11
US	56	28	40	138	17

Current liquidity ratio days

France	758	920	135	−30	1327
Germany	204	408	1311	477	1278
Italy	681	429	−164	204	421
Netherlands	163	317	130	130	181
UK	−513	316	−175	106	823
US	312	232	448	58	1020

Sales/cash

France	4	45	3	5	24
Germany	10	417	7	15	62
Italy	6	14	15	20	6
Netherlands	17	14	25	25	12
UK	12	36	23	3	34
US	9	31	39	5	92

Cash flow/sales

France	6	5	14	22	4
Germany	5	4	5	16	3
Italy	10	10	9	18	16
Netherlands	3	15	7	7	7
UK	66	6	20	27	7
US	3	10	10	24	4

Net current asset/sales %

France	−1	9	6	28	−3
Germany	11	0	−27	8	−2
Italy	28	2	2	8	7
Netherlands	5	16	−10	−10	3
UK	24	7	23	22	1
US	25	6	0	54	3

Days' inventory

France	12	42	4	210	42
Germany	46	117	3	147	87
Italy	53	35	14	157	174
Netherlands	57	59	79	79	23
UK	116	56	15	190	27
US	24	67	19	114	61

Days' receivables

France	94	45	26	77	11
Germany	55	26	38	75	7
Italy	118	46	42	69	36
Netherlands	66	47	42	42	9
UK	61	37	38	84	19
US	45	29	36	5	5

Days' payables

France	115	55	57	102	49
Germany	73	46	70	139	57
Italy	270	115	22	126	71
Netherlands	130	49	157	157	23
UK	92	67	70	517	64
US	43	45	63	113	47

Cash cycle days

France	−9	32	−27	185	5
Germany	28	97	−30	83	37
Italy	−98	−34	34	100	139
Netherlands	−8	57	−36	−36	9
UK	86	26	−17	−243	−18
US	26	51	−7	5	19

Interest cover

France	20	3	6	8	4
Germany	5	11	1	1	5
Italy	1	4	12	16	8
Netherlands	−3	11	3	22	4
UK	9	13	12	13	4
US	30	6	5	34	13

Equity/total assets %

France	16	33	39	58	17
Germany	38	32	15	42	37
Italy	33	21	46	58	49
Netherlands	22	47	39	47	40
UK	36	44	52	40	36
US	45	33	19	52	33

Debt/total assets %

France	25	24	26	28	34
Germany	22	24	28	23	11
Italy	16	21	19	17	33
Netherlands	20	20	40	28	31
UK	22	26	26	33	34
US	22	46	56	30	33

Current liabilities/total assets %

France	59	43	35	14	49
Germany	40	44	56	35	52
Italy	50	28	35	25	19
Netherlands	58	33	21	25	29
UK	42	30	22	27	30
US	33	21	25	18	34

Sales/employee $'000

France	290	284	363	303	268
Germany	377	394	339	1471	221
Italy	335	323	284	406	422
Netherlands	407	399	222	403	250
UK	543	329	128	730	281
US	728	449	346	425	372

Operating profit/employee $'000

France	11	12	13	51	8
Germany	34	38	9	199	8
Italy	16	25	17	54	57
Netherlands	4	29	13	21	11
UK	58	16	21	167	15
US	32	100	56	135	15

2 Glossary

English	French	German	Italian
assets	actif	Aktiva	attivitá
balance sheet	bilan	Bilanz	bilancio
cash and bank balances	trésorerie, disponibilités, caisse	Kassenbestand Liquide Mittel	cassa e banche
cost of sales	coût des ventes	Herstellungskoten	costo del venduto
current assets	actif circulant	Umlaufvermögen	attivitá correnti
current liabilities	dettes à court terme	Kurzfristige Verbinlichkeiten	passivitá correnti
depreciation	amortissement	Abschreibung	ammortamenti
earnings per share	bénéfice par action	Ergebnis je Aktie	utile per azione
going concern	continuité	Unternehmens- fortführung	continuitá operativa aziendale
goodwill	écart d'acquisition, survaleur	Geschäftswert	valore di avviamento
income statement	compte de résultat	Gewinn- und Verlustrechnung	conto economico, conto profitti e perdite
intangible assets	actif incorporel	immaterielles	attivitá immateriali
inventory	stocks	Vorräte	inventario
liabilities	passif, dettes	Passiva	passivitá
non-current assets	actifs non courants	Langfristige Vermögensgegenstände	attivitá non correnti
profit	bénéfice	Betriebsergebnis	utile
public company	Société Anonyme (SA)	Aktiengesellschaft (AG)	societa per azioni (SpA)
sales revenue	ventes, produits, chiffre d'affaires	Umsatzerlöse	vendite
shareholders' funds	capitaux propres	Eigenkapital	patrimonio netto
trade payables	dettes fournisseurs	Verbindlichkeiten	altri debiti, fornitori
trade receivables	créances	Forderungen	crediti

3 Abbreviations and acronyms

ADC	average daily costs
ADS	average daily sales
AICPA	American Institute of Certified Public Accountants
APB	Accounting Principles Board
ASAF	Accounting Standards Advisory Forum
CAPM	capital asset pricing model
CDO	collateralised debt obligation
CFROA	cash flow return on assets
CFROI	cash flow rate of return on investment
CODM	chief operational decision-maker
CON	Concept Statement (US GAAP)
CPA	certified public accountant
CSR	corporate social responsibility
DCF	discounted cash flow
DPS	dividend per share
EBIT	earnings before interest and taxation
EBITDA	earnings before interest, taxation, depreciation and amortisation
EFRAG	European Financial Reporting Advisory Group (EU)
EITF	Emerging Issues Task Force
EPS	earnings per share
EV	economic value
FAS	Financial Accounting Standard (US)
FASB	Financial Accounting Standards Board (US)
FCA	Financial Conduct Authority (UK)
FIFO	first-in-first-out (inventory)

FRC	Financial Reporting Council (UK)
FRS	Financial Reporting Standard
FRSSE	Financial Reporting Standard for Smaller Entities
FSA	Financial Services Authority
FTE	full-time equivalent (employees)
GAAP	generally accepted accounting principles
IAASB	International Auditing and Assurance Standards Board
IAPC	International Auditing Practices Committee
IAPS	International Auditing Practice Statement
IAS	International Accounting Standards
IASB	International Accounting Standards Board
ICAEW	Institute of Chartered Accountants in England and Wales
IFAC	International Federation of Accountants
IFRIC	IFRS Interpretations Committee (IASB)
IFRS	International Financial Reporting Standard
IIRC	International Integrated Reporting Council
IOSCO	International Organisation of Securities Commissions
ISA	International Standards on Auditing
ISO	International Organization for Standardization
KPI	key performance indicator
LLA	limited liability agreement (auditors)
MD&A	management discussion and analysis
MRP	market risk premium
NAICS	North American Industry Classification System
NBV	net book value
NCA	net current assets
NOA	net operating assets
NOCE	net operating capital employed
NPV	net present value (discounted cash flow)
NRV	net realisable value
OECD	Organisation for Economic Co-operation and Development
OFR	operating and financial review
PBIT	profit before interest and tax
PCAOB	Public Company Accounting Oversight Board
P/E	price/earnings ratio

plc	public limited company
PPE	property, plant and equipment
PTP	pre-tax profit
PV	present value (discounted cash flows)
R&D	research and development
ROA	return on assets
ROCE	return on capital employed
ROE	return on equity
ROI	return on investment
RONA	return on net assets
RONOA	return on net operating assets
ROSF	return on shareholders' funds
ROTA	return on total assets
ROTTA	return on total tangible assets
SAC	Standards Advisory Council (IASB)
SBU	strategic business unit
SEC	Securities and Exchange Commission
SIC	standard industrial classification
SIP	stock or share incentive plan
SOCE	statement of changes in equity
SORIE	statement of recognised income and expense
SORP	statement of recommended practice
SOX	Sarbanes-Oxley Act (US 2002)
SPE	special purpose entity
SPV	special purpose vehicle
SSAP	Statement of Standard Accounting Practice
SVA	shareholder value added
SWOT	strengths, weaknesses, opportunities and threats (analysis)
TSR	total shareholders' return
UITF	Urgent Issue Task Force
WACC	weighted average cost of capital
XRBL	Extensible Business Reporting Language

Index

A. H. (BOB) VAUSE is a Fellow of the Institute of Chartered Accountants and an Emeritus Fellow of Green Templeton College, Oxford, where he taught for more than thirty years. He is the author of several books and has worked as consultant to many large companies on a broad range of matters affecting performance and control.

PublicAffairs is a publishing house founded in 1997. It is a tribute to the standards, values, and flair of three persons who have served as mentors to countless reporters, writers, editors, and book people of all kinds, including me.

I. F. STONE, proprietor of *I. F. Stone's Weekly*, combined a commitment to the First Amendment with entrepreneurial zeal and reporting skill and became one of the great independent journalists in American history. At the age of eighty, Izzy published *The Trial of Socrates*, which was a national bestseller. He wrote the book after he taught himself ancient Greek.

BENJAMIN C. BRADLEE was for nearly thirty years the charismatic editorial leader of *The Washington Post*. It was Ben who gave the *Post* the range and courage to pursue such historic issues as Watergate. He supported his reporters with a tenacity that made them fearless and it is no accident that so many became authors of influential, best-selling books.

ROBERT L. BERNSTEIN, the chief executive of Random House for more than a quarter century, guided one of the nation's premier publishing houses. Bob was personally responsible for many books of political dissent and argument that challenged tyranny around the globe. He is also the founder and longtime chair of Human Rights Watch, one of the most respected human rights organizations in the world.

·   ·   ·

For fifty years, the banner of Public Affairs Press was carried by its owner Morris B. Schnapper, who published Gandhi, Nasser, Toynbee, Truman, and about 1,500 other authors. In 1983, Schnapper was described by *The Washington Post* as "a redoubtable gadfly." His legacy will endure in the books to come.

Peter Osnos, *Founder and Editor-at-Large*